A Hell of a Way to Die

Tarawa Atoll
20-23 November 1943

Dedication

For Owen and Betty

A Hell of a Way to Die

Tarawa Atoll
20-23 November 1943

Derrick Wright

Windrow & Greene

© Derrick Wright 1996

This edition published in
Great Britain 1997 by
Windrow & Greene Ltd
5 Gerrard Street
London W1V 7LJ

Designed by Tony Stocks/TS Graphics
Printed and bound by Hillman Printers
through Amon-Re Ltd

A CIP catalogue entry for this book
is available from the British Library

ISBN 1 85915 028 4

Contents

Foreword by Maj Gen Michael P.Ryan, USMC (Retd)......................7

Preface and acknowledgements...................................8

Chapter 1: A New Sun Rising
Japan's expansion in the Pacific; from Pearl Harbor to Guadalcanal;
the fortification of Betio Island 9

Chapter 2: The Best-Laid Plans
The commanders; the Task Forces; Japanese and American planning;
the 2nd Marine Division; embarkation..........................23

Chapter 3: The Red Beaches - Morning
Betio, D Day: Saturday 20 November 1943, 3am to 11.30am...........40

Chapter 4: The Red Beaches - Afternoon
Betio, D Day: Saturday 20 November, 11.30am to nightfall................64

Chapter 5: The Charnel House
Betio, D+1: Sunday 21 November 79

Chapter 6: The Day is Ours
Betio, D+2 & D+3: Monday 22 & Tuesday 23 November................100

Chapter 7: Other Islands
Tarawa - Bairiki to Na'a, 21-28 November; Makin and Apamama,
20-21 November 115

Chapter 8: Semper Fidelis
Aftermath, postmortem, lessons and conclusions...................124

Appendix 1: Japanese garrison and defences..............................138

Appendix 2: Command & staff, V Amphibious Corps
& 2nd Marine Division...........................142

Appendix 3: Ground unit campaign participation,
Operation Galvanic................................145

Appendix 4: Task organisation, 2nd Marine Division
(Reinforced), Operation Longsuit...........................147

Appendix 5: Message from Maj Gen Julian C.Smith
to 2nd Marine Division, 19 November....................148

Appendix 6: Message from Maj Henry P.Crowe
to 2-8 Marines, 15 November........................148

Appendix 7: USMC & Japanese casualties, 20-23 November.....................150

Appendix 8: Medal of Honor Awards & Citations......................................151

Appendix 9: Presidential Unit Citation..154

appendix 10: Reconnaissance & Intelligence...155

Appendix 11: Kerr Eby, War Artist..157

Select Bibliography..157

Illustrations ....after p.96

Maps   1: Central Pacific & Tarawa Atoll...14

        2: Betio Island defences...20

        3: Intelligence map, Betio defences..36

        4: Route of landing craft to beaches...42

        5: Landing beaches, Betio, D Day morning......................................52

        6: Approximate US gains, Betio, D Day, 6pm..................................74

        7: Approximate US gains, Betio, D+1, 6pm.....................................94

        8: Approximate US gains, Betio, D+2 & D+3...................................108

        9: The other islands of Tarawa Atoll..118

Foreword

by
Major General Michael P.Ryan USMC (Retd)
Navy Cross, Legion of Merit, Distinguished Service Cross (British)

The story of Tarawa is still legendary after more than fifty years, in part because President Roosevelt approved extensive film coverage of the battle. The graphic pictures stunned a nation not yet desensitized to the reality of war by television news.

For Marines, however, Tarawa represented a vindication of a doctrine and techniques developed at Quantico Marine Base in the 1930s, when war threatened in the Pacific. Not everyone believed that an amphibious invasion of a heavily defended beach could succeed. Indeed, during the assault on Betio it seemed that the doubters might be right. In the end, despite miscalculations and a suicidal Japanese defense, victory at Tarawa demonstrated that the enemy's line of island defenses could be breached.

The bitter cost of the victory, however, demanded that tactical adjustments be made. All future operations incorporated the lessons learned. Close air support from aircraft carriers was aided by better radios. Heavily armed amtracs led future invasions. Naval and air bombardments were extended in time and focused on precise targets, as well as better co-ordinated with troop landings. In addition to the usual focus on small unit leadership, training emphasised better tank-infantry tactics and the use of assault demolitions. All these actions contributed to the rapid reduction of Japanese forward island defenses, and the establishment of air bases in the Marianas and the Ryukus that hastened the end of the war.

The success of the war in the Pacific can be seen, then, as a legacy of Tarawa. For those who were there, however, what endures is the memory of the courage, determination and loyalty of every Marine.

Preface

In the opinion of Major General Holland M. Smith USMC, the commander of V Amphibious Corps at Tarawa, the invasion was a mistake: "From the very beginning the decision of the Joint Chiefs to seize Tarawa was a mistake, and from their initial mistake grew the terrible drama of errors - errors of omission rather than commission - resulting in these needless casualties." Whether he was right or wrong has been the subject of intense discussion for over fifty years.

Operation Galvanic - the invasion of the Gilbert Islands by the US Marine Corps and Army units of V Amphibious Corps - began in the early morning hours of 20 November 1943 with a huge naval bombardment of the tiny island of Betio on the western edge of Tarawa Atoll. It marked the beginning of America's "island-hopping" advance across the Central Pacific which led northward from the Gilberts to Kwajalein, Saipan, Guam, Peleliu, Iwo Jima and Okinawa, and which would - but for the dropping of the atomic bombs on Hiroshima and Nagasaki - have ended in the invasion of the Japanese mainland, at an incalculable cost in American and Allied casualties.

The atoll of Tarawa was the ground chosen for the beginning of this massive enterprise. Hard lessons had to be learned about amphibious landings on heavily defended islands, and many men died learning them. This is the story of that beginning, and of the men who - despite the blunders and miscalculations which are unavoidable in any pioneering operation - proved that it could be done. The Japanese commander on Tarawa, Rear Admiral Shibasaki, had said that "the Americans could not take Tarawa with a million men in a hundred years": they took it in 76 hours, in what proved to be - in terms of casualties suffered and inflicted for ground captured - one of the bloodiest battles of the entire war.

Acknowledgements

The most pleasant aspect of the research and writing of this book has been the unstinting help and encouragement that I have received from veterans of the battle and from fellow researchers. I would particularly like to thank the following:

Major General Michael P. Ryan, for his Foreword, and for valuable additional information on the Betio fighting; Major General Raymond L. Murray for details of the capture of the other islands of Tarawa Atoll. For their interesting reminiscences of the battle and/or valuable information, Melvin F. Swango, Joe H. Jordan, Ed J. Moore, Dr Herbert H. Deighton, Hawk Rader, Eddie Albert, Col E.J. Rowse, D.F. Khorzer, Clarence A. Shanks, Ralph Butler, W.E. Nygren, G. Blakeman, Theodore H. Stueber, Lester Hellman and Raymond Knight; Gordon L. Rottman, and Steven J. Zaloga.

Special thanks to Jim and Margaret Moran for their invaluable help. For a constant supply of information and material and for details of the exploits of his father David, many thanks to John Spencer. Throughout this venture I benefited from the constant encouragement and support of the late Bob Libby of Levin, New Zealand, whose memories of Tarawa form an important part of this book; I would much have valued his opinion of the end result.

The quotations from *Tarawa - The Story of a Battle* by the late Robert Sherrod are reprinted with the permission of the author. The charcoal drawings by Kerr Eby are reproduced by courtesy of the Navy Art Collection, Washington, DC. The wartime photographs reproduced in this book are credited to the US National Archives, Washington, the US Marine Corps, Marine Corps Historical Collection and the US Navy as individually listed. The photographs of Tarawa taken in 1993 are by courtesy of Jim Moran.

Finally, I would like to thank my wife Doreen for her patience and the exclusive use of her sitting room for two years.

Chapter 1:
A New Sun Rising

Bullets we understood: but the minds and hearts of the Japanese were beyond our understanding.

(Charles Carfrae, *Chindit Column*, 1985)

By the middle years of the nineteenth century the Japanese were just beginning to emerge from centuries of feudalism. In 1853 Commodore Matthew Perry, US Navy, arrived with offers of trade with the West, his "black ships" emphasising the obvious material superiority of a culture from which Japan's rulers had deliberately isolated her for some two hundred and fifty years. Once finally convinced that the policy of protective isolation must be abandoned if they were to survive as a nation, the Japanese made material changes at astonishing speed during the reign of the Emperor Meiji. By 1890 Japan had adopted what was outwardly a European-style constitutional monarchy complete with a form of parliament, the Diet. But democracy on the Western model - even at its rather basic late nineteenth century level - was utterly foreign to the Japanese sensibility; and for another half-century real power remained in the hands of shadowy court and military cliques operating through the *genro*, an advisory council interposed between the Emperor and his prime minister and cabinet.

Her eager embrace of the products and the military skills of the industrialised West brought Japan - the most disciplined and cohesive of Asian societies - the means of competitive expansion. By 1894 the Bonin Islands, the Kuriles and Okinawa had been annexed; and in that year Japan's lengthening reach brought her into inevitable conflict with ancient, ruined China, the disputed battlefield on this occasion being Korea. Victory in 1895 brought Japan a degree of recognized influence in Korea; the island of Formosa; and the Liaotung peninsula on the Yellow Sea coast, housing the strategically important naval base of Lu-shun (Port Arthur).

The major European powers were now beginning to view a revitalised Japan with mounting unease; and as a result of strong political pressure from France and Germany the Japanese were reluctantly compelled to relinquish their gains on the Chinese mainland. The Russians had for decades been seeking an outlet in the Far East, and promptly seized the opportunity to persuade China into leasing them Port Arthur - a piece of blatant trickery which infuriated the Japanese. Negotiations over the demarcation of Russian and Japanese spheres of activity in Manchuria and Korea broke down in February 1904; and Japan - without a declaration of war - attacked Russian ships at Inchon and Port Arthur.

The ensuing Russo-Japanese War saw Japan victorious in Korea and Manchuria, defeating Russian armies at Port Arthur and Mukden (Shen-yang); and culminated in the great naval battle of Tsushima in May 1905, when the Russian fleet was utterly destroyed for negligible Japanese loss. This decisive victory over a major European power, just fifty years after Perry's ships first forced open the gates to an apparently medieval society, shocked the world - and further fuelled the Japanese oligarchy's fantasies of invincibility. Although the Japanese had won a major victory, however, their economy was too immature to support a long war; and both empires were relieved when President Theodore Roosevelt's mediation brought hostilities to an end with the Treaty of Portsmouth (New Hampshire) in September 1905, on terms favourable to Japan.

The parallel emergence of the United States as a major power in the Far East was largely the result of the Spanish-American War of 1898. Though Cuba had been the *causus belli*, the Peace of Paris brought the victorious USA control over not only that island and Puerto Rico, but other former Spanish possessions in the Pacific - the Philippines, and the island of Guam. The seeds of mistrust were immediately sown between these two vigorous powers, America seeing Japan - with its large modern navy, built, equipped and trained largely by Germany and to some extent by Britain - as the principle threat to stability in the Pacific.

The outbreak of World War I in 1914 brought the Japanese further opportunities to expand their power without European interference. They sided with the Allies, in over-scrupulous accordance with limited pre-war guarantees given to Britain; and Japanese warships would co-operate with the Allied navies in the Pacific and Indian Oceans, and even to a limited extent in the Mediterranean. But Japan's greatest commitment by far was to successful attacks on German possessions in mainland China and the Pacific, which were subsequently endorsed by the signatories of the Treaty of Versailles in 1919. Japan was awarded trusteeship over the Marshall Islands, the Carolines, Tinian and Saipan in the Marianas, and - despite deep American concern - the former German concessions on China's Shantung peninsula.

The Washington Naval Conference of 1921-22 sought to prevent either America, Britain or Japan from becoming the dominant naval power in the Pacific by limiting the size and tonnage of their fleets; under the final treaty America and Britain were allowed larger tonnages than Japan because of their Atlantic commitments. The treaty also prevented the signatories from fortifying their possessions (although Britain's base on Singapore at the southern tip of Malaya was, oddly, exempt from this stricture).

During the 1920s and 1930s Japan became disillusioned with the treaty, seeing the larger tonnage allowed to Britain and America as yet another humiliating evidence of the West's determination to deny Japan her rightful place as one of the "governing nations" of the world. An exploding population, economic depression, and political turmoil polarised opinion between extreme left and right wing factions; and envious eyes turned towards ramshackle, divided China as a source of vital raw materials, potentially vulnerable to Japan's Kwantung Army garrisoned in southern Manchuria.

An excuse was afforded when in 1931 a section of the Japanese-owned Manchurian railway was blown up, giving elements in the army - following their own agenda in defiance of official government policy - a pretext for intervention to protect Japanese lives and property. Government attempts to crush a secret society of extremist officers who were plotting a coup were only partly successful, and several senior politicians were assassinated. Chinese protests to the League of Nations over Japan's military expansion in Manchuria were only instrumental in speeding Japan's withdrawal from the League in 1933. The following year Japan renounced the terms of the Washington Treaty; and in 1935 yet another nearly successful coup attempt further increased the army's influence over the government, and the influence within the army of the extreme nationalist faction. The Emperor Hirohito, who had ascended the throne in 1926, was worshipped as a god by his subjects but manipulated as a figurehead by his ministers and generals.

Outright war with China broke out in July 1937, the year in which a massive naval expansion programme culminated in the construction of the world's largest battleships, the *Yamato* and *Musashi* each of 72,000 tons. In China Japanese gains were swift and extensive, and reports of Japanese barbarism following the fall of Nanking shocked the world; in 1938 America began subsidising the Chinese regime of Gen Chiang Kai-shek, the leader of the non-communist resistance forces.

An interested observer of the opening campaigns of World War II in Europe, Japan profited from the fall of France in summer 1940 by successful demands on the Vichy government that Japanese garrisons move into France's colonies in Indo-China (Vietnam). Over the 18 months which followed the USA and Britain - unprepared for war in the Far East - conducted an escalating campaign of diplomatic and trade sanctions against a Japan whose bellicose intentions were increasingly evident. Formally allied to Germany and Italy in the Tripartite Pact of September 1940, Japan freed herself from an old threat when she concluded a non-aggression pact with the Soviet Union in April 1941.

That July Japanese assets in the United States were frozen, and Britain and the Dutch East Indies co-operated in a total ban on oil exports to Japan which denied her 90% of her required supplies. Although these measures were designed to discourage Japanese belligerence, in reality they only strengthened the hand of the war party within the ruling class and accelerated the rush towards open hostilities; and in October 1941 the extreme nationalist Gen Hideki Tojo became prime minister. It had not escaped the attention of the Imperial Japanese Navy that in the middle of 1940 America had embarked on a new naval construction programme. It was calculated that by 1944 the USA would enjoy a superiority of 10 to 3 over Japan in warships - if a war was inevitable, the decision to attack must be made soon.

★   ★   ★

That the attack on Pearl Harbor came as a surprise to America at large seems in itself surprising. The only country in the Pacific area capable of attacking US possessions, and the only one with a reason for doing so, was Japan. For decades the US Navy had carried out their exercises in accordance with "Plan Orange" - a thinly disguised codename for war with Japan. Ever since the acquisition of her new territories in the Marshalls, Carolines and Marianas, Japan had been building a series of island fortresses in the Central Pacific. A large naval base was constructed at Truk in the Carolines; and indeed, the threat of the fortification of the Marshall Islands in 1940 was the reason that the US Pacific Fleet was massed at its Hawaiian anchorage on Oahu in December 1941.

The attack on Pearl Harbor was the brainchild of Admiral Isoroku Yamamoto, who had been appointed Commander of the Combined Fleet in 1939. A veteran of the battle of Tsushima in 1905, the extremely able and thoughtful Yamamoto was an advocate of naval air power, who had spent time in America as a naval attaché and as a student at Harvard University in the 1920s. He always maintained that it was futile for Japan to go to war with America; having seen the vast industrial potential of the USA, he knew that although there would be short term gains the industrial might of America would eventually prevail. Despite these misgivings, Yamamoto's sense of duty to the Emperor convinced him that he must obey whatever commands the military and naval hierarchy deemed fit. The thinking behind the overall Japanese strategy was that simultaneous attacks on the Philippines, Malaya, the Dutch East Indies and China's lifeline through Burma would neutralize the Allied forces in the region while providing access to all the raw materials - oil, rice, rubber and metal ores - that Japan needed; and that the Allies would sue for a negotiated peace rather than embark on a long and bloody war. The Japanese high command concluded that with Britain fighting for her life against Germany the Royal Navy did not pose a serious threat to Japanese operations against Malaya. But the US Pacific Fleet, if committed in strength to the defence of the Philippines, could frustrate the lightning conquests upon which ultimate Japanese success depended, dragging out hostilities until the superior resources of the USA began to tell decisively.

Yamamoto, a compulsive gambler, urged that the only way to neutralize the US Navy was to mount a carrier-based attack on Pearl Harbor at the very outset of the offensive; if the American fleet was allowed to disperse into the vast Pacific, Japan would begin to lose the initiative gained by her lightning invasions. The spectacular success of the Royal Navy's Fleet Air Arm at Taranto in 1940, when a substantial proportion of the Italian fleet had been sunk or disabled by a few obsolete biplane torpedo bombers, had convinced him that carrier-launched attacks on land and sea targets were destined to play a major role in forthcoming operations. So, as the American and Japanese diplomats wrangled in Washington, Yamamoto gathered a strike force organised around Japan's six largest aircraft carriers.

The attack on Pearl Harbor, codenamed Operation Z, was originally scheduled for 17 November, but had to be put back because the Imperial Navy were having problems adapting their torpedoes for the shallow waters of the anchorage. Yamamoto knew that he was taking an enormous risk in committing six of his eleven aircraft carriers to an operation against an objective nearly 3,500 miles away whose success depended on achieving surprise. The attacks on Malaya, the Philippines and the Dutch East Indies, scheduled to coincide with the Hawaiian strike, would commit much of the Imperial Fleet to operations with theoretically insufficient air cover; but recent information suggested that only the Royal Navy battleship HMS *Prince of Wales* and the battlecruiser HMS *Repulse* posed any threat to their plans in the western Pacific.

The Pearl Harbor strike force, commanded by Vice Adml Chuichi Nagumo, sailed from the remote Kurile Islands north of Japan on 26 November 1941. Between them the six carriers - the *Akagi, Kaga, Hiryu, Soryu, Shokaku* and *Zuikaku* - carried a total of 423 level, dive and torpedo bombers and nimble Zero fighters; they were escorted by two battleships, three cruisers, nine destroyers and eight tankers. On 2 December the coded final confirmation for the attack was flashed from Tokyo. Admiral Nagumo received the latest report on the situation at Pearl Harbor, which indicated that at least eight battleships lay at anchor around Ford Island but that the expected aircraft carriers appeared to be missing.

Contrary to Japanese expectations, the American carriers were well dispersed. The USS *Saratoga* was undergoing repairs in the navy yard at San Diego, California; the *Yorktown* was operating in the Atlantic; and the *Lexington* and *Enterprise* were delivering aircraft to the Marine garrisons on Wake and Midway islands. However, the US fleet in port that weekend after exercises at sea presented the enemy with more than enough targets: eight battleships, two heavy cruisers, six light cruisers, 29 destroyers and five submarines, together with a mass of other vessels - auxiliaries, repair ships, tenders, oilers and hospital ships - which made a grand total of 70 ships moored in the sunshine under the clear morning sky of Sunday 7 December. They lay anchored in peaceful rows, without torpedo nets rigged or barrage balloons raised, with anti-aircraft ammunition carefully stowed under lock and key, and with many of their crews ashore on weekend leave.

At 6am, from some 230 miles north of Oahu, Adml Nagumo launched his first wave of 43 fighters, 49 level and 51 dive bombers and 40 torpedo bombers; the whole force got airborne in only fifteen minutes. At about 7.50am the first blows fell on Oahu's airfields, Hickam and Wheeler Fields, where scores of neatly parked aircraft were destroyed. Next the torpedo planes swooped on "Battleship Row" near Ford Island; and finally the bombers, with their armour-piercing ordnance, completed the mayhem. The Zeros, almost unopposed in the air, came in low to strafe targets at will. By 8.30am Battleship Row was a blazing shambles: the USS *Oklahoma* had rolled onto her side, the *West Virginia* was sitting on the bottom of the harbour, and the *Arizona*, whose magazine had exploded, was a flaming wreck with over a thousand of her crew dead. A second wave an hour later - of 35 fighters escorting 78 dive and 54 other bombers - met more organised anti-aircraft fire and suffered 20 losses, but damaged another battleship and wrecked three destroyers. In all five battleships - including *California* and *Pennsylvania* - and two light cruisers were destroyed, together with almost every US aircraft on the island; eleven other warships were disabled; and more than 2,300 US servicemen died.

Another strike by the entire force was urged, but the cautious Nagumo decided that with the US carriers unaccounted for the potential risk of retaliation was too great. He withdrew his force - leaving the vital carriers, and the main oil tanks on Hawaii, unharmed. Nevertheless, Yamamoto's faith in naval airpower had not

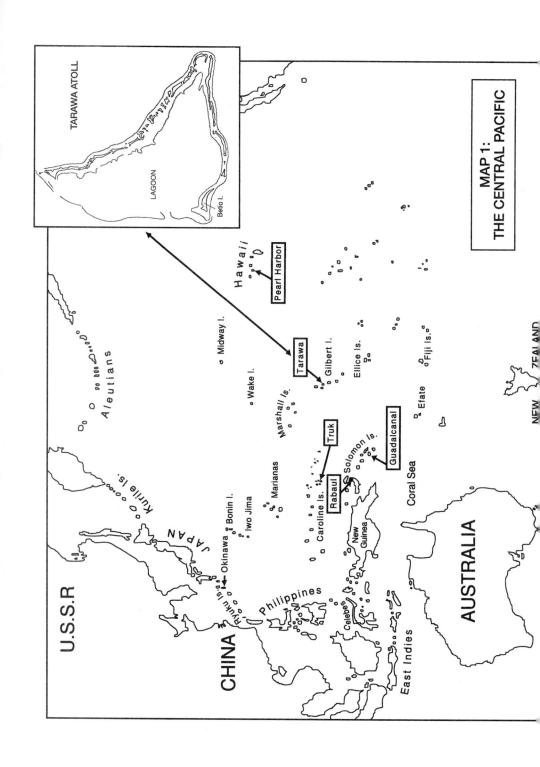

MAP 1:
THE CENTRAL PACIFIC

been misplaced; the Japanese were amazed at the scale of their victory, and at their modest losses of 29 aircraft and 55 aircrew.

News of the attack, and President Roosevelt's broadcast speech marking the "date that will live in infamy", sent shockwaves throughout America and finally disarmed the isolationist school of opinion. The US declaration of war against Japan on 8 December, and Germany's and Italy's answering declarations of war against the USA on the 11th, marked the great turning point of World War II. Britain no longer stood alone, and the final end was not in realistic doubt; but the Allies could only hope to reach that end by a long, bloody, and often heart-breaking road.

⋆   ⋆   ⋆

Pearl Harbor unleashed a tide of Japanese expansion that was not contained until 1943, and the first year of the Pacific war was an almost uninterrupted catalogue of disasters for the Allies. On the day after Pearl Harbor bombers flying from Formosa carried out heavy attacks on American airfields in the Philippines; the swift establishment of Japanese air superiority over the whole of the islands paved the way for amphibious landings on Luzon later in December. Caught in a classic pincer movement from Lingayen Gulf in the north and Lamon Bay in the south, the American garrison were forced onto the Bataan peninsula where they eventually surrendered on 9 April 1942, although resistance continued on the island of Corregidor until 6 May. This pattern - of rapid, fluid advances, often through terrain which complacent colonial commands had considered practi-cally impassable, under complete local air superiority - was to be repeated right across the region in the early months of 1942.

The British warships HMS *Prince of Wales* and *Repulse*, sailing from Singapore to intercept Japanese landings in northern Malaya, were caught without fighter cover and sunk by Japanese aircraft on 10 December; Churchill said that "in all of the war I never received a more direct shock", but worse was soon to follow. Guam was captured the same day, and Wake Island on the 23rd; Hong Kong fell on Christmas Day 1941. The vital British base at Singapore, with its massive seaward defences, fell to the Japanese 25th Army on 15 February 1942 as the final prize for Gen Yamashita's brilliant campaign down the length of Malaya, which had completely outclassed a numerically stronger defence. On 15 January the Japanese invaded Burma to threaten the vital Allied supply route into China; and on the 25th Japanese troops landed on New Guinea, the last Allied outwork north of Australia. The Dutch East Indies, with their huge oil reserves, were overrun by 7 March 1942; and late in May British and Chinese troops were driven out of Burma into Assam, India.

It was May of 1942 that brought the first encouragement to Allied arms, however. The Japanese overstretched themselves when, on the 7th, an invasion fleet heading for Port Moresby in south-east New Guinea was located by the US Adml Fletcher's Task Force 17. In the ensuing Battle of the Coral Sea, fought almost entirely by the naval aircraft of each side, the Americans achieved a strategic victory - the indefinite postponement of landings at Port Moresby -

although tactically the contest could only be regarded as a draw, each side losing a carrier (the USS *Lexington* and the *Shoho*).

Between 4 and 7 June 1942 the Japanese suffered their first major defeat of the war north of Midway, the remote but highly strategic speck of land far to the north-east of Hawaii. Thanks largely to the efforts of the American cryptanalysts who had succeeded in deciphering a high proportion of the Japanese naval codes, a numerically smaller US Navy force under Fletcher and Spruance was able to intercept Nagumo's task force, sinking four aircraft carriers (*Akagi, Hiryu, Soryu* and *Kaga*) and a cruiser with the further loss of 322 aircraft and some 5,000 men. US losses were one carrier (*Yorktown*) and a destroyer, 150 aircraft and some 300 men. This blow to her naval air assets forced Japan into a defensive posture at sea, since she could no longer risk a major fleet action.

The period from summer 1942 to February 1943 would also see Japanese troops first held, and finally defeated - after many months of savage fighting in appalling conditions - by Australian and US troops on New Guinea. Simultaneously, in an equalling harrowing epic fought out largely by the US Marines though with heroic Army, air and naval support, victory was finally achieved on the strategic island of Guadalcanal in the Solomons.

By early 1943 Adml Ernest King, Chief of Naval Operations, and Adml Chester W.Nimitz, Commander-in-Chief Pacific Fleet, could look forward to the establishment of a new and powerful striking force. Nimitz had been promised twelve of the new 27,000-ton *Essex* class fleet carriers capable of operating 80 or more aircraft; and the US Navy's submarines were operating with increasing efficiency against enemy transports along Japan's long and vulnerable supply lines. But in war the luxury of simply waiting in the expectation of favourable developments can be a fatal trap.

At the Casablanca conference in January the Allied leaders had decided that the first objective was the defeat of Germany, but meanwhile the Joint Chiefs needed to settle on a strategy to exploit the increasingly favourable balance of opportunity in the Pacific. At a Pacific Military Conference in Washington in March 1943 Gen Douglas MacArthur, Commander-in-Chief South-West Pacific, urged a south-to-north advance on Japan via New Guinea and a campaign of liberation on the Philippines - although combined operations by all services would obviously be required, the size of the land task would make this, inevitably, an Army-centred campaign.

Admirals King and Nimitz favoured an "island-hopping" strategy through the Central Pacific, starting in the Marshalls and continuing via the Carolines, the Marianas, and on to Iwo Jima and Okinawa, pushing American airfields ever nearer the Japanese home islands. Each of this series of incremental advances - largely by the Navy and Marine Corps - would demand more manageable scales of resources and involve more acceptable risks than a premature attempt on the Philippines. There were not enough ships or troops available to support both options; and - while declaring that he did not yet have the forces to attack anywhere - Nimitz, with the assistance of Adml Raymond A.Spruance, moved matters along his chosen road by starting to prepare plans for the first of their island objectives: an attack on the Marshall Islands for November 1943.

Like Dwight Eisenhower in the European theatre, Chester Nimitz had a gift for dealing with volatile colleagues, and his stormy relationship with Gen MacArthur was only made tolerable by his patience. When MacArthur began ranting about what he considered the impracticability of Nimitz's "island-hopping" strategy - as he would many times during the war - the admiral assumed an air of detached calm, and continued to conduct his campaigns as he saw fit. He was a man who habitually rose at 5.30am for a long walk, and finished his working day with a hard game of tennis before indulging a love for classical music - a man with a hinterland, who exuded calm and confidence in front of subordinates even when the news was desperate. It was a confidence based on solid achievement and varied experience.

Born in Fredericksburg, Texas, in 1885, Chester Nimitz was the son of a small hotel-keeper and the grandson of an 1840s immigrant from Bremen, Germany; by his sixtieth birthday in 1945 he was a five-star fleet admiral in command of 21 other admirals and generals, six Marine divisions, 5,000 aircraft, and the biggest navy the world had ever seen. He had originally favoured the Army as a career, settling for the Naval Academy only when unable to obtain a vacancy at West Point. He joined the submarine service in 1908 and remained in that branch until the end of World War I, reaching the rank of commander before assignment as an aide to Adml Robinson, C-in-C US Fleet. After various inter-war postings Pearl Harbor found him in Washington as chief of the Bureau of Navigation; and after the debacle he was selected in preference to Adml Kimmel's immediate replacement, Vice Adml Pye, as C-in-C Pacific Fleet. With responsibility for operations over a vast area of the earth's surface - from the Aleutians in the north to New Zealand in the south, and almost to the Philippines in the west - he had to concede that "if anything is bigger than Texas, it is the Pacific Ocean".

Like many others, he considered the Battle of Midway to have been the turning point: "never again did I have any doubts about the outcome of the Pacific War". It was during the Nimitz era that the whole nature of naval tactics was transformed; Midway proved that the aircraft carrier had replaced the battle-ship as the capital asset of the Navy. Although the US continued to build new battleships, the production of 27,000-ton fleet and small 11,000-ton escort carri-ers (the latter built on cruiser hulls) progressed at an astonishing rate - 18 in 1942, and no less than 65 by the end of 1943. In all amphibious operations thereafter, air supremacy was assured by an umbrella of carrier aircraft over every beachhead. Of Tarawa, Nimitz was to say a decade later: "I have great pride in the thought that never before was such a tough job done so completely in such a short time. With the passage of time my admiration for the US Marines grows and grows."

*   *   *

Some time earlier President Roosevelt had become intrigued by the exploits of the British Commandos in Europe, and asked his Chiefs of Staff why some such elite group was not available within the American forces. He received a terse reply from the Marines to the effect that they were already an elite force, and could do anything that the British could do. One outcome had been a raid on Makin Island in the Gilberts group in August 1942. The 2nd Marine Raider Battalion - "Carlson's Raiders", commanded by Col Evans Carlson with Maj James Roosevelt, the President's son, as his Executive Officer - embarked in Hawaii on the submarines USS *Nautilus* and *Argonaut*, and after a cramped two-week voyage arrived off Makin on 16 August. During the ensuing raid some 200 Japanese were killed, a transport ship was destroyed and 1,000 barrels of fuel were burned. Twenty-one Marines were lost and nine left behind, later to be executed by the Japanese.

Hailed as a great victory by the American press, who in August 1942 were desperate to have some good news to report, the raid was of limited tactical value. However, the Japanese general staff reacted with some energy. Seeing the raid as a precursor to an all-out invasion of the Gilbert Islands, they gave the highest priority to a major reinforcement of Tarawa, the most important atoll in the group. Over 1,100 crack naval infantry arrived on Tarawa less than a month after the Makin raid, to be followed by 1,200 pioneers of a construction unit; and by January 1943 an airfield became operational on Betio Island, the largest in the atoll. The Makin raid may have given the American public a boost to morale; one can only speculate by what percentage it increased the casualties during the subsequent battle for Tarawa.

★   ★   ★

In the years before the war the islands and atolls of the Central Pacific were little known to anyone other than the crews of the small trading ships which made their infrequent visits to deliver essential supplies and to collect cargoes of copra. In 1788 a Captain Gilbert, master of the *Charlotte*, had come upon a group of atolls 1 degree 13 minutes north of the equator, and celebrated the event by naming them after himself; but it was not until 1892 that Captain Davis of HMS *Royalist* proclaimed the islands a British protectorate. In 1915 the Gilbert Islands and the nearby Ellice Islands were officially deemed to be part of the British Empire, though the imperial yoke lay very lightly upon the inhabitants.

The islanders had become a self-governing people under British jurisdiction, and small industries were developed based upon phosphate deposits and coconut plantations, but the islands were never considered to be completely self-sufficient. Before the war the natives were 78% Christian, the remainder being semi-pagan; education was provided by the numerous missions which maintained the village schools and enlisted the native teachers. Before the Japanese arrived there were about 2,000 natives and 20 white men on the Gilberts, whose inhabitants continued to live their lives and follow their customs much as they had always done.

The writer Robert Louis Stevenson, who lived in the islands for a number of years, wrote of the ruler of Apamama that "he maintained a household consist-ing solely of women who performed the duties of cooks, guards and labourers", but a guilty conscience may have caused him to maintain that they were all his sisters. The Gilbertese were Micronesians ("people of the small islands"), and the pre-war islander was described as being well built, standing about 5ft 6ins, with good shoulders and strong legs; the women were stated to be "comely". Fishing was one of the main occupations of the islanders, along with the collection of copra - the dried kernel of the coconut, a tradeable resource. Houses were built from the trunks of the palm trees, with the fronds providing the roof; the fibre from the coconut husks could be woven into a cloth, although a great deal of material was brought to the islands by traders. The men of the Gilberts were expert mariners, with a deep understanding of tides and currents and an almost instinctive ability to navigate without charts.

Tarawa, one of sixteen atolls which form the Gilbert Islands, lies 80 miles north of the equator. The atoll is roughly triangular in shape, the eastern and southern sides being made up of 47 coral islands - 42 on the eastern side and the remaining five along the southern base. The third, western side of the triangle is a submerged reef with a half-mile wide navigable passage leading into a lagoon. The largest island of the group is Betio (pronounced Bay-sho), the most westerly of the five islands of the southern base. Betio has a total area of about one square mile, being two and a half miles long and 800 yards wide at its widest point. Nowhere does the island rise more than twelve feet above sea level.

The first Japanese raid on Tarawa Atoll occurred on 10 December 1941, when a token naval force surveyed the various islands and declared an "occupation", although a garrison was not installed until September 1942. As a reaction to the attack on Makin Island by Carlson's Raiders the Gilberts were reinforced, and Betio Island on Tarawa was selected as the main base since it afforded the best site for an airfield. On 15 September 1,100 men from the Yokosuka 6th Special Naval Landing Force (re-designated the 3rd Special Base Force in February 1943) arrived to garrison the island. Later, in December, they were joined by the 1,250 pioneers of the 111th Construction Unit, shipped in to begin building the island's airfield and defence system. Reinforcements in the form of the Sasebo 7th SNLF, some 1,500 strong, arrived on 17 March to augment the 3rd SBF; and in May 1943 a detachment of nearly 1,000 men from the 4th Fleet's Construction Department completed the garrison.

Most of the British administrators on the Gilberts had left by the time the Japanese arrived, but the occupation forces showed their customary brutish attitude to the islanders. There was wholesale impressment of local slave labour, and a number of women were raped. The inhabitants of Betio were removed to the other islands of the atoll, only being allowed back as and when they were required as labour.

The primary task of organising the construction of the defences and the airfield fell to Lt Murakami, as commander of the 111th Construction Unit more of an engineer than a sailor; and he performed his duties brilliantly. Once the decision had been taken to make Tarawa the keystone of the Gilbert Islands defences no effort was spared in turning the tiny island of Betio into what was probably, yard for yard, the most heavily defended position in the world at that time.

The object of Murakami's plan was to prevent the enemy from reaching the

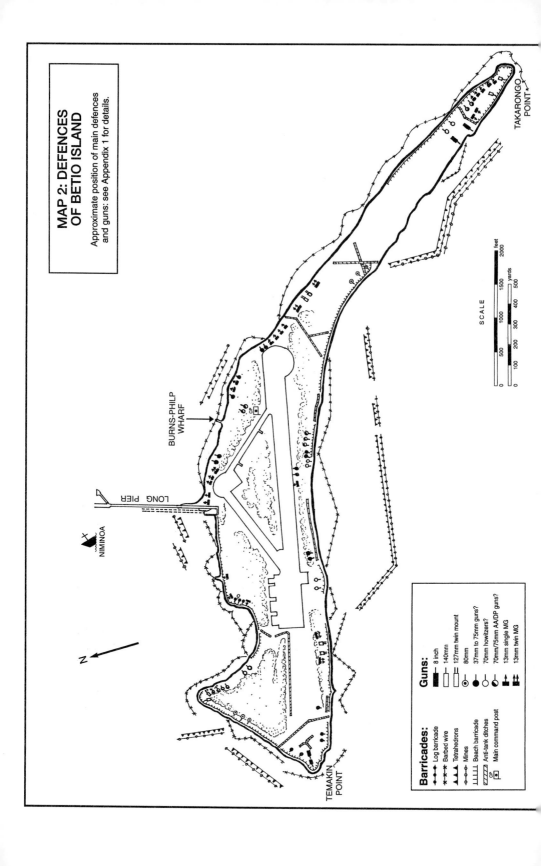

MAP 2: DEFENCES
OF BETIO ISLAND

Approximate position of main defences
and guns: see Appendix 1 for details.

TAKARONGO
POINT

BURNS-PHILP
WHARF

LONG PIER

NIMINOA

N

TEMAKIN
POINT

SCALE

feet
0   500   1000   1500   2000

yards
0   100   200   300   400   500

Barricades:

→→→ Log barricade
⊁⊁⊁ Barbed wire
▲▲▲ Tetrahedrons
⊙⊙⊙ Mines
⊔⊔⊔ Beach barricade
⫽⫽⫽ Anti-tank ditches
CP Main command post

Guns:

■■ 8 inch
█ 140mm
▯ 127mm twin mount
⊙ 80mm
● 37mm to 75mm guns?
○ 70mm howitzers?
⊥ 70mm/75mm AA/DP guns?
▲ 13mm single MG
▲▲ 13mm twin MG

beaches - the Japanese knew that if the Americans could establish a landing force in substantial numbers anywhere on the island, then it was only a matter of time before the defenders would be overwhelmed. Betio is surrounded by a shelflike reef extending to between 800 and 1,200 yards off shore; here was the first natural obstacle - one that was to prove almost catastrophic to the Marines - and its improvement by the addition of pyramid-shaped concrete obstacles to the submerged coral would continue right up until the eventual US landings.

The Japanese cut down hundreds of palm trees from the adjoining islands to construct the various gun emplacements, barriers and shelters which their defensive plan required. Murakami expected the main attack to come from the open sea to the south of the island; and he had a ten-foot-high barricade, of coconut logs secured with wire and steel clamps, constructed off this shoreline in the shape of a wide, shallow V, one leg being 700 yards long and the other 300 yards. The purpose of this barricade was to channel landing craft into killing zones under heavy fire from artillery and machine guns. On the beach the Japanese constructed another barricade of coconut logs, three to five feet high, which extended around virtually the entire perimeter of the island; behind this wall were rifle and machine gun emplacements covered with logs, coral and sand, and concrete was poured to build enfilading pillboxes at intervals along it.

Anti-tank ditches were dug on the south shore and to the east and west of the airfield; these were only five to six feet deep, because the water table on the island was only eight to ten feet below the surface, but they were usually about fourteen feet wide and covered by enfilading machine gun posts sited at the ends. Mines were sown on the south and west coasts between the barricade and the shore, about 20 yards apart and in a double lane.

Sited at various strategic points around the island were fourteen heavy coastal defence guns, ranging in calibre from 8in (205mm) to 80mm; nineteen dual-purpose anti-aircraft guns of between 127mm and 70mm; more than 30 other artillery pieces ranging from 75mm mountain guns (pack howitzers) down to 37mm quick-firing light field guns; some 30 heavy 13mm machine guns; and an unknown but high number of 7.7mm infantry light machine guns, and mortars - the latter a type of weapon in whose use Japanese troops excelled.

Work had begun at an early date on the airfield, which dominated the centre of the island. This had a 4,000-foot main runway complete with taxiways and revetments for aircraft, and a second runway was still under construction at the time of the US landings. The main command post stood in the centre of the island just north of the airfield, an impressive reinforced concrete structure measuring 60ft by 40ft by some 25ft high, further protected by heaped sand and coral, with a twin 13mm machine gun post on the roof. It was from here that a number of steel pillbox mini-command posts were controlled by radio; these, situated at intervals of about 300 yards all round the perimeter of the island, controlled in turn the dozens of rifle and machine gun positions which lined the beach barricades[1].

In September 1943 Rear Admiral Shibasaki - a young, ambitious and ruthless

---

(1) See also Appendix 1 for a more detailed description of the Japanese defences.

commander - took over command of the island and its defenders. The Special Naval Landing Forces - the *rikusentai*, who are still commonly, if inaccurately, referred to as "Imperial Marines" - could trace their origins to the earliest days of the Imperial Japanese Navy. Initially they were deployed as small infantry units attached to naval ships, but over the years they developed into much larger combat units of highly trained and specialised amphibious infantry. With the outbreak of the war in 1941 they became Japan's shock troops, leading the invasions of Guam, Wake Island and the Solomons. By 1942 there were some 50,000 *rikusentai* based at various locations throughout the Pacific theatre. Their experience of amphibious warfare gave their commanders an expertise in this demanding discipline that no other power possessed. (Indeed, the only other large scale opposed amphibious operations up to that time had been the Gallipoli landings in the Dardanelles during World War I, which led to a stalemated ten-month campaign before withdrawal at a cost of over 162,000 British and Australian casualties.) On Betio the US Marines would face not ordinary Japanese Army units, as many of them believed, but the *rikusentai* of the Yokosuka 6th and Sasebo 7th SNLF - elite troops, familiar with the problems of amphibious operations, and specially trained in the use of a wide variety of weapons including artillery, machine guns, mortars and tanks; led by skilled and highly motivated officers; and imbued with the *bushido* philosophy of death before dishonour - the greatest dishonour being to allow oneself to be captured alive.

The orders of the Japanese forces were unambiguous: in the event of any Allied landings they were "to wait until the enemy is within effective range and direct your fire on the enemy transport group and destroy it. If the enemy starts a landing, knock out the landing boats with mountain gunfire, tank guns and infantry guns, then concentrate all fire on the enemy's landing point and destroy him at the water's edge."

Chapter 2:

The Best-Laid Plans...

Only by great risks can great results be achieved.

(Xerxes, 480 BC)

Shortly before the Battle of Midway in summer 1942 Admiral William F."Bull" Halsey, the commander of Task Force 16 in the South Pacific, was forced to go into hospital with a skin infection. When asked by his C-in-C Pacific, Adml Chester W.Nimitz, to name his temporary replacement Halsey chose Vice Adml Raymond A.Spruance. Nimitz was surprised at the choice - as was Ray Spruance. Born in Baltimore, he had graduated from the Naval Academy in 1906. In contrast to the extrovert Halsey, Spruance was noted for his austere and self-effacing character; he hated publicity, maintained only a small staff, and would usually fly his flag in a cruiser rather than a battleship. (After his victory in the Battle of the Philippine Sea in 1944 he would hide copies of *Time* magazine when they arrived on board with his picture on the cover.) Before Midway many more senior officers balked at the choice of a cruiser division commander to lead an aircraft carrier task force; but Halsey knew his man, and Spruance showed a remarkable aptitude in handling the carriers under his command. During the battle he came in for some criticism for turning from the pursuit of the remaining enemy warships as night fell; in fact Spruance showed an intelligent restraint, as the true strength of the Japanese force was unknown and his isolated command was running low on fuel. Nimitz's chief of staff for much of the war, Spruance's intelligence and ability would bring him command of most of the Central Pacific operations from Tarawa in November 1943 to Operation Iceberg, the invasion of Okinawa in April 1945.

Nimitz knew that the quiet, introverted Spruance was the man to organise what was now codenamed Operation Galvanic; he would fully appreciate the problems posed for the US Navy and Marines by their first major amphibious assault against a heavily defended island. Named for this operation as admiral commanding the US 5th Fleet (Fleet Flag, Central Pacific Force), Spruance was given an office at Pearl Harbor and began the selection of his planning team - but first he called in a squad of carpenters and, within a couple of days, visitors were astonished to find the admiral standing behind a makeshift wooden lectern from which all conversations were conducted. Gone were the tables, chairs and even the coffee pot; Spruance had his lectern, a telephone and wall maps - the rest he considered superfluous.

The Marshall Islands had originally been chosen for the start of the drive through the Central Pacific - certainly Maj Gen Holland M.Smith, commander of V Amphibious Corps and thus of all US Marines in the Central Pacific, favoured a direct attack on the Marshalls, leaving the Gilbert and Ellice Islands to wither on the vine. But Ray Spruance's caution prevailed: the Marshalls were too much of an unknown factor. Ceded to the Japanese in 1919, they had been virtually closed to foreigners ever since. US intelligence about the islands was vague, and the large Japanese naval base at Truk in the Carolines was too close for comfort. The Gilberts, only a few hundred miles south, were within easy reach of Funafuti, the US base in the Ellice Islands, and thus vulnerable to extensive aerial reconnaissance. As importantly, since the islands had until recently been British territory the Americans had access to a wide range of up-to-date information from British, Australian and New Zealand expatriates in the area. The Gilberts were the easier option for an operation whose novelty was already quite demanding enough.

Admiral Ernest King, the 63-year-old Chief of Naval Operations, was probably the most unpopular man in the US Navy; rude and humourless, he was warmly detested by - among others - both Winston Churchill and US Secretary of War Henry Stimson, and even Gen Eisenhower would write that "one thing that might help win this war is to get someone to shoot King". When he saw the plans for Operation Galvanic, King gave his general approval; but he also wanted the island of Nauru, 380 miles to the west of Tarawa, included in the programme. Spruance was horrified: aerial photographs had shown Nauru to be of no strategic value, and the Marines estimated that they would need a division to take it. His main worry was that if the Japanese mounted a naval counter-attack from Truk he would not be able to defend such a widely dispersed invasion fleet; and "one troopship sunk by a submarine could cause more casualties than the amphibious landings".

At a conference held in Hawaii on 24 September 1943, Holland Smith circulated a memorandum saying that Nauru was not a suitable target. "What would you substitute for Nauru?", growled Adml King after glancing at the paper. "Makin", said Smith and Spruance almost in unison. King remained silent, and the meeting continued; but on the 27th word came down from the Joint Chiefs of Staff - substitute Makin for Nauru. Both Smith and Spruance heaved sighs of relief, and the final choice of objectives for Galvanic was made: Tarawa, Makin, and Apamama - a small island 75 miles to the south-east of Tarawa.

★   ★   ★

Spruance could now set about selecting his team. At this stage of the war experienced field commanders were in short supply.

For the assault force, Task Force 54, he chose Vice Adml Richmond Kelly Turner; subordinate to this command would be Task Force 52, the Northern Attack Force for Makin led by Turner himself, and Rear Adml H.W.Hill's Task Force 53, the Southern Attack Force for Tarawa. "Terrible Turner's" experience of amphibious operations went back to 1935 when he had first begun to show an interest in what was then a rather obscure branch of the Navy curriculum. At the outbreak of war Turner had begged Adml King for the South Pacific amphibious command, and by June 1942 he was organising the Marines to land on Guadalcanal. Many hard lessons were learned in the early days; a shortage of amphibious craft, and of warships to protect them, led to severe losses, but Turner did the best that was possible with the available resources.

The mounting of an amphibious operation was a monumental task: the escort and protection of the lumbering, vulnerable troopship convoys; the co-ordination of air strikes by both land- and carrier-based aircraft; the timing of the shore bombardments by battleships and cruisers; the disembarkation of the Marines from transport ships into the frail craft which would carry them to the beaches, and getting them onto the right beach at the right time - each aspect of the commander's responsibilities carried with it the seeds of general disaster, while success depended upon every part of the plan dove-tailing.

By 1945 Adml Turner, as Commander of Amphibious Forces, Pacific Fleet, would be the world's leading practitioner of this demanding discipline, having organised and directed the landings on Guadalcanal, New Georgia, the Gilbert Islands, the Marianas, Iwo Jima and Okinawa. A hard taskmaster with an explosive temper, Turner had a phenomenal memory, amazing his staff with his ability to memorize sheaves of documents at a single reading - as at Iwo Jima, where he read some 3,000 messages a day which passed through his command ship. At a conference shortly before the Okinawa operation one senior officer was heard to remark to another, "They can replace me, and they can replace you, but there is no one to replace Kelly Turner."

The overall command of V Amphibious Corps was held by USMC Maj Gen Holland McTyeire Smith - "Howling Mad" Smith to his Marines. Here was another man with a short fuse who did not suffer fools gladly. He had set out on a career as a lawyer, but by 1905 he had had enough; in a dramatic rejection of his original path he joined the Marine Corps. America's entry into World War I found him as a captain, and he served with I Corps in France at Soissons, Champagne and St Mihiel. By the start of the war in Europe in 1939 the now Brig Gen Smith was involved in an amphibious training programme with the 1st Marine Brigade. He was associated in the development - with Andrew Jackson Higgins - of fast, shallow draught landing craft, and - with Donald Roebling - of an amphibious tractor; both of these craft were to prove invaluable in the Pacific theatre. In 1940 Smith carried out experiments in beachhead landings in the Caribbean, and built up a sound understanding of the problems involved in this highly specialised form of operations. Even before Pearl Harbor he was training both Marine and Army units, and in 1942 he ran courses in amphibious tactics on the West Coast.

By 1943 "Howling Mad" had managed to secure the transfer to combat duty which he had long sought; and would go on to command both Marine and Army personnel from the Tarawa landings right through to Iwo Jima. This Marine general's fiery temperament often got him into trouble, particularly for his uninhibited criticism of Army units during the Makin and Saipan landings; but although he had frequent clashes with Kelly Turner, these two large calibre personalities always managed to reconcile their differences.

The command of the 2nd Marine Division (Reinforced), charged with the assault on Tarawa, was given to Maj Gen Julian C.Smith in May 1943, just six months before the Gilbert Islands operations. A quiet, unassuming man who was highly respected by his fellow officers, Julian Smith had been born in 1885 in Elkton, Maryland; he was a graduate of the University of Delaware, and became a Marine Corps officer in 1919. Although he would serve in the Corps until 1946, retiring as a lieutenant general, Tarawa would be the peak of Julian Smith's military career.

The Makin operation, for which the troops would be provided by the 27th Infantry Division, would be led by yet another Smith - the US Army's Maj Gen Ralph Smith. Minor irritations surfaced soon after Spruance named Kelly Turner as the overall commander: Holland Smith resented being placed under the command of the Navy, while Ralph Smith was not happy about being subordinated to a Marine general. Spruance stood aside and watched with detached interest while the rival factions settled their turf wars.

To provide air cover and ground support, Task Force 50 was created under Rear Adml C.A.Pownell; this force was sub-divided into four groups. Task Group 50-1, with the carriers USS *Lexington, Cowpens* and *Yorktown*, three battleships and six destroyers under Pownell's direct command, was an Interceptor Group whose aim was to prevent any Japanese naval forces from the Marshall Islands from attacking the assault groups at Makin and Tarawa. Task Group 50-2, the Northern Carrier Group with the *Enterprise, Belleau Wood, Liscomb Bay* and *Monterey,* three battleships and six destroyers under Rear Adml A.W.Radford, was to operate in direct support of the Makin operations. Task Group 50-3, the Southern Carrier Group under Rear Adml A.E.Montgomery, would support the Tarawa operation with the carriers *Essex, Bunker Hill* and *Independence,* three heavy cruisers and five destroyers. Task Group 50-4, the Relief Carrier Group, had the *Saratoga* and *Princeton,* two light cruisers and four destroyers under Rear Adml F.C.Sherman; this force was to stand off ready to assist any of the other groups if required. It is something of a tribute to American industry that little more than eighteen months after Pearl Harbor they could field eleven aircraft carriers for the Gilberts operation.

★   ★   ★

Realising that sooner or later the Americans could be mounting attacks in either the Marshall or Gilbert Islands, the Japanese high command decided that as many reinforcements as possible should be brought out from the home islands. At a conference held in May 1943 at the naval base of Truk between the Commander-in-Chief South-East Area, Vice Adml Kusaka, and the C-in-C Second Fleet, Vice Adml Kondo, the decision was taken to bolster the existing air detachments in the Solomons and to increase the number of troops in both the Marshalls and the Gilberts. It was considered that the existing Second Fleet detachments at Truk would provide sufficient naval assets to cover any eventuality in those areas.

In the event of an invasion of the Gilbert Islands the admirals decided that they would initially employ long range bombers based in the Bismarck Islands, north of New Guinea, to attack the American invasion fleet as soon as it approached the area. Following up these attacks short range aircraft, dive bombers and torpedo bombers would be assembled at Truk from various outlying bases on Guam, the Palau group or the Marianas, and staged through to the Marshalls to attack the Americans. It was anticipated that it would take about four days to assemble this force. Warships of the Second Fleet would meanwhile sortie from Truk and meet the American invasion force off the Gilberts. With the assistance of six or seven submarines, which would be vectored from the Bismarck Islands, it was hoped that they could prevent the invasion force from landing.

This contingency plan was part of a comprehensive strategy for defending the outer limits of the Japanese Empire as it stood in 1943. Relying upon the rapid deployment of the Japanese fleet from Truk, the ability of the air forces to shuttle to any of the far-flung islands of the Central Pacific at short notice, and the ability of island garrisons to hold their positions long enough for the naval and air reinforcements to come to their assistance, it was a supremely optimistic strategy - particularly in view of the rapid increase in American land, sea and air power in the second part of 1943.

The vulnerability of the Japanese strategy was demonstrated when the US forces mounted a series of offensives in the Solomon Islands in the early days of November 1943. The 3rd Marine Division landed on Bougainville on 1 November. If Bougainville were to fall then Rabaul, the major Japanese base in the Solomons-New Guinea area, would be seriously threatened. Japanese air forces in the region had been suffering such heavy losses that reinforcements had to be drawn from as far afield as the Marshalls, the Marianas and even Celebes. The threat to Rabaul was considered so serious that the Japanese high command were prepared to weaken their defences in the Central Pacific in order to resist it. A large number of naval vessels were transferred from Truk to bolster the Rabaul defences; and while this force, consisting of cruisers and destroyers of the Second and Third Fleets, was refuelling at Rabaul, aircraft from the *Saratoga* and *Princeton* of Rear Adml F.C.Sherman's Task Group 50-4 carried out an early morning attack on 5 November. The Japanese warships immediately weighed anchor and attempted to escape to the open sea, but seven of the nine cruisers were so badly damaged that they had to return to the shipyards of Japan for repair. A further attack by TG50-4 a week later inflicted heavy damage on a number of cruisers, destroyers and supply ships.

As a result of the deployment of these naval and air forces to the Rabaul area, the 22nd Air Flotilla in the Marshall Islands and the naval forces based around the Marshalls and Truk were so weakened that they would be incapable of repelling any major landings in the Central Pacific islands. If an invasion came it would be up to the island garrison to resist the Americans as best they could.

*   *   *

In the temporary headquarters of the 2nd Marine Division at the Windsor Hotel in Wellington, New Zealand, detailed planning was under way in what was known as "Room K". In particular, aerial photographs of the whole of Tarawa Atoll and of Betio Island were being studied minutely.

Lt Col David M. Shoup had been appointed divisional operations officer; and to this stocky, aggressive, cigar-chewing 38-year-old (from the aptly named town of Battleground, Indiana) fell the task of planning the assault on Betio down to the finest detail. It was Shoup who devised a remarkable method of determining the number of Japanese on the island. Because Betio covered a total of only one square mile of land, the Japanese had built their latrines on wooden structures out over the reefs. By making a simple equation of the ratio of toilets to backsides, he came up with a figure that in retrospect proved to be amazingly accurate.

It was in Room K that the vital question of tides was first broached. Betio is surrounded by sloping reefs which extend from 800 to 1,200 yards out from the beach. A careful assessment of the Japanese defences had convinced the planners that they must attack from the lagoon side of the island on the northern shore. Three landing beaches were allocated: Red 1, from the north-western tip of the island eastwards across the width of the north-west cove; Red 2, from the end of the cove to the long wooden pier; and Red 3, from the pier to a point in line with the eastern end of the airfield (see maps). The depth of the water over the reef at the time of the landings was probably the most important single factor in the whole operation. A group of sixteen men who were familiar with the islands had been gathered to assist the Americans with their planning. Known as the "Foreign Legion", they were mainly British, New Zealand and Australian expatriates who had worked, lived or navigated around the Gilberts before 1942. Julian Smith and David Shoup were determined to extract every last bit of information that they could get from these local experts, and the state of the tides came top of the list.

There are two kinds of tide which change with the lunar cycle: spring tides and neap tides. Both of them have high and low daily tides, neap tides having less depth than spring tides. Neap tides occur during the first and third quarters of the moon; and Betio was due to be attacked during the neap phase. However, in some parts of the world - Tarawa included - there are "dodging" tides, and a low dodging tide is even lower than a low neap tide. The attack was scheduled when a dodging tide might occur.

Opinions varied among the "Foreign Legion": some thought that there would be ample clearance for all boats to reach the beaches, some thought that it would be touch and go. But one consistently dissenting voice was raised from the very beginning - that of Maj Frank Holland. Holland had lived on Tarawa for fifteen years before the war; various sources describe him as resident commissioner or as headmaster of the secondary school on Bairiki - the next island to Betio - and as either British or New Zealand by birth. Whatever his antecendents, there was no disputing his knowledge of the tides around Tarawa Atoll. Life during fifteen years on this remote speck in the endless ocean had proved more than a little boring at times, and to occupy his mind Holland had made a detailed study of the various tides all around the atoll. When he heard that the Marines were planning to make a landing on Betio on 20 November he was appalled; he knew that there would be a "dodging" tide at that time, giving no more than three feet of water over the reefs.

★   ★   ★

In one respect the depth of water might be - theoretically - irrelevant. The first three waves of 1,500 men were due to hit the beaches in what Navy nomenclature had christened LVTs (Landing Vehicles Tracked), known commercially as Alligators, Crocodiles or Water Buffaloes; in official Marinese, as "amphibian tractors"; but generally, and hereafter in this book, as "amtracs".

These remarkable vehicles, of which the original commercial model was designed by Donald Roebling as a rescue craft for the Florida Everglades, had impressed sharp-eyed Marine officers as early as 1937, and at their urging were finally ordered by the Navy's Bureau of Ships in 1941. The 1st Amphibian Tractor Battalion of the 1st Marine Division had completed organisation in February 1942; at that time its mission was seen solely as carrying supplies from ships off shore to the beach, and crawling up and a little beyond it - the caterpillar tracks would not stand up to much use on hard ground, and the LVT had an official service "life" of only 200 hours.

The LVT-1 model was 25ft long by 10ft 8ins wide and weighed around 10 tons; driven on land and water alike by caterpillar tracks powered by a 120hp engine, it was simply a floating open-topped box flanked by buoyancy compartments and tracked suspension, with a partly enclosed cab area above the snub-nosed bow, and made throughout from mild, unarmoured steel. It was capable of carrying about 20 men and a crew of four at a maximum of 4 knots in the water and 15mph on land. The LVT-2 model, which entered service in June 1942, featured an improved powertrain, suspension, and treads giving better traction; the carrying capacity was also increased by 1,500lbs; but it was still unarmoured. Although later variants would be better protected (and indeed, would include armoured LVT(A)s mounting tank turrets for direct fire support of the personnel carriers), the LVT always suffered from the disadvantage of having no landing craft style lowering ramp; all equipment had to be lifted over the side, and troops were vulnerable when disembarking during an opposed landing.

The divisional amtrac battalion had an establishment of 100 LVT-1s; but after hard service at Guadalcanal only 75 war-weary vehicles were actually available to the 2nd Division at Wellington. Very concerned by the conflicting opinions they were hearing about the tides, David Shoup and Julian Smith made their top priority the procurement of more amtracs, which seemed to offer the only certain way of getting their men onto the beaches. If Maj Holland was right, then only the first wave, in amtracs, were going to make it over the reef; the following waves of ramped landing craft - LCMs (Landing Craft Medium) carrying the tanks, and "Higgins boats" (LCVPs - Landing Craft Vehicle/Personnel) ferrying the rest of the infantry - would probably ground far from shore. The Marines would either have to be transferred to amtracs return-ing from the initial landings to run a shuttle service to the beach - or wade the rest of the way. . . . All in all, the more amtracs they had, the better[1].

Convinced by his divisional commander, "Howling Mad" Smith then contacted Adml Turner and demanded that more amtracs be made available. Kelly Turner - like most Navy officers at that date - had a poor opinion of the tractors: they were not "proper" craft, they were weak and unseaworthy, and the Marines' enthusiasm for them perhaps implied an irritating disregard for Navy expertise in such matters. He did not appreciate the need for any extra landing craft, and told Holland Smith that he considered that the boats already allocated would have to suffice as there was no time to go looking around for additional tractors. Feeling that his Marines were being short-changed, "Howling Mad" lived up to his name, and in the ensuing showdown gave Turner a simple ultima-tum: no extra amtracs, no Marine landings. Even Turner had to capitulate in the end, and urgent messages flashed between Hawaii and the USA. Eventually it was discovered that 50 of the improved LVT-2s were available on the West Coast; but time was too short to ship them out to Wellington and then to work up the unit with them before Galvanic.

An elaborate scheme was devised whereby the amtracs would be sent to American Samoa, where crews from New Zealand would meet them, train with them, and then ship out with them to rendezvous at sea with the Gilberts invasion force. On 14 October Capt R.D.Horner and the crews of the 2nd Amphibian Tractor Battalion's newly formed and at that date wholly theoretical "Company A1"[2] were sent to Samoa to collect their brand new tractors. In the meanwhile the battalion commander, Maj Harry Drewes, scoured the Wellington area for extra plate to provide some armour protection for his 75 worn-out LVT-1s. Eventually a supply of 9mm boiler-quality plate was found, and this was cut and welded onto the front cab area of the amtracs by the local General Motors plant in time for the invasion. To give the crews some means of hitting back under enemy fire mounts were also added for .50cal and .30cal machine guns. Major Drewes then followed his men to Samoa to familiarise Horner's company with the plans for Operation Galvanic. He received a shock when he arrived.

Due to the poor mechanical condition of the "brand new" vehicles, the company was only able to train for five days before leaving for the Gilberts. The LVT-2s had been standing in the open at San Diego for four or five months, and their poor state of maintenance cost Horner's company most of the three avail-able weeks in Samoa. During that period, however, they were able to add 40in x 26in sheets of 3/8in boilerplate to the cab fronts, and to mount a .50 cal and a

(1) The LCVP had a displacement of 11.5 tons loaded, measured 36ft x 10ft 6ins, had a loaded draught of 3ft 6ins, and carried 36 men or one 3-ton truck. A loaded LCM displaced 52 tons, measured 50ft x 14ft, had a draught of 4ft 6ins, and carried one 30-ton tank or 60 men. The larger LCTs were produced in various classes, from 322 to 2,160 tons loaded displacement, carrying from three to eighteen tanks and drawing from 4ft 6ins to 9ft 6ins.
(2) Identified in another source as Company D.

.30cal machine gun forward and a second .30cal aft. After their hasty few days' training the company were embarked aboard three LSTs (Landing Ships Transport) on 8 November, though not without difficulty: the elevators in the LSTs were unable to lift the amtracs to the upper decks, and they had to be stowed on the tank decks. The convoy arrived at Funafuti in the Ellice Islands on 12 November, where Maj Drewes conducted the only practice operation that time would permit. The company proceeded to Tarawa Atoll, arriving in the early hours of 20 November - D Day.

★　　　★　　　★

At his meeting with his corps commander Julian Smith also brought up the question of artillery support for the Betio landings. He wanted artillery to be landed on Bairiki - the island next east in line to Betio - to provide fire support for his Marines, and to prevent any Japanese evacuation of Betio to other islands of the atoll. This request was turned down on the grounds that the Japanese were thought capable of launching a combined air and submarine attack on the invasion fleet within three days of the attack; Holland Smith was not prepared to risk having a second assault force lying offshore and partially loaded. Julian Smith was unhappy with this decision, even to the extent of having the operational plan worded to show that the 2nd Division had been directed to seize Betio before turning their attention to any other island of Tarawa Atoll - he was not going to have it said that this was his decision.

★　　　★　　　★

The 2nd Marine Division was born at Camp Elliott, California, on 1 February 1941, and it could be argued that its lineage could be traced to the famous 6th Marine Regiment of the Great War. At Chateau Thierry the collapsing French Army expected the newly arrived Marines to retreat with them under the weight of a fierce German offensive, but the words of a Marine captain aptly conveyed the feelings of the 6th: "Retreat, hell! We just got here." At Belleau Wood the 6th suffered casualties of over 1,000 killed and wounded in 24 hours.

In May 1941 the division's 6th Regiment was shipped to Iceland to take over the defence of that barren land from the British. The 2nd and 8th Regiments and the gunners of the 10th Marines remained in California, while the engineer batallion were sent to Hawaii to work on the construction of Camp Catlin, halfway between Pearl Harbor and Honolulu. When the attack on Pearl Harbor caused near-panic on the American West Coast the 2nd Division Marines from Camp Elliott were dispersed to defend California from what many thought would be imminent invasion.

Once the hysteria had subsided the Marines regrouped; and on 6 January 1942 the 8th Regiment sailed from San Diego for American Samoa. The trip afforded the Marines a touch of unaccustomed luxury when they departed in three cruise liners, with civilian steward service and comfortable beds. On Samoa they were hastily put to work building artillery emplacements, an airfield and coastal defences to repel an expected Japanese invasion; but as the months passed the only attackers who materialised were the mosquitoes. Meanwhile the rest of the 2nd Division remained in California, and were dubbed the "Home Guard" by their comrades in the 6th and 8th Regiments, respectively shivering in Iceland and sweating in the tropics but at least on active service overseas. When it became obvious that the Germans had no intention of attempting an invasion of Iceland, the 6th Marines returned to Camp Elliott, to be followed by the engineers after they had completed their work in Hawaii.

The tide of war in the Pacific turned at Midway, and America went onto the offensive. On 7 August 1942 the first troops of the 2nd Division landed in the Solomon Islands in what was initially intended as a limited offensive aimed at the capture of Rabaul, the Japanese stronghold on the northern tip of the island of New Britain. The 1st Marine Division were given the task of capturing the unfinished airfield south of Lunga Point on Guadalcanal, while the 2nd Division attacked Tulagi and Gavutu Islands to the north. Although the first landings on Guadalcanal were unopposed, very heavy Japanese naval and land counter-attacks resulted in the temporary withdrawal of US naval forces, leaving the Marines to fight on their own. In a protracted campaign which lasted until February 1943 the 2nd Division - who sent part of their force over "the Slot" to Guadalcanal to reinforce the 1st - had 263 men killed in action and 932 wounded. Tropical diseases accounted for the indisposition of at least 95% of the force: malaria and dengue fever were rife, as were fungal complaints caused by prolonged sweating and the chafing of their filthy uniforms.

The 2nd Division have always resented the fact that this campaign was largely credited to the 1st Division, whose defence of the airfield on Guadalcanal at the Battle of Bloody Ridge in September 1942 attracted the attention of the news media, who referred to the 2nd Division as "reserves."

By February 1943 Guadalcanal was declared secure; the Marines said goodbye and good riddance to the rotting jungles, weeping sores and mosquitoes of the Solomons, and on 1 March they reassembled in New Zealand. After six months of bitter combat against a fanatically brave enemy, strength-sapping heat, inadequate food and voracious insect life, the lush coolness of New Zealand seemed something like paradise to the Marines of the 2nd Division. As their ships sailed into Wellington harbour the sight of neat houses, green parks, smart hotels and friendly people was a shock that most had difficulty absorbing; to many of them the New Zealand capital, with its hills rising steeply from the bay, was reminiscent of San Francisco, and to all of them it was a joy.

With nearly 20,000 men the division was far too large to be housed in any one location, so camps were erected at various points in the Wellington district. The 8th Marines were only three-quarters of a mile out of town; the 6th and 2nd Regiments went to Camps Russell and McKay, two miles out, and the 2nd Tank Bn and Special Weapons Bn were located at Titahi Bay. The 18th Engineers went to Judgeford Valley and the artillerymen of the 10th to Pahautanui, eighteen miles from Wellington, while the divisional HQ was set up in the centre of the city in the Windsor Hotel.

After six months in the Solomons there were still many sick and wounded, with the malaria cases far exceeding the walking wounded; and for quite a time the hospitals at Anderson Park and Silverstream would be working at full capacity. Initially the Marines were allowed a period of relaxation after their rough time on Guadalcanal and Tulagi. The New Zealanders opened their homes and their hearts to the visitors; the Marines began to learn the English ritual of afternoon tea, and faced up to unchilled beer like men. Romance was in the air, and over the months that the division spent in New Zealand hundreds of Marines married local sweethearts. There was time to look around and explore this remotely beautiful country; trips were organised to see the geysers at Rotorua, and four or five hundred troops went each week to the South Island. Despite wartime rationing the New Zealanders were even given a special allowance of petrol to enable them to show their visitors around. Clubs were set up in Wellington, and USO concerts were arranged - a visit by the famous bandleader Artie Shaw was particularly well received. The camps for the Marines were pretty makeshift affairs, mainly tented with a few wooden huts; but there were few complaints.

After a few months the euphoria gradually faded as the business of preparing for the next battle got under way. Training became the order of the day. Replacements arrived to fill the gaps - in some units these new faces made up 55% of the total strength - and the Marines sensed that action was not far away. Amphibious assault exercises were carried out at Hawke Bay, and the Amphibian Tractor Bn made practice landings under fire from live ammunition. The newly arrived Sherman tanks for the additional medium company attached to the 2nd Tank Bn were put through their roaring, clanking paces. There were also changes at command level, as names which were to become very familiar in the forthcoming battle for Tarawa took over their units. When Julian Smith became commanding general in May, Col Leo Hermle was promoted to the rank of brigadier general as assistant divisional commander, with Col Merritt ("Red Mike") Edson as chief of staff. During August the senior staff were informed that Tarawa was the division's next destination, and the lights burned ever later in the Windsor Hotel.

★   ★   ★

In late 1943 the strength of the basic US Marine division (with assigned Navy personnel such as medical corpsmen, the "SeaBees" of the Naval Construction Bn, etc.) was officially 19,965 men. A headquarters battalion controlled and co-ordinated the various elements, which were organised in a "triangular" manner: in three-strong series, so that support and service units could be split at need for attachment to combat units right down the chain of organisation.

The core of the division's fighting strength was provided by three infantry regiments (in the 2nd Division, the 2nd, 6th and 8th Marines) each officially with 3,242 men. Each regiment had a headquarters and service company, a weapons company with 37mm and 75mm anti-tank guns, and three numbered battalions each of 953 all ranks; the abbreviated form used in this book is e.g. 2-6 for 2nd Battalion, 6th Marine Regiment. As in most armies, above the level of his immediate buddies in the platoon the individual's highest practical focus of loyalty - the extended family throughout which he might recognize familiar faces, names and reputations - was the battalion. Each battalion had an HQ company, plus three rifle companies and a weapons company each identified by a letter (A-D in 1st Bn, E-H in 2nd Bn, and I, K, L, M in 3rd Bn, the weapons companies normally being D, H and M). The battalion weapons company in 1943 comprised an anti-aircraft platoon (four 20mm cannon), a mortar platoon (four 81mm tubes), and three machine gun platoons each with four heavy, water-cooled, belt-fed .30cal Browning M1917A1 guns.

Each rifle company had a headquarters element, three rifle platoons and a weapons platoon. The company weapons platoon had five .30cal M1919A4 air-cooled, belt-fed light machine guns and three 60mm mortars. The rifle platoon at full strength numbered 42 men. The platoon headquarters consisted of a second lieutenant platoon leader, the platoon sergeant, and five radio operators and runners. Each of the three nine-man rifle squads was led by a sergeant, seconded by a corporal, with two scouts, three riflemen, one automatic rifleman, and a rifle grenadier; the fourth, automatic rifle squad had a squad leader, two automatic riflemen and five riflemen or assistants.

The basic personal weapon of the infantryman was the M1 .30cal Garand rifle, a trail-blazing semi-automatic weapon which fired eight rounds as fast as the soldier could pull the trigger. This gave the US infantryman much superior firepower to his Japanese enemy armed with a five-shot Arisaka rifle which had to be reloaded by working the bolt after each shot (although the tactical realities of assaulting against a well dug-in enemy often rendered this advantage fairly academic). Some snipers and rifle grenadiers still carried the slower-firing, simpler M1903 .30cal Springfield bolt action rifle. The squad automatic was the .30cal M1918A2 Browning Automatic Rifle, fed by 20-round magazines.

Some junior leader ranks, and enlisted men with encumbering duties (e.g. members of heavy weapons crews) carried .45cal semi-automatic pistols and/or .30cal M1 carbines: the latter were light and handy, but notoriously lacked stopping power. Hollywood notwithstanding, the issue of .45cal M1/M1A1 Thompson sub-machine guns was officially limited to divisional scout and MP companies, though individual enthusiasts in line units sometimes obtained them. Another "exotic" weapon was in fact allotted on a relatively generous scale of 100 to each regiment: the 12-guage Winchester M1897 or M1912 pump-action shotgun, popular with the USMC since the Latin American "Banana Wars" of the 1920s-30s, for close combat and clearing trenches and bunkers. At least four hand grenades were also issued to be carried by every infantryman.

This was the theoretical shape and firepower of the Marine assault units; but it is important to remember that this neat pattern of organisation and equipment seldom survived the beginning of a hard-fought infantry action for long. Men fell - often, the junior leaders - to be replaced by the next man in the chain of command, or simply by an individual whose courage and leadership qualities rose to the moment of challenge. Vital equipment was destroyed or lost, or simply malfunctioned; individuals and small groups, sometimes whole platoons, went astray in the disorienting confusion of battle, and lost their chain of command. The ranks, skills and tools available to any particular group of fighting men quickly became almost random. The men left standing at a given place and moment had to do what needed to be done with what was to hand. That has always been the reality of combat; and that is what reveals the character and temper of men and battalions, upon which the outcome will always turn on the red day of battle.

* * *

Supporting the infantry, and doomed to be subject to the same varying confusions once ashore (aggravated by the greater bulk and complexity of their equipment), the division also had an integral artillery regiment - in the 2nd Division, the 10th Marines - with five battalions: in 1943, three of 75mm and two of 105mm howitzers, each fielding a headquarters and three six-gun batteries. The integral engineer regiment (18th Marines) incorporated one each engineer, pioneer and US Navy "SeaBee" construction battalions. The division's battalion of M3A1 Stuart light tanks had three companies each with a three-tank headquarters and three five-tank platoons; and Co D, the scout company, which for Operation Galvanic would leave its armoured scout cars and motorcycles behind and would fight as infantry. The division also had its own integral service, transport, medical, special weapons (anti-aircraft and anti-tank), and amphibious tractor battalions, normally bearing the division's number; and smaller units of signals, military police, and other specialist categories.

For battle, experience had shown that the division's units were best organised into separate and to some degree self-sufficient "combat teams" (late in 1943 the term "regimental landing team" was substituted). For Operation Longsuit on Tarawa it was intended that the 2nd Marine Division (Reinforced) should send its assault troops ashore in RLTs each comprising a number of infantry battalions with an attached artillery battalion and tank, engineer, pioneer, medical and amphibian tractor companies under command. Some additional assets from V Amphibious Corps - such as the M4A2 Sherman tanks of Co C, 1st Corps Tank Bn (Medium) - would also be attached for this operation[1].

* * *

As preparations matured for the division's departure, secretly scheduled for 1 November 1943, elaborate plans were hatched to disguise the real nature of the operation. Rumours were deliberately circulated that the men were just off on a routine landing exercise to Hawke Bay, and fake arrangements were even made for their return to the various camps. Julian Smith took Col Shoup on a courtesy visit to the Governor General to inform him of their imminent departure, and to thank him on behalf of the Marines for the kindness of the New Zealand people. For any Marine walking his Kiwi girlfriend along Lambton Quay, the sight of the ever-increasing number of troop and supply ships could have only one, ominous meaning.

(1) See Appendix 4 for details of task organisation.

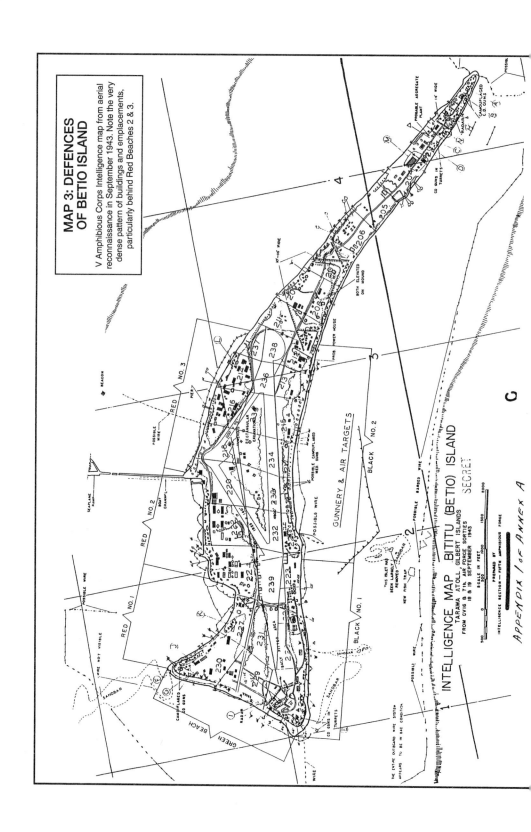

MAP 3: DEFENCES OF BETIO ISLAND

V Amphibious Corps Intelligence map from aerial reconnaissance in September 1943. Note the very dense pattern of buildings and emplacements, particularly behind Red Beaches 2 & 3.

INTELLIGENCE MAP, BITITU (BETIO) ISLAND
TARAWA ATOLL, GILBERT ISLANDS
FROM CV16 & 7th AIR FORCE SORTIES
18 & 19 SEPTEMBER 1943

SECRET

PREPARED BY
INTELLIGENCE SECTION— FIFTH AMPHIBIOUS FORCE

APPENDIX I OF ANNEX A

Sergeant Raymond Knight of the 3-8, who sailed from New Zealand in the troopship *Monrovia*, remembers the last night in Wellington harbour:

"We were all restricted to ship, no one could get liberty. Since a lot of the Marines had steady girlfriends there, a lot of them slid down the ropes that were holding the boat to the docks to spend one last time with them. I remember I had Sergeant of the Guard and was on the quarterdeck with the Officer of the Day at about daylight. I happened to walk over to the port side of the ship, and noticed four men out of my squad on the dock with the idea of slipping back aboard. They were in dungarees because we had stowed our dress uniforms in our seabags, so all any of us had was our camouflage dungarees. I saw the Officer of the Day looking the other way and motioned them not to come aboard yet while he was there. He was a Navy officer, and not in our outfit. He told me after a few minutes that he was going for a cup of coffee. As soon as he left I hollered down and told them to pick up some garbage cans and carry them aboard. It was a good decision, because as they were coming up the gang plank he came back and inquired who these Marines were coming aboard. I said 'Garbage details, Sir', and he let them pass. . . ."

Although the people of Wellington had become used to seeing masses of shipping in the port, there still seemed to be something unusual about the movements in the harbour on 1 November. Those with a good view could see the troopships in a single column, led by escorting destroyers, heading for the open sea. The Marines who had become a part of New Zealand's wartime life were leaving their shores, and though they did not at once know it, never to return; in what seemed an extraordinarily short time not a ship was in sight.

New Zealand is a small country, and Wellington a little city; for eight months something like a holiday spirit had prevailed, and now it had come to an abrupt end. These young Americans had won the hearts of the Dominion, and had been proudly proclaimed as "New Zealand's own Marine Division" - the only one they ever had. Now Wellington seemed almost deserted; and although some sensed that they were seeing history in the making, a sadness settled over the country as life returned to normal.

Quietly lining the rails of the troopships, the Marines of the 2nd Division gazed upon the receding New Zealand coastline, little knowing that hardly any of them would be returning there. After Tarawa they would be going on to Hawaii to prepare for the next island on the road to Japan. Many would get no further than Tarawa.

Major Frank Holland, the old Gilberts hand, was still accosting anyone who would listen with his forebodings about the dodging tide; but the consensus had been that the planning was too far advanced to put back the landings until December, when the water would be deep enough to satisfy all opinions. The masses of ships and troops could not be kept waiting around for another three or four weeks. The forlorn corpses of scores of Marines would bob in the milky waters of Tarawa lagoon in silent condemnation of the intransigence of the men who ignored Frank Holland's warning.

On 6 November the convoy reached Efate in the New Hebrides. Here the final amphibious rehearsals were carried out, with landings at Mele Bay while the support ships practiced their gunnery on Pango Point. It was during these manoeuvres that Col William Marshall, the designated leader of Regimental Landing Team 2 - comprising the three battalions of the 2nd Marines and the 2-8 - suffered a minor heart attack. Despite his protests he obviously could not be allowed to continue in such a responsible position; and he was replaced by the obvious choice. David Shoup, who had planned so much of the operation, was now given the task of implementing its most critical phase. The Task Force weighed anchor at Efate on 13 November, and on the 17th met up with the convoy sailing from Hawaii with the Army's 27th Infantry Division bound for Makin.

The Transport Group of the Southern Attack Force bound for Tarawa and Apamama - TG53-1 - comprised Transport Division 4 carrying the reinforced 2nd Marines aboard the *Zeilin, Heywood, Middleton, Biddle, Lee* and *Thuban*; TD18, carrying most of the 8th Marines and divisional troops aboard the *Monrovia, Sheridan, Lasalle, Doyen, Virgo* and *Ashland*; and TD6, carrying the 6th Marines aboard the *Harris, Bell, Ormsby, Feland*, and *Bellatrix*.

Task Group 53-4, Adml Kingman's Support Group, comprised the battleships *Tennessee, Maryland* (Adml Hill's flag) and *Colorado*; the heavy cruisers *Indianapolis* (Adml Spruance's flag)[1] and *Portland*; the light cruisers *Mobile, Birmingham*, and *Santa Fe*; and the destroyers *Bailey, Frazer, Gansevoort, Meade, Anderson, Russell, Ringgold, Dashiell* and *Schroeder*.

As the armada sailed northward towards the equator the Marines were finally told of their destination. Many had laid bets that they were about to recapture Wake, the small American island overrun by the Japanese in December 1941; now they were told that their objective was the Gilberts, although the island of Betio was referred to by the codename "Helen".

✦　　　✦　　　✦

In the early hours of 20 November the troopship *Arthur Middleton* lay still in the water some six or seven miles north-west of Betio. Bob Libby, a 21-year-old private first class in the mortar platoon of M Company, 3-2, had decided to come topside for a little air. "It was pitch dark, so dark in fact that it was impossible to see the outline of any object against the sky. Groping my way to the rail, I leaned against a davit and listened to the drone of the ship's ventilators. I knew that we must be near to our objective, and was glad to be up in the fresh air away from the hot, stuffy troop compartments."

In the silence he remembered the good times that he and his buddies had

---

(1) Notoriously, sunk by a Japanese submarine on the night of 30 July 1945 while sailing alone from Guam to Leyte. Of the crew of 1,196, some 900 took to the water; but due to the secrecy of her outbound mission - delivering one of the atomic bombs - and through failures of reporting procedures, no one knew that she had been sunk for four days. Only 300 men survived injuries, thirst and shark attacks to be rescued after a chance aircraft sighting.

enjoyed in Wellington, but thought mostly of the new bride that he had left behind there. Suddenly his reverie was shattered by a brilliant flash and the thunder of a naval gun opening fire on the islands to their stern. He watched the solitary shell explode in a fireball on the island. Within moments ships of all sizes - battleships, cruisers and destroyers - joined in a crescendo of fire that heralded the beginning of one of the heaviest and most concentrated naval bombardments of the war. The ship's speaker system called all troops to lay below to their stations and, with a last look at the fires that were now raging on the island, Libby made his way below decks. It was a scene of turmoil, with Marines moving their heavier equipment towards the ladders in preparation for the call to their boat stations on the upper deck.

"Then the action began - each platoon of troops was called to move topside and to their boat stations. Gradually the compartments emptied, and as I looked around I couldn't help wondering how many of these men I would see again. For some inexplicable reason, I had no doubts about my own survival - I don't think that a soldier going into action ever does, you know that people are going to get killed but you have to believe that it isn't going to be you.

"Ours was the next group to get the call, and hoisting our gear we proceeded to the deck - it was now daylight and the water astern of the troopships was a mass of landing craft, circling and manoeuvring to their allocated positions. Off to the south we could see great columns of oily smoke rising from an island - 'Helen', presumably. I guessed that it was around twelve miles away.

"We had practiced time and time again this phase of our disembarkation from ship to sea, and had no problems. Around this time the Japanese began to bring their guns to bear on us; one shell landed pretty close to. . . the troopship that we had just left, and immediately the ship moved further out to sea. The enemy gunfire only lasted for a short time, we all assumed that our naval gunfire had silenced them in short order. I got the impression that someone was having problems getting the show organised, as the landing time was altered several times; then eventually the circling stopped, and I noticed that we were all strung out in columns and heading for the point of departure."

Chapter 3:

The Red Beaches - Morning

In landing operations, retreat is impossible.

(Gen George S.Patton)

In the pre-dawn darkness of Saturday 20 November the invasion fleet lay in position off the shores of Betio Island, waiting to launch Operation Longsuit. The optimists were still in high spirits; as yet there was no sign of life on the island. Robert Sherrod, a war correspondent with *Time Life*, was aboard the troopship *Zeilin* with the 2-2; he recalled, "Try as I might I never got over the feeling that the Japs had pulled out of Tarawa - not until the first bullet whizzed by my ear." The capital ships of Adml Kingman's Support Group had taken up their positions off the west end of the island to enable the battlewagons and cruisers to fire right down the two-and-a-half mile length of Betio, the way their forefathers had raked the whole gundeck of an enemy man-o'-war by sending broadsides through her stern. The nimbler minesweepers - USS *Requisite* and *Pursuit* - and the destroyers *Ringgold* and *Dashiell* were stationed off the entrance to the lagoon, ready to clear a passage for the landing craft and to give close fire support.

During the planning of the operation B24 Liberator heavy bombers of the 7th Air Force operating from Funafuti in the Ellice Islands had carried out photo-reconnaissance sorties over Tarawa, providing invaluable information on the reefs, beaches, gun emplacements and other details to the teams in the Windsor Hotel. The Liberators had also carried out heavy bombing raids during April, destroying many Japanese aircraft on Betio airfield together with other military targets.

Shoup had requested that the B24s drop "daisy cutters" - 500lb bombs fused to detonate a few feet above ground level - all along the beaches on the north side of Betio early on D Day. Both he and Merritt Edson were confident that such an attack would cause major casualties among the Japanese personnel manning the many gun emplacements covering the proposed landing beaches. It was a sound idea, but unfortunately the raid never materialised; for some unexplained reason the Marines' request never reached the 7th Air Force, and a wonderful opportunity to cut back the enemy firepower on the Red Beaches was lost.

"As we drew nearer to D Day, I remember there was no great apprehension; it seemed the prevailing attitude was that this was going to be an easy one. 'The naval bombardment alone would probably sink the island' was the phrase I most remember - considering the size of Tarawa, that didn't seem so far-fetched", recalls Ralph Butler, who was among the 3-2 aboard the *Arthur Middleton*.

By 3am the seventeen transports had finally assembled in the planned formation, and the laborious task of disembarking the troops could get under way. The amtracs and box-like LCVPs were put into the water, and found their places in the cab ranks to come alongside the troop transports. Although the Marines had practiced this manoeuvre many times before there were still some casualties from falls and crush injuries. Climbing over the side of a tall troopship in almost complete darkness, down scrambling nets and into landing craft which are bobbing up and down in a choppy sea, is not the ideal way of leaving a ship.

This feat had to be performed under the burden of anything up to 100lbs of equipment; apart from their own packs and rifles, BARs or carbines many Marines were carrying extra items for the assault - radios, mortars and machine guns broken down into man-loads, the huge quantities of ammunition which crew-served weapons consume, flame throwers, demolition charges, boxes of grenades. Photos show Marines in the Tarawa landing force encumbered with gasmasks, and with life preservers - inflatable rubber rings worn round the waist, whose value was more psychological than practical. Thus burdened, the Marines clambered awkwardly down the nets, gripping the vertical ropes of the mesh to avoid having their hands trampled by the boots of the man above, and keeping a wary eye downwards on the black gap which opened and closed like crushing jaws between the landing craft and the ship's hull.

The battalions committed to Operation Longsuit on 20 November wore a mixture of two different sets of uniform: some units in the old 1941 sage green utilities, and some with the new 1942 camouflage-printed outfit, both made of herringbone twill - shapeless jackets and loose-cut trousers in material roughly similar to modern denim. Both green "dungarees" and the new camouflage uniform - originally exclusive to snipers and Raider battalions, but by late 1943 on general issue in some infantry units - bore the familiar black USMC and "bird-on-a-ball" stencils on the left breast. Photos show some men on Betio wearing camouflage jackets with green trousers if they could not get a complete set; it seems to have been a desirable novelty. The camouflage uniform was reversible, one side printed with a pattern of spots in greens and browns on pale drab, the other with browns only on a beige background.

Like so many ideas dreamed up in peaceful design shops, it seemed sensible at the time: the Marines could wear exposed whichever side best matched the local vegetation (the designer was a learned horticulturalist). Unfortunately, blending into dappled jungle twilight was not an option on most Pacific beaches, where a man in a spotted suit stood out rather starkly against sand and sea; and after the Tarawa and Bougainville fighting in late 1943 its use by assault units declined. These suits were normally worn green-side-out; in wartime photos men wearing them brown-side-out stand out much paler.

One part of the camouflage uniform which was already very widely worn and would become for many years a Marine trademark was the printed cloth cover for the M1 steel helmet. This had deep flaps all round, trapped between the steel shell and the fibre helmet liner, which some men untucked at the back to make a sun curtain. On his feet the Marine wore "boondockers" - ankle length brown leather boots made flesh side out for a matt finish. He was also supposed to wear canvas web leggings extending from instep to calf; but these were unpopular in the Pacific and by now often discarded - they were hot, they trapped water, and the many eyelets of the fastening laces made them difficult to get off when trying to treat wounds. Marines sometimes wore them under the untucked dungaree legs.

The web equipment - to the Marine, "782 gear" - comprised his basic fighting harness and his subsistence load; usually only the upper haversack of the M1941 two-part pack system was carried in the assault. His rifle belt held ammo clips in eight snap-fastened pockets; a field dressing pouch; one or two aluminium or steel water canteens in their web carriers, and perhaps a K-Bar sheath knife. Shoulder suspenders supported the belt front and back and linked it to the web haversack, worn behind the shoulders and containing eating and washing kit, combat rations, utility cap, spare underclothes, extra ammunition, and anything else that could be crammed in. The bayonet, and the entrenching spade or other assigned tool, were hooked to tabs on the haversack; some men carried hatchets or machetes, some the medical corpsman's huge "bolo" knife. The pack had straps for stowing a rolled blanket, raincoat and/or shelter half; in November

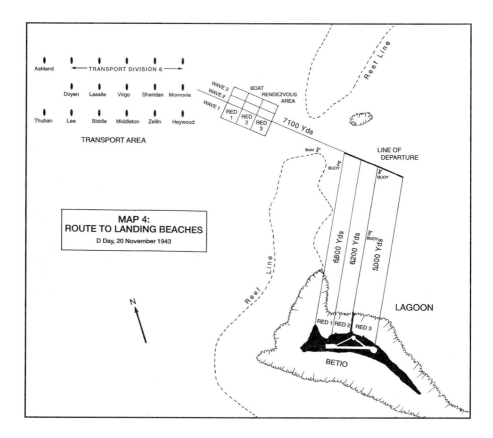

MAP 4:
ROUTE TO LANDING BEACHES
D Day, 20 November 1943

1943 the usual item visible here was the rubberized canvas poncho printed in the same reversible camouflage patterns as the pattern 1942 utilities.

In his limited pocket space - the dungarees lacked the big cargo pockets of later patterns - the Marine carried grenades, and probably an extra field dressing, his smokes, perhaps chewing gum or hard candy; and whatever small but desperately important mementoes of home and loved ones he clung to on the eve of battle.

★   ★   ★

Many eyes on many ships were keeping watch on Betio - at 4.41am all heads turned as a single red star shell sped into the sky from the centre of the island, hung in the air for what seemed to be minutes, and lazily dropped to earth. Any lingering hopes that the Japanese had pulled out of Tarawa were gone.

All remained quiet on the island for the time being, and off shore the disembarkations were well under way. As each landing craft collected its load of Marines it chugged away to join a circling pattern to the rear of the transports. Dawn was due at around 5am, and there was no time to waste.

At about 5.05am Adml Hill's flagship, the battleship *Maryland*, launched its Vought Kingfisher spotter plane; its task was to observe the imminent naval bombardment and to radio back any necessary corrections to the fall of shot. Seeing the red flash from the ship's launch catapult, the commander of the Japanese 8in guns at Temakin Point on the south-west headland of Betio opened fire on the *Maryland*, and the first shell erupted in the sea 500 feet beyond the huge ship. The US Navy battleships and cruisers swung around, and one battleship fired a salvo from its 16in guns at the island. The Marines in their landing craft listened and watched in awe as the massive shells - each as tall as a man and weighing over a ton - howled over their heads and crashed down into the lagoon just short of the island. From the *Maryland* orders were given for an all-out bombardment to commence, her captain signalling the rest of the Support Group, "Commence firing, the war is on."

On the flagship the aft 16in guns fired with a blast that made the old ship shudder; dust spurted from every crevice, crumbled insulation showered down from the deckheads, and as the forward turrets joined in the bombardment several lights went out - and the radios began to malfunction. . . Other battleships and cruisers opened fire, lighting up the sea with monstrous flashes, and the noise became unimaginable as salvo after salvo thundered across the water. Within minutes there was a massive explosion near the centre of Betio as an ammunition dump exploded, flame-lit black clouds billowed skyward, and for minutes the palm trees were starkly silhouetted against the blaze.

At 5.42am, as suddenly as it had started, the bombardment ceased. Admiral Hill had learned that the troopships were in the wrong position; a strong current had been carrying them southwards, and now they were not only shielding the field of fire of the warships but were within range of the enemy guns on the western end of the island, which would drop several shells dangerously close to the transports *Lasalle* and *Harris*. As the troopships laboriously worked their way northwards to their newly allocated positions the landing craft raced behind them like ducklings trying to keep up with their mothers.

As yet nobody seems to have realised to what extent these manoeuvres would delay the timing of the whole operation. As time passed, and no more shells fell on the shattered island, Adml Shibasaki took advantage of the respite to move troops and such guns as could be manhandled from the southern shore to the defences facing the lagoon, from which it was now obvious that the landings would come.

*　　　　*　　　　*

Throughout the whole of Operation Galvanic, Adml Spruance was naturally preoccupied by the possibility of a major Japanese naval and air counter-attack. By late 1943 the desperate days of Midway, when the security of the Hawaiian Islands depended upon just three aircraft carriers, were just a memory. American yards were turning out warships for the Pacific at a phenomenal rate; Spruance's total command for Galvanic was an enormously powerful battle fleet by the standards of two years before, and he was confident that he could repel any enemy force in a set-piece engagement. But he was not free to fight a fleet action - his responsibility for the invasion forces was paramount, and it weighed upon him. Once the process of disgorging troops and supplies got under way the transports, with their thousands of precious lives, were extremely vulnerable to air and submarine attack.

The two senior commanders with the most experience in amphibious tactics - Kelly Turner and Holland Smith - had both elected to be with the landing force for Makin; this was the less important and hazardous of the two main objectives, but the two officers presumably felt that an operation by untried Army troops required closer personal supervision. Although Adml Spruance was present at Tarawa - off the south shore of Betio aboard *Indianopolis* - his duty was the overall command of Galvanic, and his mind was understandably turned not towards the lagoon, but outwards towards the horizon over which any threat to the totality of his operation might come. The conduct of local operations had been properly delegated, and his command presence at Tarawa was at best unobtrusive.

*　　　　*　　　　*

On the bridge of the *Maryland* Adml Harry Hill and Maj Gen Julian Smith were scanning the skies for the carrier-based aircraft which were due to launch a preparatory strike at 5.50am. They were late; but Hill found that he could not contact the carriers because of the problems with his radio equipment.

At around 6.12am the minesweepers USS *Pursuit* and *Requisite* began to sweep the entrance to the lagoon; the former was piloted by Lt Forbes of the Royal New Zealand Navy, who was familiar with these waters.

At 6.15am, just as Adml Hill was about to decide that he could delay no longer, the carrier aircraft arrived. The Dauntless and Avenger bombers and Hellcat fighters ranged the length of Betio for seven minutes - the planning had called for a much longer strike - before wheeling away to re-group and fly back to the

Essex, Bunker Hill and *Independence.*

Once a clear passage had been swept the destroyer USS *Ringgold* (also conned by a New Zealand pilot, Lt Gordon Webster) entered the lagoon and immediately engaged Japanese shore batteries which had been shelling the minesweepers. The *Pursuit* now took up station at the "line of departure" - the final assembly and jumping-off point for the assault waves - and shone a searchlight to guide the little landing craft through the smoke and dust that was drifting over from the fires on Betio.

Inside the lagoon the *Ringgold*, protected only by her power to manoeuvre, was soon fighting her own deadly little battle. Within minutes she had been hit by a 5in shell in the port engine room, and seconds later another shell hit the forward torpedo mount, deflected through the sick bay and on into the emergency radio room. Luckily, neither shell exploded - one was carried on deck in the arms of a seaman and dumped overboard. Locating the shore battery that was causing the trouble, the *Ringgold* sent a well-aimed salvo into its ammunition dump and the battery and its crew vanished in a massive explosion.

It was at about 7.35am that the main bombardment of Betio by the Support Group recommenced. For an hour and twenty minutes three battleships and four cruisers blasted the tiny island from end to end. Great gouts of sand and coral erupted into the sky, and palm trees were ripped up and tossed apart as the ground was churned over yard by yard. More ammunition dumps exploded, and a great pall of black smoke from a fuel store rose to thicken the shroud of dust hanging over the island. This was the most concentrated pre-invasion bombardment, per square yard of ground, in naval history so far. The bombardment of Betio was nothing if not spectacular to the Marines circling around in their amtracs and those still aboard the troopships. The Navy sailors' boasts about "obliterating the island" seemed if anything to be understated. The whole of Betio became engulfed in smoke and dust, lit up from within by sinister orange-red eruptions.

However, for all the pyrotechnics the bombardment failed in its prime objective: to destroy the Japanese strongpoints, particularly those on the north shore. When the first wave of amtracs cleared the reef they would find a high proportion of the enemy batteries intact. Many of the shells missed the island altogether and landed in the lagoon or on the reefs beyond the south shore; others, because of their low trajectory, hit their targets but glanced off into the sea. Nor did the bombardment kill many of the garrison; most of the Japanese sat out the storm in their well prepared bunkers and dug-outs.

The carrier air attacks were of little value. The Avenger and Dauntless pilots, who had practically no experience of close air support against land targets, could do little but blind-bomb the identifiable areas of Japanese fortification, while the Hellcats' strafing runs had little effect on dug-in troops with overhead cover. By far the most useful contribution in the air was afforded by the *Maryland's* Kingfisher spotter, flown by Lt Cdr Robert MacPherson.

It was now broad daylight, and on shore the heat was building. Undisturbed by the generally inaccurate Japanese fire, the amtracs completed their loading, formed three columns, and followed a control boat towards the rendezvous area.

In the crowded landing craft the sea breeze was welcome after the oppressively sour heat of the troop decks, but for some Marines the constant pitching and rolling was playing hell with the steak and egg breakfast that they had eaten earlier.

It was a long haul for the landing craft. First they had to form up in a rendezvous area between the transports and the entrance to the lagoon. Once correctly assembled, they had a three-and-a-half-mile voyage from the rendezvous area to the line of departure just inside the lagoon entrance; and once released for the final assault, they had another three miles to cross from the line of departure to the beaches. By the time they landed some of the Marines would have been pitching about on the sea for nearly six hours. They would be happy to land and fight anybody, just to get off this stomach-churning switchback.

From the cockpit of the Kingfisher Lt Cdr MacPherson had a spectacular view of the bombardment; ranging the length and breadth of Betio, he ignored the sporadic anti-aircraft fire and continued to relay a running commentary back to the *Maryland.* Before long, however, he became worried about the progress of the landing craft. By 7.48am the leading group were still laboriously ploughing through the swell half a mile from the line of departure. The minesweeper *Pursuit* had also been tracking their progress on her radar, and confirmed the delay to Adml Hill. He had no option but to delay H Hour - the time the landing craft were due to hit their allocated beaches - by fifteen minutes, and this order was passed at 8.03am; but after another brief discussion aboard *Maryland,* a second signal at 8.13am further delayed H Hour until 9am.

Exact relative timings are hard to confirm - as they were on the day, due partly to various radio malfunctions which dogged the operation. All three waves of amtracs were held up at the line of departure for approximately half an hour before they all made a right flank movement and headed for the beaches. The first wave crossed the line of departure at 8.24am; and at this point control passed from Adml Hill to divisional commander Julian Smith.

Admiral Spruance was still off the south shore of Betio, where his flagship *Indianaopolis* was engaged in an independent fire mission as part of the overall bombardment. He had heard intermittent radio communications, and witnessed the air attacks. As far as he was aware everything was going to plan; he did not know of the delays in the bombing, the movement of the transports, or the postponements of H Hour.

The original schedule called for a second air strike up and down the beaches just as the landing craft were approaching the shore. The *Maryland* ceased firing, and radio contact was re-established with the carriers. The naval gunfire was lifted onto targets well away from the beaches as the re-scheduled air attack took place at about 8.55am; but as the planes banked away to the west, with the leading amtracs still well off shore, the Support Group's turrets fell silent. A cloud of dust from the pulverised coral still hung over the whole island, and the thick column of oily smoke from the blazing fuel dump rose hundreds of feet into the morning air. Admiral Hill was afraid that because of the curtain of coral dust his gunfire might fall among the LVTs now approaching the beaches; so at 9am he ordered the end of the bombardment, over the protests of Julian Smith and

Merritt Edson.

The result was that the Japanese had a vital ten minutes' respite in which to consolidate their positions, restore communication, and bring their guns to bear on the rows of lumbering landing craft now approaching the end of the pier; and that apart from this brief strafing run by carrier planes, and the gallant but necessarily limited gunfire support of the destroyers inside the lagoon off Red 3 - where the *Ringgold* had since been joined by the *Dashiell* - the amtracs had to approach the beaches without any fire support for the final and most dangerous 1,500 yards of the whole operation.

In the first three waves were the amtracs, straining to hold their four-knot speed in the choppy sea, while the Higgins boats - the LCVPs making up the other three waves - butted along behind, trying their best to keep in contact. In all 87 amtracs carrying some 1,500 Marines were heading for their allocated beaches.

In the first wave were 42 LVT-1s each carrying eighteen infantrymen; 24 LVT-2s made up the second wave, and 21 the third, each carrying twenty Marines. The interval between each of the first three waves was 300 yards. In addition there were eight empty amtracs following the first wave, and five behind the third wave, to act as pick-ups for any tractor which might break down. If they were not required their mission was to demolish barbed wire on the reef just off the beach.

A small amount of fire was received at the point of departure, and some difficulty was encountered in keeping the proper distance between waves; but by the time the amtracs were about 300 yards off shore all were in their correct positions, and formation was held all the way to the beach. Machine gun fire was received by the first wave from the end of the long pier when they were 700 yards from the beach, but all the amtracs cleared the reef successfully. (Indeed, at least two LVTs would manage to negotiate the obstacles and beach wall and proceed inland as far as the airfield before discharging their troops.)

Braving anti-aircraft fire in his bulky little floatplane, Lt Cdr MacPherson dived in ahead of the flotilla and took a look at the reef; and what he saw filled him with horror. Instead of the four or five feet of water that had been expected, the sea was so low that in places large stretches of coral were drying in the sun, while elsewhere it looked as if three feet would be about all that could be expected. The pilot knew that the amtracs could scramble over the reef and on to the shore; but the fourth, fifth and sixth waves in their Higgins boats were inevitably going to ground hundreds of yards out. Major Frank Holland's predictions were going to haunt many people before the day was over.

*   *   *

The three landing beaches were designated - from west to east - Red 1, 2 and 3. The 3rd Bn, 2nd Marines (3-2) under Maj John Schoettel had been given Red 1: a deep cove, its eastern half protected by a log barricade, and covered from both sides by clusters of heavy machine guns and artillery. Red 2 stretched for about 500 yards from the eastern end of the cove to the quarter-mile-long wooden pier; assigned to the 2nd Bn, 2nd Marines (2-2) under Lt Col Herbert

Amey, this beach had a three to four foot high log sea wall along its entire length. From the pier eastwards to a point level with the end of the airfield runway, Red 3 stretched for some 800 yards, intersected by the short wharf of the Burns-Philp South Seas Trading Company; 2nd Bn, 8th Marines (2-8) under Maj Henry ("Jim") Crowe would land here. Admiral Shibasaki's huge concrete command bunker stood about 100 yards to the south-west of the Burns-Philp wharf.

As the rows of landing craft butted towards the beaches, long white wakes trailing behind them through water which the bombardment had churned to milk with pulverised coral, a lone boat was surging ahead of them. A few hundred yards in front of the first amtracs, Lt William D.Hawkins and a section of his specially trained Scout Sniper Platoon were heading for the end of the pier. Their task was to clear off it any Japanese who could fire on the waves of landing craft which would shortly be passing by it on either side.

The boat slammed against the Y-shaped seaplane dock at the seaward end of the pier at about 8.55am, and Hawkins and five others clambered up among the dozens of steel drums that had been placed as a barricade. A round of mortar fire from near the beach landed on the seaplane dock and ignited some fuel drums, but no one was hurt. A machine gun had already opened up on the approaching first wave from a shed yards from the end of the pier. A Marine with a flame thrower triggered a jet of billowing orange fire and the whole shed disappeared in a crackling, popping inferno. Hawkins and his men then proceeded to shoot, grenade and burn their way down the quarter-mile length of the pier, clearing snipers from small barges moored alongside it and a machine gun nest from a platform under the trestles.

With all opposition on the pier now silent, Hawkins and his men scrambled back into their boat and headed away from the ruptured fuel drums. (Once they had left the Japanese again started swarming back onto the pier from the shore end, and Capt Aubrey Edwards of 2-8, whose amtrac had just arrived on Red 3 in the first wave, had to grab a group of Marines and start all over again.) A full account of Lt Hawkins and his Scout Snipers, dated 15 December 1944, reads in part:

"For the Tarawa operation the Scout Sniper Platoon was divided into two groups and allocated two boats. Lieutenant Hawkins was in command of the first section and the headquarters team, this unit was in one boat. Gunnery Sergeant Hooper, in tactical command of the second and third sections, was in the other boat. On D Day, Lieutenant Hawkins' boat cleared the ship at 0345 hrs and circled around until 0830. This boat gained the pier at 0855 and put into the jetty at the left of the pier. Lieutenant Hawkins, accompanied by Lieutenant Leslie (A Co, 18th Marines) and four men landed on the jetty. Working their way toward the ramp, they encountered sniper fire. When Lieutenant Hawkins was satisfied the ramp had been secured, the rest of the men in the boat were then ordered to land. Before the men could unload, Japanese mortar shells began landing in the gas dump and the boat was moved about a third of the way inboard toward the beach. While this boat was making its way alongside the pier, Lieutenant Hawkins and his men were setting fire to two houses with flame throwers and cleaning out sunken Japanese landing craft.

"Lieutenant Hawkins had by this time reached his men in the boat and because of extremely heavy enemy mortar and machine gun fire decided to gain the beach by using the channel alongside the pier. Halfway down the channel the boat grounded. The boat backed down and proceeded to the end of the pier to await amphibious tractors. Whilst waiting, the boat drew machine gun fire which seemed to be coming from the pier. Lieutenant Hawkins ordered the coxswain to circle the end of the pier to determine from where the machine gun fire was coming. After circling four times Lieutenant Hawkins came to the conclusion that the fire was coming from the beach and not the pier. This was about 1030. All amphibious tractors were stopped to determine whether they could be used to get his men to the beach. The few that were serviceable were filled with wounded".

★   ★   ★

The lines of landing craft were now on the final approach, slapping through the low waves as the long wooden pier slid past, clouds of dense smoke still billowing from the raging fires near the end. In the first wave of amtracs carrying 3-2 into the cove on Red 1, Ralph Butler remembers that everyone seemed in high spirits; there was even a sense of adventure. "After what seemed like hours of milling about, jockeying for positions, we all seemed in proper alignment and proceeded shoreward. Each tractor was equipped with two .50cal machine guns mounted in front, and at a certain point the first wave were to start firing shoreward. I don't recall how far we were from shore when all hell let loose. The amtrac started getting hit and our first reaction was that the tractors on our flanks had lost control of their guns. The sudden realisation that there were Japs still alive on the island and capable of resistance snapped everyone out of their joviality. I remember a violent, turbulent trip shoreward - explosions, detonations, bodies slumping and bloody, and finally crunching to a stop; somebody screaming 'Get the hell out, fast!' - throwing equipment out and scrambling over the side onto the beach."

All hell had certainly been let loose. As the rows of amtracs entered the cove heavy machine guns and artillery opened up from ahead and both sides. Within moments amtracs were burning as bullets found their unarmoured fuel tanks; others spun and wallowed as their drivers fell dead or wounded; some erupted in balls of flame as they were blown apart by shells at point blank range. The noise was almost unbearable, and the men dived for the illusory shelter of the LVTs' deck plates in a vain attempt to escape the fusillade.

The first amtrac trundled onto the shore of Betio at 9.10am: No 49, "*My Delores*", driven by PFC Ed Moore. They had had a rough trip in, and were being riddled by machine gun fire from a coconut log bunker just to the left of their landing point at the western end of Red 1. A couple of Marines jumped out as they ground ashore, and knocked out the emplacement with a few well-aimed grenades; but almost at once another machine gun sent a hail of bullets into the front of the amtrac as it climbed the sea wall, shattering the instrument panel and bringing the LVT lurching to a halt. More Marines scurried out and silenced the second machine gun with another shower of grenades. "How my radio operator and myself got out of that riddled cab without being hit at that time remains a mystery to me to this day", recalls Moore.

Ed Moore was later hit by mortar fire and, along with other wounded Marines, was put into an amtrac to be evacuated to the troopship *Arthur Middleton*. As the LVT left the end of Green Beach it came across an exposed coral reef some 150-200 yards out into the lagoon where a number of Marines were lying within range of enemy rifle and machine gun fire from Red Beach 1. In charge of the amtrac was a Navy captain - who, Moore thinks, had perhaps been in charge of the Navy LCVP landing craft at the original morning point of departure. Seeing the silent Marines on the reef the captain told everybody to stay where they were while he investigated, and to get the hell out of it if he got hit. While Ed and the crew chief looked on, along with the few others who were able to stand, the captain checked each and every one of the Marines on the reef. After making sure that all were dead, he climbed back into the amtrac and gave the order to get under way again. Ed Moore still remembers his courage with admiration.

★   ★   ★

The neat pattern of landings planned for Red 1 was already degenerating. In the face of the furious barrage amtrac drivers were taking the line of least resistance and putting their passengers ashore as far away from the enemy guns as they could get. Fire from a Japanese strongpoint at the eastern end of the cove between Red 1 and Red 2 was particularly effective, and more and more landing craft were veering away to the west to avoid the devastating fire from this part of the shore. Company K of 3-2, who were designated this eastern area of the beach, were particularly hard hit; amtracs were being knocked out wholesale, and the survivors were cut to pieces as they waded ashore.

To their right Co I were having a slightly easier time, although their company commander was killed within minutes of landing. "Where we landed there was no sea wall, it was an open stretch of beach", recalls Ralph Butler. "We were raked with fire from all directions. . . later we found that the Japs were using a half-sunken freighter in the lagoon. People were getting killed wholesale; those of us who could leapt into shell craters, holes and whatever for cover. Every once in a while someone would attempt to return fire with whatever he had, but if exposed would be immediately killed".

The old inter-island steamer *Niminoa*, which had been run aground in 1941 about 100 yards west of the end of the long pier, and abandoned after an air strike on 19 November, now concealed at least one machine gun and many snipers - the misery of the Marines on Red Beach 1 was being compounded by fire from the rear. A survivor of the landings on Red 1 writes of the perceived impossibility - which must have been felt by many men that day - of doing anything much more than cling to survival; and of the speed with which the day seemed to pass:

"At each step I marvelled at still being alive; by the time I had reached a point where the water was only knee deep I felt that surely I would reach the sanctuary of the sea wall - I had cried like a baby and prayed aloud, and somehow felt that I was receiving divine assistance at that moment. Throwing myself behind the low sea wall I gazed out over the lagoon; the sound of battle came from every direction but at that moment I felt quite secure where I was. At this stage the beach was littered with burning wrecks, a few men were still milling about out there, and dead and wounded lay all around. An officer moving along the beach passed by me and met his end a few yards away. Amtracs along the beach from where I sat stood at crazy angles part way over the sea wall, others were blazing. Lying just offshore a destroyer provided fire support, while further to my right a rusting hulk of a ship held fast on a reef.

"Medical teams were frantically dealing with casualties; every attempt was being made to evacuate the more seriously wounded - I saw an amtrac, one of the few that seemed to have survived the initial assault, loaded with wounded. It trundled off over the reefs towards the troopships beyond the lagoon. I was pinned down at this point just beyond the beach for nearly two hours; all that I could do was rest after the labour of getting ashore with my heap of equipment, dry my gun and wait to see if anyone was going to join me.

"As the time passed a few more Marines came along, all from different outfits to mine; and around 4pm an officer appeared on the scene and told us that he was forming a skirmish line across Red Beach 1 and that we were to advance towards the southern side of the island. He then moved off to the east towards Red Beach 2 and we didn't see him again. We decided to move forward, and met some opposition which resulted in some brisk exchanges of rifle fire. By now it was rapidly becoming dark, so we formed a perimeter roughly 150 yards in depth from the sea wall and secured ourselves for the night. We took turns to keep guard while the others tried to grab a little shuteye; when my turn came I was aware of bodies moving around in the trees ahead, whether they were ours or theirs I didn't know - unless someone decided to get too close to my position I wasn't going to bother them. I didn't sleep that night, but it was nice to dump my gear for a while and just relax."

*   *   *

Major Michael Ryan, commanding officer of Co L of 3-2, headed for Red Beach 1 in the fifth wave:

"The landing plans called for the assault to be made from the lagoon side, with three battalions abreast; 3rd Battalion, 2nd Marines [was] on the right to land on Red 1. The 3rd Bn consisted of I, K and L infantry companies, M company with heavy mortars and water-cooled machine guns, and supporting logistical and medical units. I and K companies were to land in amphibious tractors. We had a long distance to go to the line of departure, since the ships were not to enter the lagoon, either because of their draught or because of the coast defence guns. The amtracs moved slowly, so they were to leave the ships first and precede the boats by enough time to allow all waves to arrive at the line of departure on schedule and avoid excessive milling around before moving in to the

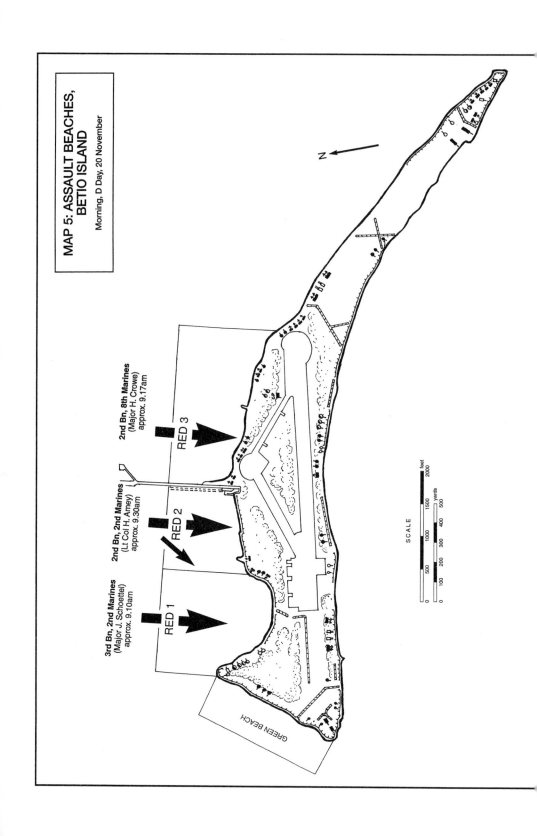

MAP 5: ASSAULT BEACHES, BETIO ISLAND

Morning, D Day, 20 November

N

3rd Bn, 2nd Marines
(Major J. Schoettel)
approx. 9.10am

RED 1

2nd Bn, 2nd Marines
(Lt Col H. Amey)
approx. 9.30am

RED 2

2nd Bn, 8th Marines
(Major H. Crowe)
approx. 9.17am

RED 3

GREEN BEACH

SCALE

0   100   200   300   400   500
yards

0   500   1000   1500   2000
feet

beach.

"It was early morning when the last waves started over the side. As our loaded boats moved in circles near the ship it started to move away. We took off after it, since all the boat waves had not yet disembarked. I was told later that the ship moved to be out of range of the coast defence guns, but this movement delayed our arrival at the line of departure and may have given the enemy time to man their defences after the preparatory bombardment stopped. The landing was scheduled for high tide, so it was full daylight by the time we came to the break in the reef that was the entrance to the lagoon. I can still remember how clear the water was and how impressive the coral formations of the reef.

"As we entered the lagoon, we could see the continuous naval gunfire explosions and the planes diving to deliver the heavy bombs they carried. Fire and smoke seemed to engulf the island. The coast defence guns ashore had been silenced; the destroyers were moving in to concentrate on the beach defences. I felt confident that such softening up of the enemy defences would enable us to move across the island in short order.

"Soon, however, we could see the amtracs were taking heavy fire, especially those on the left half of the beach. Because of the smoke and haze we could not see the beach itself, but it soon became apparent that most of the amtracs had been hit and were dead in the water. Ahead of us was a kaleidoscope of destruction. Many of the amtracs were burning with the shimmering heat of burning diesel fuel. Two Marines crawled out of a burning tractor with their clothing on fire; they stood erect on the side of the tractor, outlined against the smoke for a few seconds; then slowly, ever so slowly, they fell face down into the water. I have never since heard the word 'deadfall' in any context without visualising that scene. Men from I and K companies were climbing out of disabled tractors and trying to wade in under heavy machine gun fire. With the first troops nearing the beach, the ships were unable to fire on the beach defences.

"As our boats neared the fringing reef it was clear that few, if any, amtracs would be able to come back for us to tranship and ride to the beach. As we prepared to get out and wade in, O'Brien from the next boat shouted 'Hey, Mike, what do you want to do?' What I wanted to do was turn around and go back to the ship, but I couldn't think of a good explanation. My orders were to land in the centre of the beach, but it was obvious that if we continued straight ahead through the enfilading machine gun fire we would have nothing left to land. O'Brien's question alerted me to look for another alternative, and through the smoke I saw a Marine jump over the parapet on the western end of the island - it seemed that some troops were getting ashore there. I told O'Brien that we'd go around a sunken Japanese ship on the reef and wade into the western tip of Red Beach 1.

"As the boats moved to the west, no longer in a line but in a large bunch, we hit the reef and started to disembark. The Japanese fire shifted from the disabled amtracs and started to concentrate on our troops. General Shoup later said about his move to the beach that he 'couldn't remember dreams very well'. I know what he meant, because our move into that beach seemed to take forever, just as in a nightmarish dream, and the shore seemed to be a haven that kept moving further away. We were up to our waists in water initially as we left the boats, so movement was slow. Looking back, I saw that the men were leaving the boats without hesitation; the courage of these young men, many of them not out of their teens, still is a source of pride to me. These were not fanatical and seasoned troops as the Japanese were, but ordinary young people faced with an unimagined horror, but determined not to let their fellow Marines down.

"On the beach at last, we found two wounded Marines propped up against the log parapet watching our advance; years later a Marine from either I or K company told me that he had dragged them from the water and placed them there to wait for help, then hurried on to join the attack. O'Brien came out of the water saying, 'Mike, I did my Hollywood act coming in'. At my puzzled look he explained that every time the machine gun splashes came close to him he would ostentatiously 'die' and fall into the water to divert the fire. He did this several times, but still the clips of carbine bullets on his belt were shot off. As I watched the Marines trying to wade to the beach there were only one or two upright, and the rest appeared to keep as much of themselves as possible covered in the water to escape the bullets splashing around them.

"O'Brien and I went over the parapet and encountered the survivors of I and K companies. They had assaulted the beach defences on the right half of Red 1 and were moving inland. These two companies had come ashore in the few tractors that had made it to the beach, or had waded in from disabled machines. They had sustained heavy casualties, since they had absorbed the initial heavy fire, but in their reduced state they had attacked the enemy defences on the right of Red 1 with grenades and rifle fire. They overran the coast defence guns and cut down a Japanese officer and an NCO who had led a rush out of the gun shelter. Their heroic actions were what made it possible for the rest of us to get ashore.

"As the men from the boat waves struggled ashore I looked for the command element of the battalion - it never arrived, and I was later informed that the command[er] believed that our waves were completely destroyed in the water and had moved his boat to another beach. After some hours we were convinced that the battalion command was not coming ashore and had probably been destroyed in the water.

"The company radios we had were bulky, pre-war models that were not very reliable at best and inoperative when wet. All the radios from the 3rd Battalion, 2nd Marines were lost in the water. We had no way to contact battalion headquarters and were completely separated from regimental headquarters, unable to let them know how we were doing or to learn what was happening on the rest of the island. As the only major in our area, I was forced to assume command of the three rifle companies and the machine guns from M company. As heavy fire on the left of Red 1 caused individuals to drift over to our beach, including some from the battalion on our left [2-2], our battalion became a composite unit.

"Captain George Wentzel from battalion headquarters tried to organise evacuation of our wounded in some of the amtracs, but he was killed by enemy machine gun fire. Since our senior medical officer had been killed in the initial assault his assistant, Dr Warrick, established an aid station in the lee of the parapet on the point and our casualties were carried there. The battalion surgeon was sorely missed when we were able to treat the wounded; I decided then that it was a mistake for doctors to land with the first waves, and that it would be better for them to come in after the initial waves were ashore."

★   ★   ★

PFC Bob Libby, from the 81mm mortar platoon of 3-2, should have been in the third wave of assault troops heading for Red 1, but it was not to be. About 500 yards out the launch rammed into the reef and everyone was ordered over the side. "I recall leaping over the gunwale of our landing craft into water well over my head, having missed the actual coral reef due to the launch being held up against it. Looking up, I could see in the clear water the underside of the launch now drifting in over the edge of the reef - with less weight aboard it continued to drift shoreward. Kicking myself from the bottom, I rose to the surface, finding a footing on the reef itself. A quick look around revealed nightmarish activity around me. I noted our launch still drifting toward shore; I struck to my right, my intention being to keep the launch between me and the heavy fire coming from shore for as long as possible. This gave me time to assess the situation and plan on reaching shore.

"As I advanced, now finding myself out in the open, it was possible to keep a watch for machine gun fire skipping off the surface of the water coming in my direction. A move to one side or the other allowed passage for this while still moving slowly toward the beach, the depth of water still hampering movement so it was painfully slow going. Of course you could not watch for mortar or other heavy weapon fire, but keeping your wits about you and making as small a target as possible assisted your chance of survival. . . .

"It was all too obvious that the landing operations were not going to plan - it had been envisaged after the amount of attention that this island had received in the days leading up to the invasion that there would be minor opposition to hold up our landing. Everywhere and anywhere I looked there were knocked-out amphibious tractors burning fiercely, landing craft being blown apart. . . those still operable [were] taking on nearby wounded men and backing off into deeper water to escape the deadly fire being sent from ashore in every direction. One moment I was among a group of advancing men, the next I found myself alone with my own thoughts and prayers; we had no answer to what was taking place around us - we were live targets in a shooting gallery.

"Still in chest deep water, a stream of skips on the water revealed machine gun fire being directed at me; as I moved to my left out of the line of danger I noticed a number of other men lined up in a neat row. The machine gun fire passed inches from me and took out a number of these men, our platoon commander among them. The walking wounded moved in the opposite direction to the advancing troops, making their way to drifting landing craft in the hope of getting medical help. The water around me, blood red, was a churning mass of spouting geysers through which those of us still able to continued to make our way shoreward. Bodies were floating on the surface everywhere we looked; here a man moving along nearby was suddenly no longer seen, and there the faltering steps of another told the story of a wounded man determined to reach dry land.

"The sound of screaming shells passed overhead, the unmistakable crack of rifle fire zipped around our ears, heavy explosions on shore, burning amtracs destroyed and lying at crazy angles. . . the screams of the wounded were lost in this cacophony of sound - all the while we who survived so far still made our way to the beach to find some haven of safety, if such existed. About half an hour had elapsed since leaving the landing craft before I put foot on dry land. It is doubtful if anyone who survived the 500 yards wade into the lagoon waters on that day could possibly give a coherent picture of what happened, it was all too confusing to methodically record everything you saw. Every step of the way was a life and death situation; how anyone ever reached the shore is still a mystery to me as the enemy fire seemed to cover every inch between the reef and shore - there was no hiding place, no protection, our only armour was the shirt on our backs.

"I had done time on Guadalcanal and thought that I had seen some pretty rough situations, but I don't think that there was anything like this even at places like Peleliu or Iwo Jima. If anyone can think up a picture of hell, I don't think that it would match up to that wade in from the reef to the shore at Tarawa, with the floating bodies and bits of bodies, the exploding shells and burning landing craft.

"To say a man's chances were 50-50 may sound ludicrous, but in the lagoon, in chin deep water to begin with, a man's head was a very small target indeed. At this point you could see skips on the water surface indicating machine gun fire from a certain direction; an eye on such points could give an indication as to where the fire was coming from and evasive action allowed them to pass harmlessly. What you could not foresee were the mortar shells or anti-boat gun shells sizzling slightly above your head.

"In fact, [once on shore] one Marine raised himself up from a hole in the ground just in time to have an anti-tank shell glance off the front of his helmet. The Marine was knocked for six, did a backward somersault back into the hole where he had just been hit; he lay momentarily, yet apart from a headache there was not a mark on him - he came to, picked up his helmet and breezily showed one and all the dent in it - one of those freak incidents that happen from time to time.

"Speaking of freak incidents, another Marine must have been looking directly towards a sniper without actually seeing him. The sniper fired, the bullet hit fair and square in the centre of his helmet, went through the steel outer shell,traced a path up over the inner lining, and tore its way through the steel outer covering at the back - the Marine was not injured in the slightest. . . quite a souvenir of his brush with death - he was proud of it.

"M company of the 3rd Battalion, 2nd Marines was a heavy weapons company; I was in the 81mm mortar section. My gear for the landing was comprised of the usual combat green clothing and helmet, a light pack containing rations for at least two days, spare socks, underwear, a shelter half strapped to the pack, a carbine rifle, a cartridge belt with 120 rounds of ammunition plus two full clips. Hanging off the belt were two full canteens of water and a medical kit; over my shoulder as a gunner on our mortar I carried the gun sights, a gas mask, and the portable individual plastic gas shelter. I was only 147 pounds to begin with, but with all of this equipment hanging off me I was now carrying close to 100 pounds.

"Once I was out of the landing craft and up to my chin in water I was handed out the bipod of the mortar weighing around 46 pounds - try wading about 500 yards with that lot, never mind the bullets. This was about the average load that I carried wherever I made a landing - Gavutu, Guadalcanal, Tarawa, Saipan and Tinian. Incidentally, I forgot to mention an entrenching tool and the usual rain cape; no wonder I ended the war bow-legged.

"An incident that I recall as we headed for Red Beach 1 concerned a corporal in our outfit called Edgar Best. Edgar was one of those people with a peaches-and-cream complexion and a voice to match, maybe as a kid they kept him in diapers too long. However, he was here in the lagoon and wading some distance ahead of me and to my left front and, like all of us, keeping a weather eye out for machine gun bursts in the water, and making sure that he wasn't too close to anyone else so as not to present some Jap with an easy target. As he waded forward, Edgar looked over to his right for some reason or other and at exactly the same time some Jap cranked off a shot at him. The bullet passed under the visor of Edgar's helmet and continued on its merry way with both of Edgar's eyebrows. The first that I knew of his problem was when he yelled out in his soprano voice and began staggering towards me with his face covered in blood. We had all been warned before we disembarked not to stop for anyone who was wounded, but Edgar was clearly disorientated so I grabbed him by the collar, swung him round in the direction of one of the landing craft that was drifting past, and told him to jump aboard and wait until someone could come to his help. I was in no position to dilly-dally about, so I turned my attention to getting to the shore. I believe that he did make it to a landing craft and was duly picked up and returned to the nearest transport. Someone told me that he made it OK, although I never met him again."

*   *   *

The situation of the assault troops was a little less desperate on Red Beach 3, where Maj "Jim" Crowe's 2-8 made the next landing at 9.17am. The destroyers USS *Ringgold* and *Dashiell* had remained off shore and maintained a constant barrage of 5in shells all along the landing area. They were so close to the shore that they were both in serious danger of running aground on the reef. One Marine, looking back after disembarking from an amtrac which had found a gap in the sea wall and ground to a halt just short of the airfield taxiway, said "Hell, those destroyers were that close I could have sworn they were sailing down the beach."

From 3,000 yards out to within 200 yards, Crowe's men had been hammered by 3in shells from the shore. Crowe himself - who would be the only one of the three assault battalion commanders to reach the shore on D Day - had to wade in from the reef when his Higgins boat ground to a halt. Taking cover behind an amtrac that had almost reached the shore, he was suddenly knocked flat when the vehicle struck a mine, but continued unhurt to the sea wall.

PFC Joe Jordan vividly remembers the trip ashore. "As the amtrac reared up when we hit the reef they let go with what I think was a 77mm right through the front bottom, and boom - a hole just a few inches big in the bottom metal and an explosion in the troop compartment. Several of the guys were killed or seriously injured but I was lucky not to be scratched. The momentum carried the tractor forward into deeper water and it began to fill and sink. Needless to say everybody was excited and attempted to get away.

"After a couple of feet we discovered that the water was too deep to wade and we would have to shuck gear and swim for it. About this time another tractor came to our rescue, and threw grab ropes into the water to use in dragging us to shallow water. The orders had been to ignore anyone that was down and move toward the objective, but thank goodness those young men defied the order. When the rescue tractor was a little way off the beach it got hit and the motor died.

"Everyone again bailed out, and as I got to the side of the machine I recognised one of the machine gunners as the young man that lived next door to me as we were growing up. He was bleeding pretty good but was alert enough to hang onto my neck as I waded in to the beach. Finally we hit dry ground and he turned loose so that a corpsman could look after him. Four years later he was best man at my wedding."

Seventeen of the amtracs ended up at the far west of the beach near the pier, and two of them found a gap in the sea wall and advanced for about 100 yards to the north-east taxiway of the airfield. By the standards of the day this was good going; but as soon as the Marines disembarked and tried to consolidate their positions the Japanese began filtering back between them and the shore, and they had no option but to withdraw to the sea wall or face being cut off. Company F of the 2-8, on the left flank, had meanwhile managed to reach the short Burns-Philp wharf.

Correspondent Robert Sherrod came ashore with the fifth wave. "I looked around the ramp to see what was on the beach. For the first time I felt that something was wrong. The first waves were not hitting the beach as they should. There were very few boats on the beach and these were all amphibious tractors which the first wave used. There were no Higgins boats on the beach, as there should have been by now."

*   *   *

In the waters off Red Beach 2 a disaster was shaping up. As Lt Col Amey's 2-2 was the last of the first wave assault battalions to reach the shore the defenders had plenty of time to prepare themselves. F Company were supposed to land on the left and E Co on the right, with G Co in support; but many coxswains put their vehicles ashore wherever they could find a space, some ending up on Red 1. The first wave were 500 yards out when machine guns and artillery - the guns that few Marines believed could have withstood the raging naval bombardment - caught them in a murderous crossfire from behind the log sea wall which ran the length of the beach. Drivers tried desperately to coax more speed from their screaming engines as Marines - many already exhausted and seasick from hours of pitching and heaving in the heavy swell - waited helplessly, crowded in their flimsy craft, for the chance to get ashore and take cover.

As the amtracs shuddered to a halt at last the troops leapt over the sides and rushed for the shelter of the log barricade, only yards up from the edge of the water - the only cover they could see. But the first ashore were the lucky ones. Looking back, the Marines huddled behind every available foot of sea wall were horrified to see the next waves clambering out of the Higgins boats that were already grinding to a standstill on the reef, splashing into the sea and wading ashore. This was Flanders and the Somme all over again - troops burdened with masses of equipment walking inexorably forward towards entrenched machine guns; but this time they were struggling through waist-deep water.

Lieutenant Colonel Herbert Amey, the commanding officer of 2-2, was only 200 yards from the shore when the amtrac carrying his headquarters group became entangled with a heavy barbed wire barricade west of the pier. The driver butted and reversed the tractor, but it was firmly stuck; Amey ordered everyone over the side, and they crouched alongside the stricken amtrac to escape the hail of bullets lashing the water around them. Moving inshore, they went down on hands and knees to present a smaller target; but when the water became too shallow Amey stood up and shouted "Come on - these bastards can't stop us!", and splashed towards the beach. He was hit by a burst of fire in the chest and stomach and was killed instantly.

A member of Amey's command group was Lt Col Walter Jordan from the 4th Marine Division, who had come along as an observer; being the senior officer, he now found himself the acting commander of 2-2. As soon as he got ashore he radioed the *Maryland* to clarify the situation; but he had difficulty in identifying himself, as he was not on the 2nd Division roster and nobody knew who he was.

*   *   *

Staff Sergeant William Bordelon, a tall Texan from the 1st (Engineer) Bn, 18th Marines, had been coming ashore in an early wave of amtracs when a direct hit shattered the tractor, killing all but four of the eighteen Marines aboard. Bordelon mustered the dazed survivors and led them to the shore. Making up two satchel demolition charges, he leapt over the sea wall and silenced two of the enemy pillboxes that were causing havoc among the incoming boats. Coming back for more explosives, he returned to the fray and blew up a third emplacement, but in the process received wounds to his chest and stomach from enemy machine gun fire.

Back on the beach, Bordelon not only refused medical aid, but charged out into the water to rescue an injured Marine who was calling for help, assisting another wounded man back at the same time. The intrepid sergeant, armed with more satchel charges, then moved forward again towards the Japanese emplacements, but was shot again and killed before he could reach the enemy. His was the first of four Medals of Honor to be won during the 76 hours of the battle.

⋆　　　⋆　　　⋆

Aboard their LCVP out in the lagoon, Col David Shoup and his Regimental Landing Team 2 headquarters group were anxious to get ashore. Even at this early stage it was obvious that things were not going well on the beaches. He hailed an amtrac that was returning from the island, only to find that it was filled with wounded. Transferring them to his boat and taking over the amtrac, he and his group headed for Red Beach 2. They were only about 100 yards from the shore when two LCMs, carrying light tanks, came under heavy fire only yards ahead of them. One of the landing craft immediately sank, and the other wheeled around and withdrew badly damaged. "This is no place for a command post", said Shoup, and told his driver to move back into the lagoon.

At his second attempt, Shoup headed in alongside the western side of the pier; but about halfway along the engine spluttered and died, and everyone piled out and took shelter under the trestles. To their surprise a Higgins boat came along-side: someone had discovered that there was a dredged channel alongside the pier deep enough for one boat at a time to sail its full length. Commandeering the boat the group headed for the landward end of the pier, only to be met with such a hail of fire that that any further movement would be suicidal.

A few yards away Shoup saw an amtrac and splashed over to investigate. The vehicle appeared to be filled with wounded men, but closer inspection showed that nearly all were dead. Foregoing delicacy for necessity, he ordered the driver and gunner to dump the bodies over the side, and returned to collect the members of his headquarters group. Finally reaching the beach in this, their fourth craft since leaving the transport, they were sprinting for the shelter of the sea wall when a mortar bomb exploded nearby and Shoup received shrapnel wounds to the leg.

Waving off the men who rushed forward to help him, he climbed over the sea wall and limped inland about 50 yards, where he came across a low air raid shelter beside a row of palms, their foliage blasted away by the shelling. He decided that this was as good a place as any for his HQ, and instructed his communications team to set up their equipment. After a few minutes one of his Marines rushed over in a state of high excitement to tell him that the shelter seemed to be full of Japanese. "Get rid of 'em!", he yelled, his mind on more important matters. Informed that "We can't, without blowing you up", Shoup ordered his men to plug up all the holes in the shelter with whatever they could find, and set someone to stand guard over the entrance. Having got ashore and established some kind of HQ at long last, even if only feet away from the enemy, he decided that he had neither the leisure nor the inclination to wander around looking for a better spot.

Aboard the *Maryland*, Maj Gen Julian Smith was having serious communica-tions problems; parts of the radio equipment had been so badly shaken up by the vibrations from the 16in guns that only intermittent signals were being received.

All that he could do at present was stare at the smoke-covered island and wonder what the hell was going on.

While Maj Mike Ryan was rallying the mixed gang of Marines from 3-2 and 2-2 which he had inherited at the western end of Red Beach 1, his battalion commander, Maj Schoettel, was still out in the lagoon with the fourth wave. A witness to the carnage as the first three waves had entered the cove, he took it upon himself to hold back the fourth and fifth waves, believing that any further landings on Red 1 would be suicidal. Sadly, his contribution to the battle from then on was minimal.

At around 9.59am he managed to contact Shoup by radio, and sent the message "Receiving heavy fire all along beach, unable to land, issue in doubt". This was followed eight minutes later by: "Boats held up on reef of right flank Red 1, troops receiving heavy fire in water." Shoup responded with: "Land Red Beach 2 and work west". The reply shocked all who heard it: "We have nothing left to land".

Schoettel did, however, intercept and order back to Red 1 two LCTs carrying M4A2 medium tanks from the *Ashland*, which were turning away from the shore. The ramps came down and six Shermans wallowed into the sea, engines roaring, hundreds of yards from the beach. The churned-up water concealed many deep shellholes from the naval bombardment, and one Sherman flooded and stalled when it lurched into one of these. Three others suffered the same fate while moving through the shallows in an attempt to find a path ashore through the scores of dead and wounded Marines who lined the water's edge. Two tanks - "*Chicago*" and "*China Gal*" - managed to struggle onto dry land, but again were unable to head directly inland because of the infantry and casualties lying thickly along the narrow beach. Making a tortuous journey around the shore, they finally got forward behind Green Beach. "*Chicago*" was knocked out; but "*China Gal*", her turret ring jammed by a lucky hit from the only one of the Japanese *Ha-Go* tanks to leave its dug-out, promptly charged and rammed it. With her 75mm main gun out of action "*China Gal*" returned to the beach, supporting the infantry thereafter with her hull machine gun.

After sending the LCTs back towards the beach Maj Schoettel returned to the lagoon, and again raised Shoup on the radio to tell him that he had lost contact with his men. Before Shoup could reply, a terse message came through from *Maryland*, where Julian Smith had overheard the conversation: "Direct you land at any cost, regain control of your battalion and continue the attack". In view of Schoettel's conduct during the landings on Red Beach 1, it is interesting to read a report on the operation which he submitted to Julian Smith in December 1943:

"In attacking a well fortified beach frontally, it is recommended that the frontage assigned each landing team be reduced to 350 yards." Bearing in mind his inability or unwillingness to land most of his command on D Day, he goes on: "Fire should be continued over the landing craft until the last moment. This may be controlled from the air. Simultaneously, fire should be placed directly against unused beaches on the flanks, and the enfilading fire should lift to a line just outside of the initial beachhead, in other words the troops land inside of a box barrage." He probably had in mind the deadly fire of the Japanese strongpoint at the junction of Red Beaches 1 and 2 when he wrote "Give special attention to prominently placed objects such as outlying points of land, jetties, docks or hulks."

Too much has perhaps been made of Maj Schoettel's failings: after the battle he was transferred to the 22nd Marines, and was recommended for a Bronze Star while serving on Eniwetok. He was later wounded while commanding a rifle battalion on Guam, and on 16 August 1944 he was killed in action.

★   ★   ★

Once he was finally established at his makeshift command post David Shoup began to assess the situation. Communications were still the overriding problem; many of the man-pack radios had been submerged in sea water during the struggle to get ashore, and the waterproofing was proving to be inadequate. Runners were despatched in an attempt to contact the company commanders to his left and right, but many never returned - probably falling victim to the scores of snipers who had strapped themselves into palm trees which had survived the initial bombardment. Slowly, however, news began to filter through.

Jim Crowe's men on Red 3 appeared to be in the best shape; some forward positions were near the airfield taxiways, and further east a few Marines were nearly 200 yards inland. Lt Col Walter Jordan had managed to contact Shoup, who instructed him to retain command of 2-2; most of the troops on Red 2 were huddled beside the sea wall, with a few scattered positions no more than 75 yards inland. From his own CP behind Red 2 Shoup could verify the tenuous hold on the beachhead from the mortar and rifle fire all around him. Despite the strange messages which he had received from Maj Schoettel, whom he knew was still out in the lagoon, Shoup was aware that some troops had indeed managed to get ashore on Red 1; but no one could get through to give him a first-hand report, and he was unaware of Maj Ryan's gallant rallying of the stragglers at the western end of the beach.

Shoup had already committed his reserves - 1st Bn, 2nd Marines under Maj Wood Kyle - with instructions to land on Red Beach 2 and attempt to work their way westward to link up with Red 1. At the line of departure the surviving amtrac crews, who had already made the hair-raising trip to Betio and were now returning, told Maj Kyle that it was suicide to try to reach the shore in Higgins boats. Kyle had difficulty in rounding up enough amtracs, and the two companies which finally headed for the beach were met with such heavy and accurate fire that many of them had to veer sharply to the west onto Red Beach 1, where the survivors - four officers and 110 enlisted men - were gratefully accepted by Maj Ryan.

★   ★   ★

As the 6th Marines were still aboard the transports off Betio and could not be committed without V Corps authority, Julian Smith was left with only two battalions in reserve - the 1st and 3rd Bns, 8th Marines. At 10.18am he decided to send the 3-8, under Maj Robert Ruud, to the line of departure, where they would be available to David Shoup as and when he needed them. Still suffering from a virtual communications blackout between the flagship and the troops ashore, and not realising the potential disaster that was facing his division, Julian Smith radioed to Holland Smith with the Northern Task Force off the coast of Makin: "Successful landings on Beaches Red 2 and 3. Am committing one landing team from divisional reserves. Still encountering strong resistance throughout." The V Corps commander was disturbed by the signal; he knew that it was not usual to send in reserves this early in a battle.

Aboard the USS *Indianapolis* it must have been becoming clear to Adml Spruance, too, that the operation was faltering. The naval and air bombardment had not devastated the Japanese defenders as had been expected; the enemy were full of fight. The landings - what little he knew of them from the chaotic communications and the smoke and haze that still covered large areas of Betio - were unco-ordinated and scattered; the tides had been badly miscalculated; all the ingredients of a disaster were to hand. These were probably among the worst hours of Ray Spruance's career. His worried staff were of the opinion that he should step in and take control. Spruance declined: he had selected his commanders, and they must be allowed to fight their battle as they saw fit, without his interference.

Chapter 4:

The Red Beaches - Afternoon

It was at around 11.30am when Maj Ruud received Shoup's order to land his 3rd Bn, 8th Marines in support of Jim Crowe's 2-8 on Red Beach 3. There were no amtracs available to shuttle them to the beach - they were going to have to get there the hard way. The LCVPs turned for shore in neat rows, their ramps thumping into the swell and green water sloshing over the sides. The Marines stared forward in apprehension, but at first their advance seemed undetected on the smoke-hooded shore.

The Higgins boats were within yards of the reef when the first shells arrived - the heavy guns at the eastern end of Betio had found their range, and amid huge water-spouts landing craft began to explode all along the line. Whole boatloads were vanishing in a roar of flame; heavily burdened men were hurled into deep water, screaming as they grabbed for anything that might support them; some thrashed in a welter of blood, others simply disappeared in silence.

At last the ramps came down as the landing craft ground to a halt on the almost exposed reefs, and the Marines charged out, with only one thought in their minds - to get out of their floating coffins and across the shallows to the doubtful haven of the beach. As they plunged into the water they were met by a criss-cross of machine gun and rifle fire, and fell by the dozen. Some coxswains lost their nerve and lowered the ramps too soon; "This is as far as I go", yelled one, and the Marines rushed forward into fifteen feet of water, many drowning before they could disentangle themselves from their equipment.

Those who survived the chaos at the edge of the reef now began the slow struggle to the shore, straight into the murderous fire from the entrenched Japanese positions. Everywhere around them dead fish floated on the surface, killed by the concussion of the morning's shelling - and not only fish. Marines killed during the first landings were already bloating, their corpses bobbing high in the water; men who had died more recently were still limp and supple. Overhead in the Kingfisher spotter plane, Lt Cdr MacPherson watched the agony of the 3-8 Marines impotently: "The water never seemed clear of tiny men - their rifles over their heads, slowly wading beachward - I wanted to cry."

★   ★   ★

Raymond Knight of L Co, 3-8 thought that he was to be part of the reserves, perhaps to land on the second day, but instead found himself heading for the beach at around noon of D Day:

"As we hit the line of departure we were taking shelling from the 20mm type Japanese guns; we would glance up and see a boat being blown up on our right or left." The Higgins boats laboured towards the shore, their largely plywood construction offering no protection against the hail of machine gun bullets, or shells from as far as Takarongo Point at the extreme eastern end of the island. "We hit the reef when we got about 500 or 600 yards from the beach; we were being raked with machine gun fire and took a hit in the bow of our boat. We had to go over the side not knowing where we were, and being pinned down in our boat by small arms fire. I thought that we were on the beach, and was really surprised when I jumped over the side into about three or four feet of water.

"There was steady machine gun fire, and every once in a while you would hear the anti-boat shells go over and see a boat beyond you go up. I had no more than hit the water when one of my riflemen, Wayne Carlton, got hit in the throat and was bleeding, he was stumbling about in the water; a BAR man by the name of Austin helped me get Wayne back into the boat, which was still hung up on the reef. After we all unloaded and got the weight out of it, I found that Wayne made it back to the ship and got medical attention that saved his life.

"After we hit the water the Japs were hitting us with machine guns - I spotted the pier about 100 yards to my right and decided, as several other Marines did, that it offered more protection than wading straight in, because the water was hard to walk in and it gave the Japs more time to pick you off. From experience gained from fighting on Guadalcanal, I knew the Japs didn't use traversing fire as we would have - had we set up a final protective line, we would also have had a crossfire - so I made my way toward the pier. . .and when the Japs would squeeze off a burst I would dive under the water and come up and watch for his next burst, hoping another gunner wouldn't join in.

"I made it to the pier and worked my way in to the beach, which was under heavy fire. There was about 15 yards of beach and then the sea wall where I landed. This was where Colonel Shoup was, he was running up and down the sea wall urging Marines over the wall. We went over the wall into heavier fire, as the Japs had pillboxes staggered to protect one another, and big sand fortresses that were virtually bombproof."

Out in the lagoon Maj Ruud took a courageous decision. Seeing his men facing what he saw as total annihilation, he took it upon himself to order the fourth wave back from their approach to the beach. Shortly afterwards, and much to Maj Ruud's relief, his regimental commander Col Elmer Hall, who was watching the debacle from the troopship *Monrovia*, sent the message "Land no further troops until directed." On Red Beach 3, Jim Crowe got a message from Shoup: "Ruud is landing to your rear and catching hell." Crowe and his Marines did not need to be told; they had watched the slaughter for themselves.

★   ★   ★

Tanks and artillery had been intended to play an important part in the assault on Betio, but the chaos on the beaches meant that they were not deployed where and when originally planned. Lieutenant Colonel Presley Rixey, commander of the 1-10 artillery battalion, had ordered the landing craft carrying the 75mm M1A1 pack howitzers to remain on standby in the lagoon. Having seen the appalling losses suffered during the initial landings he was not prepared to subject his troops, manhandling heavy equipment, to the scourge of enemy fire.

The M4A2 Sherman medium tanks had been specially prepared for the amphibious landing. Metal stacks, six to eight feet high, had been fitted to the air intakes and the exhaust, to be dumped when they got ashore, and every other opening below the anticipated water line was sealed with a tar-like composition. Special reconnaissance platoons had been assembled to guide the almost blind tank drivers from the landing craft through the maze of shellholes and bomb craters that would inevitably cover the reefs. A system of brightly coloured orange floats was prepared to mark safe corridors for the passage from landing craft to shore. Melvin Swango was a member of one of these reconnaissance platoons on Red Beach 2:

"Ahead we could see the land rapidly approaching, and between us and the beach we could see the turbulence at the edge of the reef. This is where we would begin our assignment. In the 700 or 800 yards between the edge of the reef and the beach we would attempt to plot a safe route for the tanks that would follow; how well we were able to perform our task would mean life or death to our friends within those tanks - it was an awesome responsibility. As we approached the edge of the reef projectiles and machine gun fire began ripping through the bulkheads of our landing craft, and several of our group fell to the deck wounded. There was no time to administer first aid, and we began dividing the floats of those who would not be leaving the boat.

"The Navy coxswain who piloted our craft was a very brave man, he never wavered for a moment and rammed the fragile craft solidly onto the edge of the reef. It was imperative that we get into the water as quickly as possible; to pause even for a few minutes would provide the Japanese machine gunners with a stationary target and we would surely die. We cast a parting glance at our wounded comrades and plunged over the side of the boat and into the shoulder-deep water. We would only have a limited amount of time in which to lay our floats for the big Sherman tanks, each in its own individual landing craft, which were awaiting our signal to charge the reef.

"From the beginning it was apparent that the floats were not going to work. The ropes became soggy with salt water and could not be separated from each other, and the anchors were too light to hold the floats in place - the wash from the first tank to pass them would cause them to drift out of position. So we abandoned all the floats at the location of the first crater. We spread out in a single line, spacing ourselves as far apart as possible while still being able to see any crater that may appear between us; at each crater one man would remain to wave the tank safely by. The closer we approached the island the more intense became the enemy fire. Grimly I observed that each time I surveyed our little group there were fewer of us - a man would simply sink beneath the water and not be seen again. I prayed that when my time came the wound would be instantly fatal; it would be a horrible death to be mortally wounded and drown while thrashing about in the chalky water.

"Our tanks were watching for us as they ploughed through the water, exhausts roaring like some terrible denizens of the deep; occasionally one of the tank hatches would tilt slightly and one of our buddies would wave a friendly salute from within the dark confines. Finally all the tanks had passed; most of them made it in, a few met with mishaps or drowned out and were abandoned in the water. I looked about for other members of our group but only a handful were left."

The Shermans which landed on Red 3 were eight tanks from Co C's 2nd and 3rd Platoons. Of the former, one flooded out in a shellhole but three got ashore and went into action on Red 2; the four tanks of 3rd Platoon all made it to the beach.

★   ★   ★

There now followed a period of ever-worsening confusion at command level, as persistent radio failures obscured the situation of the 1,500-odd Marines who were holding their two separated and tenuous footholds on the western point of Red 1 and on either side of the long pier on Red 2 and 3. Julian Smith was left with only one reserve unit, Maj Lawrence Hays' 1st Bn, 8th Marines; and he now decided to place them at the point of departure to be available to Col Shoup. At 1.30pm he sent an urgent message to Holland Smith asking V Corps for the 6th Marines to be turned over to him: "Commanding General 2nd Marine Division requests release of Combat Team 6 to 2nd Marine Division - issue in doubt."

To try to clarify the situation on the island Julian Smith sent his second in command, Brig Gen Leo Hermle, to land on the pier to gather information and report back to him aboard *Maryland.* Hermle was unable to locate Shoup's command post, however, and when he tried to contact Smith by radio to give him what little information he had he was unable to get through. Hermle actually remained at the pier overnight and did not get back to the *Maryland* until the 21st, D+1 - only to find that Smith had sent a message, which he had never received, ordering him to take command on the island. One result of these multiple failures of communication was that David Shoup remained in command on Betio on D+1. Shoup, meanwhile, with similar concerns, had sent Lt Col Evans Carlson - who was with his staff group - to try to get back out to the *Maryland* to give Julian Smith a first-hand account of the situation on Betio.

At about 2.30pm, an hour after he had radioed his request for control of the 6th Marines, Julian Smith received permission from V Corps; he now felt free to commit 1-8 under Maj Hays, and sent a message to Shoup asking where he wanted them landed. This message, too, was never received. Having had no acknowledgement from Shoup, Smith ordered 1-8 to land on the extreme eastern end of the island and work their way north-west to link up with Shoup's beachhead on Red 2. Yet again, the message never got through. The 1-8 spent the rest of D Day and the whole night of 20-21 November lurching around in their boats at the line of departure, waiting for instructions.

Not all the Marines who had got ashore on Red Beach 1 were with Maj Ryan.

PFC Bob Libby, the mortarman from M Co, 3-2, had survived the murderous wade across the reef and reached the sea wall:

"Once I reached the shore and the relative safety of the coconut log barricade, I felt as if a huge weight had been lifted from me; from now on I would be on a more or less equal footing with the enemy - out in the water the Japs were invisible and somehow even more menacing. . . .Looking around we found there were precious few of us remaining. The heaviest concentration of fire seemed to be coming from our left front - even though our area had its share as well. For some moments we huddled up against the four foot high sea wall while the Japanese continued to keep us pinned down on the beach. It was soon found that there were no officers ashore in our area, we were a mixed gathering of men from many units driven together by circumstances. Catching our breath and gaining confidence during a lull in the enemy fire, we leapt over the sea wall and began some sort of advance.

"Few men knew each other, but this mattered little at this stage. We banded together and made up an attacking force of our own. Heavy sniper fire held up our advance for some time, but gaining the upper hand we began to broaden our immediate front - by about 2pm we safely held over half of the 800 yard area we had landed in. The first aid station to our rear was overflowing with wounded; the problem of getting the more seriously wounded off the island and out to the ships was acute.

"A group of a dozen or so of us had decided to make an advance as far across the island as we could go. Steadily moving from one position to another, we cleaned out isolated pockets of resistance until we had some 600 yards of territory. Suddenly, finding myself leading the advance, I reached an area of tank traps where I waited for those following me - for some reason no one appeared behind me. [Presumably these were the ditches immediately west of the airfield.] Moving to the side of the tank trap, I saw a lone Jap Marine operating a knee mortar some 100 yards away from me. I saw him loading a grenade into his launcher and pull the lanyard to fire; it was at this stage that I scrambled along the trench towards the southern shoreline - an advance preferable to retreating. The mortar he had fired landed in exactly the spot where I had been standing; having moved when I did saved me from becoming another casualty. The Jap fired several more shells in my direction; all fell some distance behind where I actually was, but he did succeed in wounding those behind me. One of those wounded had half his face blown away; his screams drew medical teams to his rescue, all were attended to and removed from the scene to be evacuated.

"Meanwhile I was in a dilemma - to continue advancing or retire from the area? I came to realise that I was now on my own; there was little point in continuing my advance, however I did move a little further along the trench. I had heard voices. . .talking quietly but close enough to be heard; I wondered if they were some of our own men or had I stumbled across a pocket of enemy troops? Heroes are said to be born, not made, and I felt that this was no time for me to find out which was true. I cleared out in the direction of our own lines and comparative safety. Arriving back to our own front line I found that the advance had fizzled out after the wounded had been evacuated from the area. I had been given up as a casualty, with no one game enough to check for certain. . . they were surprised to see me loping in all in one piece."

*   *   *

The spirits of the beleaguered Marines, jammed against the sea walls and taking continual casualties from mortar, machine gun and sniper fire, were lifted by the arrival of the seven survivors of the Sherman tanks which Melvin Swango had helped guide ashore on Red Beach 3. After weaving their way between the wrecked amtracs, yawning shell craters and strewn bodies the four tanks of 3rd Platoon reported to Jim Crowe for instructions; the three from 2nd Platoon were placed at Shoup's disposal on Red 2.

Crowe directed his tanks to the south-east in support of the infantry in that part of the tiny perimeter; one Sherman, getting too far ahead of the ground troops, was knocked out by a Navy dive-bomber. Another lumbered into an enemy fuel dump and had to be abandoned when it caught fire, and a third fell victim to Japanese artillery. The last of the four, "*Colorado*", also caught fire; but her crew saved her by driving into the sea to extinguish the flames. Scorched but still operational, she was diverted to the western flank of Red 3, and though repeatedly hit she remained in action against the enemy pillboxes and bunkers.

The commander of the tank battalion, Lt Col Alexander Swenceski, became a casualty very early in the battle. Approaching the beaches, his amtrac received a direct hit and he was blown overboard and severely wounded. In danger of drowning although the water was only a few inches deep, he spotted a pile of bodies that had become entangled on a protruding ledge of the reef. Swenceski laboriously crawled over to them and, after making sure that they were dead, climbed to the top of the pile and flopped down in total exhaustion. He remained clinging to his gruesome island all of the first day and all night before he was found.

*   *   *

Meanwhile, Lt Hawkins' Scout Snipers had finally managed to link up to co-ordinate their movements for the afternoon of D Day. In the words of the report of 15 December 1944:

"Gunnery Sergeant Hooper and his two sections cleared the ship at 0400 and proceeded to the line of departure. They then went to the edge of the reef where the Beach Master ordered them to circle. The boat circled for several hours until Lieutenant Hawkins was contacted. All the Scout Snipers were loaded into one boat and the decision was made to go in as far as possible, and swim the rest of the way if necessary. They proceeded towards the pier and commandeered three useable amphibious tractors; Lieutenant Hawkins then took command of the second and third sections, less Sergeant Morgan and his team, and landed on the pier midway to the beach and proceeded inland. This was approximately 1615.

"Gunnery Sergeant Hooper, with 1st section and headquarters team, made their way to the beach with orders to report to the Regimental CP and await arrival of platoon leader. The beach was gained by this group at 1430. In the meanwhile, Sergeant Morgan and his team boarded the third tractor and landed at the jetty on the boundary of Red Beach 1 and 2 at 1600. Because of the situation, the first section men were needed to advance the line to the south side of the airfield and the first section participated in this advance, where they remained until almost dark. A runner brought a message ordering them back to the Regimental CP [i.e. Col Shoup's command post just south of Red 2].

"Lieutenant Hawkins and his two sections (less Sergeant Morgan and his team) proceeded to the Regimental CP. Because of the time element and strong enemy machine gun fire, Lieutenant Hawkins was told to remain at the CP and set up a defence for the night. Platoon assembled at the CP about 1700, set up defence and immediately started to work on Japs in the bomb shelter near the CP."

*   *   *

At the western end of Red Beach 1, Maj Mike Ryan of 3-2 found himself in charge of a motley force from several units. He had the remains of I, K and L rifle companies and one machine gun platoon from M of his own battalion; from 2-2, who were supposed to have landed on Red 2, he had the survivors of two rifle companies and two machine gun platoons; around a hundred men from Maj Kyle's 1-2 had joined him; and an assortment of dismounted tank crews and amtrac drivers, heavy weapons men who had lost their equipment, engineers, medical corpsmen and signallers filled out his *ad hoc* battle group.

Over on the eastern side of the cove the hard knot of Japanese defence positions which had decimated the amtracs and Higgins boats at 9am were still intact (indeed, this position was one of the last on Betio to fall). Ryan decided that his best chances lay in making an attack southwards from the point along Green Beach, heading down the western end of the island. "Later in the day, as our attacks continued on enemy positions, two Japanese came running across open space by the airfield", he recalls, "with our troops on the left firing on them. How they made it I'll never know, but they did get to the area of what later was discovered to be the Japanese command post. Our front was waving forward with the open flank behind it on the left. Seeing the two Japanese moving to our left, we made a search and found a few Marines ashore there, and others on the beach, most of them from other battalions. With these additions a makeshift line was established behind the left flank of our forward units.

"During this process, a staff NCO came to me dragging his wounded hip, saluted and asked what he could do. Told of the plan, he set out to place the men along the line in the experienced fashion of the competent NCO. Through the years I have treasured that salute. He was not from one of our units and I have no idea who he was or if he lived through the operation - he could not be found after the line was established.

"Concerned about a possible suicide attack when the day was ended, I ordered the units to withdraw the forward elements to form a continuous line around the point. Few of us slept that night, but there was no attack and the night passed uneventfully."

Bob Libby of 3-2 recalls: "I was one of the remnants that Major Ryan gathered up to carry out the charge down Green Beach. . . we did relinquish our gains to fall back for the night. On that night we on Red Beach 1 set up a defensive perimeter no more than 100 yards in depth. . . .We knew the sods were all around us throughout the night, but by dawn's early light they had all scooted back to their bunkers."

★   ★   ★

On Red Beach 3, Maj Jim Crowe's enclave was ringed by fires and explosions. The US warships were still blasting the eastern end of the island, and dive bombers and fighters from the carriers were constantly pounding and strafing anything that moved around the Marines' perimeter. The survivors of Maj Ruud's 3-8 had staggered ashore and were re-grouping into some semblance of a fighting force after the slaughter on the reef. Crowe's Marines were making small incursions into the Japanese lines, as PFC Joe Jordan recalls:

"The beach consisted of about ten or twenty feet of dry sand and ended on the landward side in a sea wall of coconut logs . . . this was excellent cover for rifle and machine gun fire, but the Japs began dropping in mortar rounds, a very uncomfortable situation. If you lay there the mortars would get you, and if you went over the sea wall there was complete exposure to small arms fire. It was too far to swim back to the States or I may have tried that. Several feet down the beach from us was an amtrac that had gotten onto the wall and had been stopped; it was at an angle to the beach and gave cover for some of us to crawl after getting on top of the wall. A few feet inland was a deep ditch for an anti-tank trap and we got into it.

"There was plenty of cover from the small arms fire, but you had to expose part of yourself to attempt to return fire. The Jap positions were laid out so that at least one position could shoot into another position; this meant that if we attacked one, then we would be under fire from it and at least one more. We finally got enough firepower into the ditch to shoot into the firing ports of several of the machine gun nests at the same time. If you could stop their shooting for only a few seconds it would allow someone to get forward with hand grenades. By now the flame thrower teams were getting into action and were very effective, if they could get close enough - flame throwers are only effective for about ten or twenty yards at most; a lot of them were killed that morning. [It is recorded that the Marines had only received their flame throwers and 2.36in bazookas just before leaving New Zealand. The only training they were able to carry out was firing off the sterns of the troopships, which permitted no practice of fire and movement as teams. This greatly reduced their effectiveness, and increased their vulnerability, when they first went into action on Betio.]

"Tanks which should have landed early were blown up during the time they were attempting to get in from the reef; their trip required men to guide the tanks around the craters caused by the naval bombardment - those guys should have gotten a Congressional, the tank and the guide were under constant fire from machine guns and anti-tank weapons.

"Due to the foul-up in not knowing about the reefs, landing schedules were mangled and a group of Seabees [Navy Construction Battalions, i.e. men from 3-18] and their bulldozers arrived early. Those brave bulldozer operators thought they were driving tanks, and would pick up the blades and charge pill-boxes, using the blades as armour. When they got real close to the firing ports they would drop their blades and cover the ports with sand and coral; more than one pillbox was silenced this way - and sad to say, more than one operator was killed.

"By afternoon we had moved inland somewhere close to a hundred yards; we discovered that our flanking companies had not been as successful and the Japs could sneak behind us and re-occupy positions that we had silenced. Orders were to move back and consolidate the line; sure enough we ran into problems with re-occupied positions and had to fight our way back.

"Just before dark we were ordered to straighten the line as much as possible and dig in for the night. All hands were low on ammunition and nobody had any water left; working parties were called for to go to the beach and find both - my Sergeant volunteered me! Trip number one I managed to haul about a dozen bandoliers of rifle ammunition, trip two a five-gallon can of water, and trip three several boxes of ammunition for the light machine guns. Some rations were brought in and we had a cold supper of C-rations; everyone was starved and gulped the food down."

Joe Jordan's comment that "By afternoon we had moved inland somewhere close to a hundred yards; we discovered that our flanking companies had not been as successful" speaks volumes about the nature of the fighting on Betio. Every painful yard had to be paid for; the defence always has the advantage in infantry fighting, and here the attackers were advancing over the surface against defenders who were, in effect, lying in ambush underground. The Japanese naval infantry often only revealed themselves in the act of shooting down their attackers from the gun slits of their closely-woven pattern of dugouts.

★   ★   ★

It was some time during the afternoon that everybody became aware of a sickly smell that pervaded the air. The tropical midsummer sun had been beating down all day; Betio lay only 80 miles north of the equator, and the hundreds of dead men who were floating in the lagoon and lying on the beaches were already beginning to stink.

★   ★   ★

The combined beachhead formed by parts of Red 2 and Red 3 now stretched from a short distance east of the cove at the west, to the edge of the Burns-Philp wharf in the east, with the long pier somewhere near the centre. Major Ruud was now ordered to land the remains of his mauled battalion, and they came ashore via the west side of the pier. Amtracs were still in short supply and the men of 3-8 used any form of transport that was available - a few amtracs and a lot of Higgins boats. Once round the end of the pier many had to leave their boats and wade the rest of the way.

Colonel Carlson, on his way to return to the USS *Maryland* with a situation report for Maj Gen Smith, delayed his journey and used the few amtracs that were available to pick up as many of these men as he could - the enemy fire was still intense, and many Marines fell and died within yards of the shore that they had tried so hard to reach. Major Ruud led some of his men in, leaving his executive officer at the end of the pier to organise the flow of craft arriving from the point of departure.

This long central pier had become the main point of entry for all supplies; unfortunately, a great deal arrived in anything but the order in which it was needed. The expenditure of ammunition was enormous, medical supplies were in constant demand, and in the searing equatorial heat drinking water was at a desperate premium throughout the battle - and all of it had to be funnelled down the pier. But the transports and cargo ships were unloading their supplies as fast as they could get them ashore, regardless of priorities. Constantly aware of the possibility of a Japanese air attack, the captains were anxious to be rid of their loads and rejoin the protection of the US Navy armada lying offshore. Colonel Shoup watched in fury as amtracs struggled ashore with unwanted cargoes while his parched Marines fought for their lives, scrabbling in their emptying ammo pouches or crawling under fire to snatch bandoliers from dead comrades.

Once Ruud had his 3-8 ashore Shoup ordered him to reorganise his I and L Cos to take up a defensive position in the triangle formed by the taxiways of the airfield. The battalion had suffered so many casualties already that they were absorbed into a composite unit with Crowe's 2-8 Marines.

*   *   *

All along Red 1 and Red 2 small incursions were made into the Japanese positions, but at great cost. The landing craft in which PFC David Spencer of Co E, 2-2 Marines had been heading for Red 2 that morning had come under withering fire from the Japanese emplacements directly ahead, which forced them to veer off to their right; they ended up near the edge of Red 1, and Spencer's platoon leader was killed in the water as they rushed to get ashore and over to the sea wall.

"I went in around 9.30am and hit the beach; the guy on the left hand side got hit very badly in the water, and I went on the right side and made it to the beach and the sea wall; there were only four or five of us from the 2nd Marines in that area. Our job was to get across to the airstrip."

About four or five did make it that far, but were ordered to come back to the beach - they were probably in too isolated a position to be left alone. "It was a very rough time out there. Snipers were after me; there was a Jap next to me in another shell hole. We both took a shot at each other and we both missed - I threw a grenade and finished him off there. We started running across as snipers

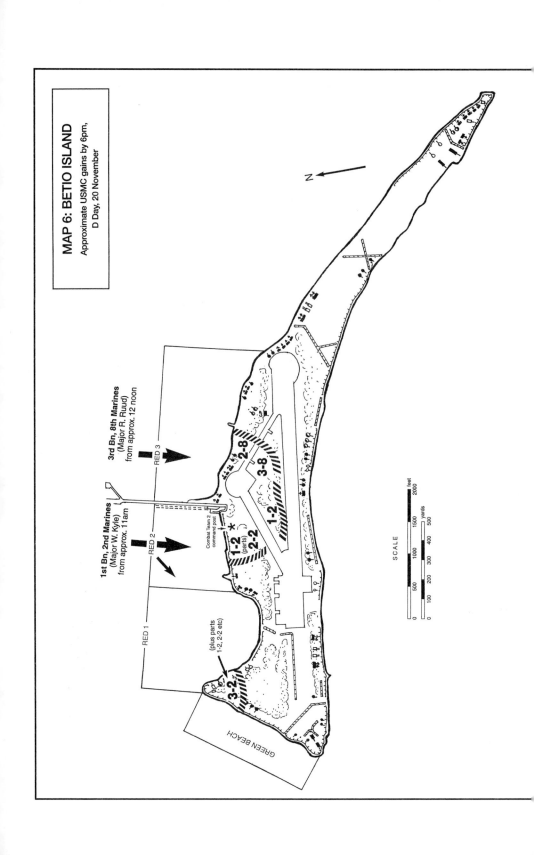

MAP 6: BETIO ISLAND
Approximate USMC gains by 6pm,
D Day, 20 November

N

3rd Bn, 8th Marines
(Major R. Ruud)
from approx. 12 noon

RED 3

1st Bn, 2nd Marines
(Major W. Kyle)
from approx. 11am

RED 2

RED 1

Combat Team 2
command post

1-2
(parts)

2-2

1-2

2-8

3-8

1-2

3-2

(plus parts
1-2, 2-2 etc)

GREEN BEACH

SCALE

0   100 200 300 400 500
0   500   1000   1500   2000
              yards
                      feet

tried getting me; I laid like I was dead - I think some other Marine got the Jap."

Private Spencer had a friend called Jack Wren; they had known each other since they were about twelve years old, they went to school together and they joined the Marines together. By one of those odd quirks of fate that sometimes occur during wartime both David and Jack were on Betio, but in different parts of the beachhead. Jack was with the 3-2, assigned to Red Beach 1; his LCVP had grounded on the reefs off the north-west end of the island, and he had to wade in towards the murderous fire from the east side of the cove. Seeing that there were survivors over to the west of him, he struggled on between the burning amtracs and floating corpses until he came across two Marines lying on a sand-bar about fifty yards offshore, and flopped down between them to rest.

"Pretty rough, isn't it?", he said to the man on his left, but immediately realised that he was dead. He turned to the Marine on his right and said, "Look, that guy's dead" - only to see that he was talking to another corpse.

Jack Wren went on to fight on the western end of Betio under Maj Ryan, whom he considered to be a great man and and a great officer; he survived the battle, and was shipped to Camp Tarawa in Hawaii with the rest of the 2nd Division. Neither Jack nor David Spencer knew at that time that the other had survived the battle; when Jack got a letter telling him that David was alive he went run-ning through the camp, yelling "Where's Spencer, where's Spencer?"

★ ★ ★

Correspondent Robert Sherrod was ashore at the landward end of the pier. After a hair-raising wade ashore from 700 yards out, during which he had faced the full fury of the Japanese fire, he could count himself a seasoned Marine:

"I do not know when it was that I realised I wasn't frightened any longer. I suppose it was when I looked around and saw the amtrac scooting back for more Marines. Perhaps it was when I noticed that bullets were hitting six inches to the left or six inches to the right." During his trip ashore he had been surprised to see an almost naked figure appear from under the water and climb into an aban-doned tank. Sherrod reported the incident to a Marine officer ashore, but he was obviously too preoccupied to do anything about it. These Japanese infiltra-tors were to give the Marines quite a lot of trouble later.

Sherrod found himself a "safe" spot behind a disabled amtrac near the sea wall: "I felt quite luxurious. Not fifteen minutes later, in the same spot, I saw the most gruesome sight I had seen in this war. Another young Marine walked briskly along the beach. He grinned at a pal who was sitting next to me. There was a shot, the Marine spun all the way round and fell to the ground dead. From where he lay a few feet away, he looked at us. Because he had been shot square-ly through the temple his eyes bulged out wide, as if in horrific surprise at what had happened to him."

Sherrod stayed for quite a time around Jim Crowe's command post, watching the wounded coming back in from the small outposts beyond the sea wall; and then decided to try to make it across to Red 1 where he was supposed to have landed. Dodging around the wrecks of the amtracs, he moved along the pier for as far as he could before making a final dash to a shell hole near Walter Jordan's 2-2 command post. Along with another correspondent he dug a foxhole; and that was as far as he got that day. He estimated that the Marines held "twenty feet along perhaps one sixteenth of one half of one side of the island, plus a few men in shellholes on either side of the airstrip" - the Japanese held all of the rest of Betio.

★   ★   ★

During the whole day the Navy had continued their shelling of the island; the battleships *Maryland, Tennessee* and *Colorado* directed their salvos away from the landing beaches, their huge 16in guns lobbing tons of steel and explosive onto the Japanese emplacements around the airfield and on the eastern tail of Betio. The cruisers *Portland, Indianapolis, Mobile, Birmingham* and *Santa Fe* poured a saturating fire into the network of coastal defences, while further out to sea the carriers *Essex, Independence* and *Bunker Hill* flew off and landed on a continual relay of dive bombers and fighters to blast anything that moved in the Japanese lines. The light carrier *Independence* was providing anti-submarine patrols on the outer limits of Task Group 50-3 when, at around 6pm, news came in from the control information centre that unidentified aircraft were approaching at very low altitude from the west. This had all the hallmarks of a Japanese torpedo attack - flying low to avoid radar, and attacking from the west late in the day when the low evening sun would be shining into the eyes of the ship's gunners. Within minutes fifteen Mitsubishi G4M "Betty" twin-engined bombers were spotted on the starboard side; they singled out the *Independence*, and assembled into line formation. Captain Johnson swung his ship 20 degrees port to present the carrier's stern to the incoming planes, but three of the bombers swung out of formation to attack from the beam. Johnson now began a series of violent evasive manoeuvres, turning first to starboard, then rapidly back to port; this not only upset the Japanese pilots' attempts to set up their attack run, but brought them within range of the escort destroyer USS *Hale*, which shot one of them down.

The remaining "Bettys" then headed in line for the *Independence*, pressing on at wavetop height through a wall of cannon and gunfire from every available turret and weapons tub. Within 60 seconds six of the bombers ploughed into the sea, three of them crashing within a hundred yards of the carrier. Five torpedo wakes were seen burrowing through the waves; four narrowly missed the starboard side of the twisting carrier, passing through her wake, but the fifth exploded against her stern.

The *Independence* rapidly took on water and listed 12 degrees, but counterflooding, and moving the aircraft to the port side, reduced the angle to three degrees. The damage was not as severe as it might have been: a 40mm gun was blown overboard, as was a fighter which was parked on the flight deck immediately above the point of impact - but the torpedo had exploded within 30 feet of a rack containing seven torpedoes for the carrier's Avengers, without detonating them. The *Independence* was detached from the Task Force and made her way back to the USA and the West Coast navy yards without further incident.

★   ★   ★

David Shoup had decided to use the three surviving Sherman tanks of 2nd Ptn, which had become available to him on Red Beach 2 sometime around noon, in an attempt to link up with the Marines that he knew were ashore somewhere on Red 1. The Japanese strongpoint on the eastern side of the cove was a major headache to Lt Col Jordan in his attempts to move his 2- 2 westwards; here the Japanese are thought to have had two 37mm and two 70mm or 75mm guns, plus a number of 13mm machine guns, all firmly entrenched in log and coral emplacements on which nothing had so far made any impression.

Neither did the Shermans have much success; and after slogging it out for about an hour they swung inland towards the airfield taxiways, to help scattered groups of Marines who had been fighting a desperate point-blank battle of attrition with the Japanese all morning. One tank slithered into a large shell hole, probably from a battleship's 16in gun, and could not climb out; a second was knocked out by a Japanese infantryman with a magnetic mine and had to be abandoned. The lone survivor continued fighting, shelling enemy emplacements and charging groups of Japanese in their foxholes.

The Marines holding this precarious triangle around the east and west taxiways were remnants of Maj Kyle's 1-2 and Lt Col Jordan's 2-2 Marines, both of which had been badly mauled that morning landing on Red 2. Their advance of a few dozen yards from the beach had taken hours of furious close quarter fighting that left them near exhaustion. Almost all these Marines were fighting in makeshift groups from different companies, even different battalions; but in true USMC fashion they had quickly and efficiently blended into cohesive fighting units.

Robert Sherrod recalled seeing one of the Marines from this group who had come to collect some cigarettes for machine gun crews across the airfield: "PFC Adrian Strange stands for a few minutes, fully exposed to the sniper who had been pecking at us. Then the sniper opens up again, the bullets rattling against the coconut logs. PFC Strange sings out, 'Shoot me down, you son of a bitch!'; then he leisurely turns around and walks back across the airfield carrying his carbine and pack of cigarettes."

★   ★   ★

The artillery, which had remained offshore all day, was finally directed to come in to Red Beach 2 late in the afternoon. As most of the 75mm pack howitzers were shipped aboard LVCPs which were unable to cross the reef, it was imperative that sufficient amtracs be rounded up. Two batteries - A and B of 1-10 Marines - were transferred to amtracs at around dusk and ordered to land on Red 2. Due to a misunderstanding, C Bty was also sent in although they had not yet been able to find any amtracs in which to transfer their equipment. This battery had to land at the end of the pier, and the Marine gunners were forced to manhandle their heavy pieces along the pier and through waist-deep water to the shore. By nightfall five batteries of artillery were ashore and ready for what the next day would bring.

★   ★   ★

And so the first day of the battle for Tarawa drew towards an end. The furnace temperatures cooled and gave way to a slight breeze, to the relief of the Marines crouching in their precarious rifle pits - it was even more of a blessing to the wounded, lying in their dozens on the narrow coral strip that passed as a beach. The American foothold on Betio was tenuous. About 5,000 men had left the point of departure that day; many were dead or wounded, and the unknown number who remained fit to fight - something over 3,000? - held no continuous lines, just a series of loosely connected foxholes, captured trenches and dug-outs.

On the right of Red Beach 1, Maj Ryan and his assorted band held a piece of the north-west tip of the island about 250 yards wide and 300 yards long, with the sea on two sides. Their supply situation was critical and they had no means of evacuation. On the combined Red 2 and Red 3 beachhead the troops on the western flank of Red 3 and the eastern flank of Red 2 were in sporadic contact; but there was a 600 yard gap between them and Maj Ryan. To the west their front line ended about 300 yards away from the pier, and to the east at the Burns-Philp wharf; inland, the lines stretched about half way to the main runway of the airfield at the deepest incursion. Colonel Shoup had no illusions; he knew that a major Japanese counter-attack could be expected - night attacks were a Japanese speciality. Could the Marines hold?

Darkness came swiftly, as it does in the Pacific; and an uneasy silence descended, punctured only by the gunfire of a destroyer out in the lagoon. The Marines kept silent, their training standing them in good stead - nobody was going to reveal their position to an enemy who in some places was crouching only yards away.

The breeze wafted the smell of decomposition all around the island. Even a thousand yards offshore, where the 600 men of Maj Lawrence Hays' 1-8 Marines had been waiting in their landing craft at the line of departure since mid-morning, the stench of death was detectable as they tried to settle down for another ten hours in their cramped, bobbing boats.

At 7.11pm Maj Gen Smith had signalled to Col Shoup: "Hold what you have, develop contact between landing teams, clear hostile machine guns still holding out on beaches, make provision to meet organised counter-attack."

Chapter 5:

The Charnel House

*"I turn to the big red-headed Marine gunner who
is standing beside me and say "What a hell of a
way to die!". The gunner looks me in the eye and
says, "You can't pick a better way".*

(Robert Sherrod, *Tarawa - The Story of a Battle*)

For Joe Jordan of Maj Crowe's 2-8 Marines, squatting in a foxhole on the outer
limits of Red 3, there would be little sleep during the night of 20-21
November. "Orders were for one man in each hole to stay awake. There was
also a good chance that the Japs would pull a *banzai* and attempt to drive us back
into the lagoon - wouldn't have been too hard to do, as we were all exhausted
and had lost about half of our forces. I do not know the name of the ship but in
just a few minutes we heard the sound of a destroyer coming our way. [It was the
USS *Ringgold*, still living up to her name - that of a famous officer of US horse
artillery in the Mexican War.]

"I thought that they ran aground to establish a firing platform, but have never
heard anything to verify this. Anyway, those gunners sat there all night and
pounded any target that we called for, and saved our rear ends. Several times we
could hear the Jap troops beginning the *banzai* chant, and would call for fire
towards that location. To this day I believe that we would have been overrun that
night if not for that naval gunfire. There was very little sleep and almost no rest
that night."

Some time during the night Japanese bombers from the Marshall Islands
to the north arrived over Betio, and attempted to bomb the shipping lying to the
west of the island. Met by heavy anti-aircraft fire, they jettisoned their bombs
and left. There was also sporadic machine gun and sniper fire from the Japanese
lines, which did not bother the Marines until they realised that some of the fire
was actually coming from their rear. It became apparent that numbers of
Japanese had swum out into the lagoon and onto the abandoned amtracs, tanks
and other assorted craft that lay scattered off the beaches, and were firing at the
Marines with the machine guns mounted on these.

Before dawn one of the big Kawanishi flying boats arrived to investigate.
It circled around for a while, dropped a few small bombs into the lagoon and
flew away. The 2nd Division Marines who were veterans of Guadalcanal remembered these flying boats by the nickname "Washing Machine Charlie" from their
peculiar throbbing engine noise.

In Maj Mike Ryan's perimeter on the western point of Red 1, Bob Libby and
four other Marines were looking for a secure place to settle for the night. "We
came across a flight of concrete steps leading to an underground bunker; cautiously we ventured down the stairway, and found the place empty. Here, we

decided, was where we would set up for the night. We worked out a guard roster that would give us one and a half hours each. When my turn came for the
watch I made my way up the stairway and took up a position where good vision
could be maintained over the clear space around the bunker.

"I knew there were Japs around us - the sound of slithering bodies in the sand
and the rustle of palm fronds attested to this fact. A voice in English would call
out for a Joe, Jack or John, or for a medical corpsman. These had to be Japanese,
as no Marine would ever give away his position after dark by talking. The discipline of our fellows was spot on, letting the Japs know that they were up against
well trained troops. Not a shot was fired throughout the night - but still the Japs
did their best to upset this discipline. Sitting snug in our little bunker, we had
quite a peaceful night as I recall."

★   ★   ★

The Japanese failure to mount a counter-attack on the night of 20-21 November
was their greatest mistake, and cost them the battle. The great majority of the
garrison were still alive; they had large amounts of ammunition and supplies
available to them; and they were the masters of the night-time *banzai* attack. The
Americans, on the other hand, were hanging on by their fingertips.

Small, dispersed pockets of Marines, few of them in contact with each other,
were scattered around the northern part of the airfield in the centre of the island,
dug in where night had found them, with no coherent defensive perimeter and
lacking many of their heavy weapons. The majority of those ashore were still
huddled behind the sea wall, many of them wounded, most of them short of
ammunition, food and water. The number of serviceable tanks could be counted on one hand (although frantic effort during the night to recover flooded
Shermans off the beach would get two more back into action on D+1). Only a
small proportion of the artillery were ashore; and the pier was jammed with
unwanted supplies of all descriptions. Over on Red Beach 1, Ryan and his men
were squeezed into a tiny pocket on the north-west tip of the island with the sea
on both flanks, almost out of ammunition and with many wounded.

Shoup, Crowe, Walter Jordan and Ryan were all certain that there would be a
counter-attack. Years of Marine training left them in no doubt as to their
predicament; the only questions in their minds were how long could they hold
on - and where did they go if they couldn't? On the USS *Maryland* Julian Smith
passed one of the worst nights of his life; he declared at the time that this was the
crisis of the battle. A general counter-attack would almost certainly have driven
the Marines back into the sea, where any evacuation could only have been
achieved with appalling losses - if at all. How could the Japanese have missed
such an opportunity?

The historians have pondered the question for fifty years without coming to a
completely satisfactory conclusion; but the death of Adml Shibasaki has always
been shrouded in mystery. The accepted theory has been that he died on the
third day of the battle when the fighting around his command post, a little way
inland from the Burns-Philp wharf, was at its fiercest. However, more recent

research by the distinguished Marine historian Col Joseph Alexander suggests that the admiral and his entire staff may have been killed on the afternoon of the first day of the battle, when a shell from either the *Ringgold* or the *Dashiell* exploded outside his headquarters while the command staff were moving to an alternative site somewhere on the south side of Betio. If this is correct - and Col Alexander's arguments are persuasive - then the Japanese failure to mount an organised, co-ordinated attack on the beachheads becomes more understandable.

Over the years it has been suggested that the massive naval bombardment of the first day, though not fulfilling its original purpose of annihilating the Japanese defences, did chew up their communications system so badly that Shibasaki was unable to organise a counter-attack. This theory has always been suspect, even if there were not a single working field telephone left in the Japanese positions. The distances involved were small, fighting had largely subsided for the night, and under cover of darkness, over ground they knew well, there is no reason why runners could not have got through with the relevant orders. But if Shibasaki and his entire staff were dead, then such orders were never given.

It was believed at the time that Japanese troops, once deprived of their leadership, were apt to become disillusioned and disorganised (as was proven on the neighbouring island of Apamama, where the entire garrison committed suicide after their commanding officer accidentally shot himself). If only junior officers of the dispersed companies of the SNLF were left to organise the defence of Betio, it is easier to see why resistance began to fragment so rapidly from the second day onwards.

*   *   *

Major Hays' 1-8 Marines were still embarked in their Higgins boats at the line of departure, and the 6th Marines combat team were on their transport ships awaiting instructions. At 2am Julian Smith sent a message to Col Elmer Hall, commanding officer of the 8th Marines (and thus of Combat Team 8), asking the location and condition of his 1st Battalion; Hall replied that they were "resting easy" at the point of departure near the USS *Pursuit*. This must have been an optimistic description of the status of men who had been cramped in their uncomfortable, unstable landing craft since mid-morning the previous day, bounding about in a medium swell, choked with diesel fumes, and without food, drink or toilet facilities.

The part played by the assistant divisional commander, Brig Gen Leo Hermle, in the landing of Hays' battalion on the second day of the battle is a matter of controversy. It will be remembered that because of the breakdown in the ship-to-shore radio communications on D Day, Julian Smith had decided to send Hermle ashore on the afternoon of the 20th to assess the situation and to get a report back to him. At around 5.30pm on that first afternoon Smith had received a faint radio message that Hermle was at the end of the pier and was under heavy enemy fire. Within ten minutes Smith ordered Hermle to proceed to the shore and take over command from Col Shoup; but once again the communications system failed. Hermle never received the divisional commander's order; more significantly, Smith was unaware that Hermle had not got his message, and confidently assumed that his deputy was ashore and in command on Betio.

Only with the arrival of Evans Carlson on the *Maryland* at about midnight (after a difficult trip via the *Pursuit* and the *Zeilin*) did Julian Smith learn that Hermle had never arrived. Believing him still at sea, Smith radioed the *Monrovia* to order Hermle to move his Divisional Forward Command Post ashore; but by then events, and the repeated radio failures, had outpaced the order.

Having had no further word from the *Maryland*, Hermle spent the night of 20-21 November at the seaward end of the pier organising the evacuation of the large numbers of casualties who were constantly arriving from the beaches, and directing the delivery and forwarding of ammunition and other supplies as they arrived from the transports - useful work, but perhaps not the best way to employ the skills and authority of the assistant divisional commander.

As night fell on D Day Hermle decided to send two of his officers inland in another attempt to contact Shoup, a mission that took them over three hours. When they finally reached Shoup at his command post they were told to inform Hermle that he urgently needed Hays' 1-8 to land at dawn of D+1 on Red Beach 3, close to the pier. The two finally made their way back to the seaward end of the pier at 3.45am on D+1; and Hermle commandeered a Higgins boat to take him out to the destroyer *Ringgold* in the lagoon somewhere off Red Beach 3, in order to use her reliable communications for his first message to Julian Smith since leaving the flagship some eleven hours earlier. The message which he eventually sent read "Shoup desires 1-8 to land off Red 2" - with no mention of Shoup's specific instructions that they land close to the east of the pier.

Hermle's signal caused consternation on the *Maryland*: what on earth was he doing aboard the *Ringgold*? Moreover, Smith had spent all night with Adml Hill and his staff organising the landing of 1-8 on the eastern end of Betio beyond Red Beach 3, where they were to secure the area beyond the end of the airfield and work westward to relieve the pressure on Jim Crowe. Air strikes had been arranged to precede the landings, and gunfire support had been laid on.

Smith immediately radioed Col Hall at 5.22am to cancel the earlier arrangements, ordering him to prepare to land his 1st Battalion on Red Beach 2 at 6.15am. Smith of course knew nothing of Shoup's request that they land close to the pier on Red 3; and consequently, when 1-8 approached the beaches, the slaughter of the previous day would be repeated.

★   ★   ★

The 1-8 finally left the point of departure around 6.15am after being embarked for almost twenty hours. The Higgins boats duly ground to a halt on the reef hundreds of yards short of Red 2; the ramps came down, and the Marines duly charged out into chest-deep water and murderous Japanese machine gun and rifle fire. This fire came not only from the beach but also from the wreck of the

Niminoa, from which vantage point at least two machine guns and many snipers were now picking off the wading Marines more or less at will.

Nineteen-year-old Hawk Rader was with the 1-8, and had been circling around in his landing craft for most of the previous day. "Came noon and we were still circling like a wagon train in the western desert ready to fend off a bunch of Indians; then came 2pm, and still circling - this went on all night. Guys would stand up to vomit, the wind would catch it and bring it back over the lot of us; guys would stand at the side of the bobbing boat and try to urinate, and the wind would bring that back over us; defecate? - forget it, you just had to hold it. By the time 1-8 got the order to proceed there were some pretty miserable Marines in our boat." After what seemed an eternity of churning around the lagoon they were finally instructed to head for Red 2.

"Our boat hit a lump of coral and the coxswain ordered us out; we were about 700 yards from the beach, and the water at this point was about five feet deep. Many times they would be in water well over their heads - many men drowned because of that, they just couldn't get out of their gear. Slowly we forged forward; bullets were coming from dead ahead, from the ship on our right flank, and from the small Burns-Philp pier to the east about the centre of Red 3. Once I got past the end of the main pier I got away from this line of fire. The ricocheting bullets on the waves churned up by so many boats made the weirdest noises I ever heard in my life. The noise was horrendous; the smoke was choking, and smelled of burning flesh and hair; men were screaming to make themselves heard, and some were trying to help others.

"I could see many, many bodies floating and washing around in the surf - the water was red-streaked with blood. I noticed when a man was hit by a sniper's bullet, or in any manner, he would go down; then another man or two would go to his aid, and a machine gun would cut them all down. I decided there and then to obey my training: do not become a casualty, it takes two others to take care of you - then there's three out of action.

"I tried not to align myself with any person in front of me, so as not to tempt a machine gunner. I saw the water kick up around me several times, which I assumed was from a sniper or rifleman, but I was not hit. I tried to make myself a scarcer target by zigzagging, and it worked. I decided that I would make it alone or die alone; I did not want anyone else getting killed because of coming to my aid."

Hawk carried on along the west side of the pier, and decided to have a rest; apart from his usual equipment he was carrying a box of machine gun ammunition and a box of spare parts. "A machine gunner, somewhere in the Red 3 area east of the main pier, was watching the pier; I would say he was somewhere in the area of the Burns-Philp pier. He saw my head and decided to have a go with a machine gun burst; by the time he had got my head in his sights I had pulled my head back - he fired a burst with very good aim, hitting the coral and knocking it all over me. So I started towards the beach again. . .

"It was at this time I saw a sight that I shall never forget, and it hurt me deeply. About twelve or fifteen Marines were dead and hanging in the barbed wire which had been placed as an obstacle on the beach. What made it stand out so was that half the Marines were American Indians. These Indian boys had been recruited for, and trained in, communications work; they spoke an Indian dialect we knew the Japanese would not understand should they cut in on our wires." Hawk continued down the side of the long pier, and finally made it to the sea wall on Red Beach 2.

⋆　　　⋆　　　⋆

The Japanese in their still-secure stronghold between Red 1 and Red 2 could scarcely have believed that the enemy were repeating the previous day's tactics; and as the hapless Marines hung up on the reef again, and wilted again under a slashing fire from the beach and from the hulk of the *Niminoa*, Shoup and the troops onshore could only watch in amazement and anger.

"From first daylight until after 8am or so on the second day, there was an uneasy lull in the battle", remembers Bob Libby of 3-2, over on the western point of Red 1. "Then the landings [were made] and all hell and bedlam cut loose as reinforcements began to come in over the reef. Why they used the same style of landing as we had was more than I could understand - the majority of Green Beach was free of enemy forces, so why a tentative landing was not attempted from this angle was something beyond belief. Such an attempt may well have saved lives; under the circumstances the Japanese would have been hard pressed to launch a defensive attack. . .On the other hand, communications from our area to Col Shoup were virtually non-existent, therefore it wasn't known what was going on on Red 1."

⋆　　　⋆　　　⋆

During that Sunday morning Shoup decided that it was time to do something about the *Niminoa*: of the 199 men in Maj Hays' first wave of 1-8, only 99 arrived on the beaches unharmed, and many of the casualties had been caused by fire from the hulk. The landings were suspended for a while, and carrier-based aircraft were summoned to make a strike on the rusting steamer. Hellcat fighter-bombers made pass after pass over the ship, raking it with their .50cal machine guns and dropping 500lb bombs, but with little effect. Of the dozen bombs dropped only one hit the ship, one of the misses falling 200 yards away.

Furiously unimpressed, David Shoup decided to send a party of Marines out to clear the ship. Approaching from the blind side, the group boarded the *Niminoa* and heard at least two machine guns rattling away on the far side. They climbed to the third deck, and could see a large number of Japanese gunners well concealed behind the steel plating on the port side. The sergeant leading the party moved his men out of earshot and radioed his report to Shoup, who decided that the patrol was too small to tackle so many enemy, and ordered them back to shore.

Eventually Shoup asked for naval gunfire on the hulk - reluctantly, because of the risk of hitting the pier or even the beaches; but the Navy provided a short, accurate barrage from the battleships *Maryland* and *Colorado* which finally left the old steamer a smoking, mangled, and silent heap of metal.

★   ★   ★

"Ten am, 21 November 1943 - I am still alive, many are not. That day dawned a beautiful South Pacific day after a miserable night of lapping water over our bodies and land crabs crawling over us. We were not allowed to move, and were to challenge anyone who did. 'Halt! Who goes there? What's the password?' - 'Ohio', repeat 'Columbus'. That was the pre-arranged code: when challenged give a state name, and when told to repeat give the capital. Later I was accused of requiring the naming of all 48 states!" So recalls artilleryman George Blakeman of 1-10, who had spent his night behind the sea wall on Red Beach 2.

The artillery that had managed to get ashore late on 20 November now began to play a part in the battle. Colonel Rixey had two of his pack howitzers moved to the western end of Red 2 and began pounding the strongpoint at the eastern end of the cove that had been responsible for so much carnage. Using delay fuses, they blasted the Japanese position for over half an hour, and this would enable Hays to land the remainder of 1-8 with fewer casualties.

At about 8am Maj Hays had reported to Shoup with what was then available of his battalion. Most of the equipment that was desperately needed ashore had been lost in the water - demolition packs, flame throwers and heavy weapons were at a premium. The 1-8 had suffered perhaps 50% dead, wounded and missing; many men were still out on the reef taking cover behind abandoned amtracs and other wrecks, and would filter in when they thought they saw some let-up in the enemy fire. Later in the day, as the tide rose, heavier equipment such as 37mm anti-tank guns, jeeps, bulldozers, and half-tracks would come ashore; but for the moment David Shoup could only make do with what he had.

Shoup was in the best position to have an overall grasp of the situation on Betio; he was in personal contact with both Jim Crowe and Walter Jordan, and radio communications had improved sufficiently for repeated, if not continuous contact with Ryan on Red 1 and with Julian Smith aboard the Maryland. At some point in the morning one of the Japanese who were still imprisoned inside the bunker beside Shoup's CP managed to dislodge the debris used to block up the vents sufficiently to poke his rifle through, and shot a Marine in the leg. More than a little short of temper, having had little sleep and being increasingly troubled by his leg wounds, Shoup sent a couple of Marines into the bunker with enough grenades to finally silence all its occupants.

★   ★   ★

The medical situation on the island was acute; because of the unexpectedly large numbers of casualties, and the confusion in bringing supplies ashore, medical equipment soon began to run short. The Navy medical corpsmen - who traditionally provide medical services for the US Marines, and who were identified by white discs painted on their helmets and dungarees - were reduced to making regular foraging expeditions to the beaches to relieve dead bodies of their first aid kits. One doctor, Lt Herman Brukardt, led a team working in a disused pillbox, attending to over 100 wounded men during the first 36 hours and only losing four. At one stage a Japanese walked in, and was dispatched on the spot by one of the walking wounded. The pillbox was only yards from the constantly moving front line, and machine gun and snipers' bullets rained all around it. There were so many casualties that the Marines who were able to walk were kept outside and only called in when room became available. Lieutenant Brukardt would recall, "When our anaesthetics gave out I had to perform some pretty painful operations, but few of them let out a whimper."

★   ★   ★

Out on the reefs the rescue operations were also proving extremely hazardous. Navy Lieutenants Edward A.Heimberger and John Fletcher - salvage officers from the transport *Sheridan* - found that many wounded Marines were on the reefs and still under fire. "It was my job to pull out boats which had been damaged and could be repaired", says Heimberger. "Since all the boats were beyond salvage, I concentrated on saving lives instead." After picking up a number of Marines from the reef he realised that more transport was needed, so he commandeered some landing craft from the lagoon and returned to the beleaguered troops offshore. With the tide now on the way in, his boats were coming under fire from both the beaches and the *Niminoa*. Waving the rest of his flotilla back, Heimberger and his crew raced to the reef, silencing a Japanese sniper who fired on them from an abandoned landing craft on the way in.

"Finally I came across a group of Marines huddled in the water and still under fire. They'd been stopped in their advance on the beach and there were dead and wounded all around them. I don't suppose there were thirty unwounded men in the bunch. I didn't have room for them all, so I called out 'C'mon, ten of you guys climb aboard and I'll take you out of here' - nobody moved. A voice from the group asked 'Did you say you were coming back, Lieutenant?' I nodded. 'Well then, bring us back some rifles - we're going in again.' Well, I got back to my ship as fast as I could; but by the time I returned those Marines had disappeared. Some of their bodies we found next day, all of them closer to the beach and the enemy."

On one of his trips Heimberger came across Col Hall of the 8th Marines making his way to the beach, and informed him about the wounded on the reef and of the heavy fire that was coming from the *Niminoa*. Colonel Hall transferred his regimental surgeon to assist the rescue group, who continued to evacuate wounded Marines from the reef for the remainder of the day. Lieutenant Heimberger is probably better known to older readers by his professional name as a film actor - Eddie Albert.

Shoup's principal objectives for D+1 were to push south across the airfield to the other side of the island, effectively cutting the Japanese garrison in two; and to link up with Maj Ryan on Red Beach 1. Major Hays' weakened and disorganised 1-8 Marines were given the task of supporting the troops on the right flank of Red Beach 2, who were expected to push across the cove towards Ryan's enclave. As happened so often on Tarawa, this force was a hotch-potch of whoever happened to be available at the time: the survivors of 2-2 under Lt Col Jordan; a party from the 2nd Marines' HQ & Service Co; Lt Hawkins' Scout Snipers; part of the absent Maj Schoettel's headquarters element, and an assortment of orphaned crewmen from the amtrac battalion. Marine training allowed for situations such as this, and one of the great achievements of the battle was the way in which scattered groups of men from different units - riflemen, gunners, drivers, engineers, radiomen - all blended smoothly into effective fighting teams to meet the needs of the moment.

Although Lt Hawkins' Scout Snipers were still fighting on Red 2, the lieutenant himself was not. The 1944 report quoted earlier continues to describe in the dryest terms how, on the western flank of Red Beach 2, William D.Hawkins had that morning become the second of the three posthumous Medal of Honor winners of Tarawa:

"During the night Lieutenant Hawkins located where the enemy machine guns were firing from and did the planning for their elimination in the morning. D+1 at 0630, Lieutenant Hawkins led two sections 75 yards west along the beach and eliminated three pill boxes and returned to the CP. He re-organised the platoon at 0830 and again proceeded west along the beach to eliminate snipers and more pill boxes that were holding up the advance. During this operation Lieutenant Hawkins was severely wounded and taken to the Regimental Aid Station. Previous to this he had been wounded, but continued to lead the platoon. The platoon stayed at the jetty at the boundary of Red Beaches 1 & 2 directing tanks until ordered back to the CP at 1200." [1]

★   ★   ★

Even with the addition of Hays' men the situation on the western flank of Red 2 was precarious. By noon the Marines had one tank to support their attack, but could make little impression on the enemy defences. Every time that the Marines broke cover they were met by a murderous hail of machine gun fire that sent them scuttling for the nearest shell hole or treetrunk. Attempts were made to co-ordinate their charges with the fire from the tank's 75mm gun, but little ground was taken; and without the flame throwers and demolition charges lost during the landings, a grim stalemate settled in.

By now the sun was high in the sky, and the dreadful stench of death hung heavy in the air. The bodies of the Marines gunned down on the reefs and beaches on the previous day were now in a distressing state. Some attempts had

---

(1) Hawkins died of his wounds. A fuller description of the circumstances, and his Medal of Honor citation, are given in Appendix 8.

been made to gather together the dead for temporary burial, but Japanese guns still covered most of the beaches, and anyone who ventured more than a few yards from the sea wall was taking his life in his hands. Robert Sherrod recalled:

"Thirty-one Marines are now laid out in a line beyond the command post: some are bloated, some have already turned a sickly green, some have no faces, one's guts are hanging out of his body. The eyeballs of another have turned to a jellied mass after so long in the water." Little could be done for those pathetic corpses bobbing in the water like so much abandoned driftwood, or strewn across the beaches, or huddled among the palm trees, until the enemy had been rolled back far enough to allow the bulldozers to scoop out a shallow trench, and the corpsmen to retrieve dog tags and personal possessions and give them a temporary burial until it was all over.

★   ★   ★

In the early afternoon young Hawk Rader of 1-8 was still pinned down on the beach just west of the long pier by relentless Japanese fire: "You just had to sit in the water below the level of the sea wall, or you would lose your head. The Japs had several machine gun pillboxes along this area, which was only about 400 yards long. They had dug down behind these large stones and were firing just over the top of them. The tops of the pillboxes were covered with concrete and had a coconut logging framework filled with sand on top of that. There was a good two feet of sand in the log frameworks, which were tied together with huge staples made of half-inch steel rods. It took a direct frontal hit with a large shell to knock them out. These were finally finished off with flame throwers and satchel charges.

"It was now about 2 or 3 o'clock in the afternoon and I was sitting with my back to the sea wall. I heard a shell go off behind me, it sounded like a 60mm mortar shell. I heard a piece of shrapnel coming - 'wheeee, smack!' - it struck me in the middle of the back. I took off my dungaree jacket and started to feel for blood. A close buddy of mine saw me and asked what I was doing. I told him I was hit in the back. He looked around at my back and said to me, 'You are not hit at all, there's no blood on your back' - he said I was just cracking up. He grabbed me and started slapping me across the face. I shoved him away so hard that he went down. While he was getting up I said to him, 'Damn it, Willie, I got hit, I heard it coming, I felt it hit me, I felt it burn, and it hurt.' He looked at me so hard and so strange I thought he was going to club me. I pulled my jacket round and looked at the back and there it was: it had scorched my jacket and was still sticking to it - it was thin and about the size of a thumbnail.

"Willie and I had a good laugh about it, and got back to business: move, stop and wait, move, stop and wait. We were now almost to the west end of Red Beach 2, where Red 1 and 2 come together. There had been a large gun emplacement hit by a bomb or large naval shell, I never did see what kind of a gun it was because there were so many coconut logs and so much sand had fallen down on top of it so that it was completely covered. We were told to set up our machine gun on the logs to cover the beach to our west, Red Beach 1. This was about 5pm; they came back about an hour later and told us we would probably move on, [but] in another hour we were told we were going to spend the night there.

"We had not seen any movement since we set up; we were under orders to open fire on anyone coming down that beach. We were told that everyone on that end of the island had been killed - that put about as much fear into us as could be put into us. Some men opened up their rations, they'd take a bite of them, look at them and throw them away. Some of these men never ate breakfast on D Day, never ate while we were circling around all day and night in the boats, and now here it was near the end of D+1 and their stomachs still would not accept food. Some of these men had not really had a meal in 72 hours; [their] eyes were red and looked as if they had sunk two inches back into their skulls.

"The wind was very light as we were right on the equator, and the smoky smell of fires on the island mixed with salt air and the stench was really terrible. About thirty feet to the back of us, behind the rock sea wall, was a [Japanese] machine gun nest which had been burned out with a flame thrower. The gunner was still sitting up with his hands – as much as was left – on the trigger end of the gun. The assistant gunner was also sitting up along with the gunner. It looked as if their muscles froze when the jellied gasoline hit them; two or three others of the gun squad had fallen over in the back of them as though they were trying to dodge the fire. This was an awful thing to look at, and now it was over 24 hours since it happened. Twenty-four hours for a corpse in the equatorial sun can result in an awful odour. . .let alone one that has been burned to a crisp."

★   ★   ★

Private Clarence Shanks of C Co, 1-8, on Red 2: "We progressed slowly to our right, which turned out to be the west, firing at rarely seen Japs, at bunkers, at what appeared to be snipers in palm trees, and throwing grenades. Navy dive-bombers came in strafing and dropping bombs in areas identified by markers and coming uncomfortably close to us. There were periods of calm in our vicinity which were suddenly broken by machine gun and rifle fire from unseen emplacements."

On Red 3, Joe Jordan of 2-8 was more optimistic: "Things had to be better today than yesterday! We were probably 50-100 yards in depth from the ocean - that was a lot deeper than day one. Water, rations and ammo were more plentiful, and we continued to work on one pillbox at a time all day; now we had some artillery on the island, at least two tanks were helping, and several half-tracks were running around. I don't mean that it was developing into a walk-away, but it was better. I do remember that we got across the airfield taxiway and re-captured all of the territory that we gave back on the pullback. Casualties were again heavy, but we were getting more speedy help from the corpsmen. No one can ever brag about the Navy medical corpsmen enough, they were the best troops around and could not do enough to help the wounded; they. . .were the bravest men I have ever seen."

The Japanese had used the first night to rectify a major flaw in their defences. During D Day some Marines had succeeded in crossing the western taxiway of the airfield and were in positions in the triangle formed by the taxiways and the main runway. The Japanese now had machine guns set up across the ends of the taxiways, and anyone who attempted to cross was facing almost certain death. This meant that the Marines inside the triangle - mainly Cos A and B of Maj Wood Kyle's 1-2 - were virtually cut off from the troops on Red Beach 2.

In preparation for Shoup's planned drive southwards across the centre of the island carrier aircraft were called in to blast the enemy positions in the south. The Hellcats and Dauntlesses wheeled in from the north-west and strafed and bombed the 125-yard wide strip between the runway and the sea; but, as with the attack on the *Niminoa*, the bombing became wild. Bullets and bomb fragments soon began to fall in the Marines' territory, and Shoup was forced to call off the planes. Meanwhile Maj Kyle had rounded up some .30 and .50cal machine guns, and a duel was going on between the American and Japanese gunners for control of the taxiways. Shortage of ammunition eventually halted this, and nobody was able to cross over to the triangle before the attack to the south was mounted.

The stalemate had to be broken; and at 1pm the Marines from the triangle - around 200 men in all - raced across the main runway of the airfield, on through the undergrowth, round the shell holes and shattered palm trees, and did not let up until they reached the southern shore of the island. Japanese fire was heavy, especially as the men crossed the runway, but to everyone's surprise the casualties were comparatively light. Once on the south side of the island the Marines occupied enemy trenches for a length of about 200 yards, where they were soon hit by a Japanese counter-attack mounted from the eastern flank. The fighting was fierce, and the Marines suffered heavy casualties before a temporary lull set in. Ammunition had become scarce, but malfunctions among the field radios prevented Shoup, Walter Jordan and Wood Kyle from keeping abreast of the situation. Colonel Jordan was worried when he heard nothing from this element, and expressed his concern to Shoup.

Shoup decided to move Jordan and his 2-2 command post over to the south side; and at about 4pm this party reached the isolated Marines and Jordan assumed command. He had brought a communications team with him, and radio contact was again established with Shoup on the northern beach. Shoup was anxious that Jordan should strike to the east and attempt to link up with Jim Crowe pushing south-east from Red 3, thus possibly sealing off the eastern half of the island. However, Walter Jordan replied that there were less than 200 men left in the position, including 30 wounded; that ammunition, grenades, food and water were in short supply; and that the Japanese were in increasing strength on his eastern flank. Given the circumstances, Shoup told Jordan to consolidate his position and arranged for the necessary supplies to be sent across in amtracs, which would return with the wounded.

At the eastern end of the beachhead on Red 3, Jim Crowe was having a frustrating time. Try as he might, he was unable to make any progress beyond the Burns-Philp wharf, where the Japanese had a group of heavily fortified positions which resisted all the Marines' efforts to clear them. Just beyond the wharf was a coral-covered steel pillbox, and slightly further inland was a large bombproof shelter; the mutually reinforcing fire from these two points had held up Co F all morning. Fierce exchanges of fire continued for most of the day, but however many of the enemy were killed there seemed to be a never-ending supply of reinforcements to take their places. "Where the hell are they coming from?", Crowe fumed: "Do they have a tunnel to Tokyo or something?"

A lone Sherman tank was available to 2-8 and was doing sterling service - it silenced one particularly troublesome machine gun post about 100 yards west of the bombproof shelter by blasting the gun port at close range. When the enemy gun fell silent a bulldozer pushed forward and buried the whole position in sand and coral. However, the tank was too valuable and vulnerable to be risked beyond the American front line. Both Co F and Co K to their right were pinned down whenever they tried to move east, and a bitter stalemate set in along the entire front.

Crowe decided that the best that could be achieved at present was to consolidate his lines and dig in until reinforcements were available, probably not until D+2. He placed a 37mm gun on the beach to provide protection against enemy tanks, and at dusk a patrol was sent forward to stop the Japanese from reoccupying the Burns-Philp wharf. During fierce exchanges during the night of 21-22 November the Marines killed 15 Japanese for the loss of two of their own men. The whole of the eastern end of Betio was still covered by a huge pall of smoke and dust; this was the only part of the island where naval, air and artillery fire could be safely directed, and the fliers and gunners were making the most of it.

★ ★ ★

Meanwhile, over on Green Beach, the most significant gains of the second day, and perhaps of the whole battle, were being made by Maj Mike Ryan and his assortment of Marines.

Ryan still had the Sherman tank "*China Gal*" (minus her 75mm gun, but still valuable as a mobile machine gun nest), and another - "*Cecilia*", which had bogged down on D Day - had now been recovered and would soon be in fighting order. During the night of D Day a naval gunfire spotter, Lt Thomas Greene, had come ashore and was now available to Ryan. The main defences on Green Beach lay in the south-west corner around Temakin Point, and although the British 8in Vickers guns had been knocked out during the preliminary bombardment on D Day the Japanese still had two medium guns in steel turrets, five other assorted artillery pieces, and a formidable array of machine gun emplacements, rifle pits, trenches and tank traps. "When we were ready to start our attack," recalls Ryan, "I sent my runner to find the officer with the radio from the adjacent battalion, and tell him that if Regiment could be contacted he should tell them that we were going to attack along Green Beach. After a while the runner came back to say that 'they said to hold on so they could call an air strike'. I sent the runner back twice requesting that the air strike be called off, since we were ready to go. He came back finally and said it was cancelled."

Lieutenant Greene called in two destroyers, later supplemented by other ships, and a bombardment started at around 10am. The Japanese emplacements were pounded from close range for nearly an hour, the shells at times falling close to the Marines' front line; the ground jumped and kicked beneath them where they lay, and some men suffered burst eardrums. "The attack that morning was well co-ordinated", says Mike Ryan; "Lt Greene controlled the naval gunfire preparation. It was quite heavy, including 5in to 8in guns; 8in fire was brought to within less than 50 yards of our front lines. In fact the fire requested was so close to where we reported our front line to be that the naval ships would not respond to the request unless the divisional commander himself approved. General Smith told me this years later. Other Marines later told me that they still remembered the explosions shaking the ground in their holes. When the naval gunfire stopped, the Marines swept forward."

The Sherman *"Cecilia"* cleared the way for the advancing riflemen, blasting pillboxes and gun emplacements and leaving the mopping up for the troops coming up behind. By not long after 11am the whole of Green Beach had been overrun; the Marines could stand by the 8in Vickers guns and gaze south to the open sea, and east along the length of the main runway of the airfield and the south shore.

"With the help of the bombardment and the tanks, the troops soon overran enemy positions to the extent that control of Green Beach was established," says Ryan. "I sent this information by runner to the radio on the beach. Large horned mines were discovered on the reef on the right half of Green Beach, and this information was sent verbally to the radio on the beach." In one short and brilliantly co-ordinated attack, Ryan had succeeded in clearing the whole of the western shore of Betio, thus providing an undefended beach for the 6th Marines to make their much-delayed landing. It is little wonder that Julian Smith would call it "the most cheering news of D+1".

Not content with the morning's success, Ryan sent a message that he was now gathering his force for an attack along Red Beach 1 in an attempt to join up with Col Shoup: "Later I sent a message back verbally to the effect that we would now organise an attack along Red Beach to re-contact Regiment. . . When my runner returned he said, 'They said stay where you are'. With that, I felt that we were back under control of Regiment; they knew we were ready and able to organise an attack along Red Beach. I expected to be ordered to do this, and waited for it."

★ ★ ★

Bob Libby, from Ryan's makeshift command, recalls the events of that day on the western end of Betio:

"With daylight at around 5am, we were soon up and about. There was no sign of any Jap activity in our immediate vicinity, so we took the opportunity to dig into our packs and find something to eat; this was our first taste of food since coming ashore. It was while we were sitting there on a coconut log that several cameramen who had spent the night on the beach came and joined us. We shared our meagre rations with them and chatted a while; it appeared that they had intended to come inland after dark but were not sure who was in control of this sector, so they had stayed put until daylight.

"A few minutes later two Marines appeared with a walking wounded Jap officer - he had been stripped of clothing except for the loin cloth that he was wearing; a rough and dirty bandage hung from his right leg. Hands in the air, he sullenly passed by to be treated at the makeshift hospital further down the beach. One of the cameramen took a shot of him, hoping that his equipment and film were in working order. . .the picture came out fine, and is one of the well known pictures of the battle. [It is reproduced elsewhere in this book.]

"Soon after this we were gathered together and given the task of sweeping to the south to cover the coastline on the seaward side of the island. . . .Before we set off on this mission we could see that reinforcement troops were having a rough time landing from the lagoon. We got the distinct impression that the Japs were not particularly concerned with the Americans who had already landed on Betio, but were hell bent on stopping any more coming ashore - perhaps they thought that if they could stop any further landings they could deal with us at their leisure.

"We made extremely good time in crossing the island, we came across a few pockets of resistance but swiftly overcame them. . . Bending our flank, we headed towards the centre of the island, but were halted when we reached the boundary of our area - something I never quite understood. Maybe it was thought that any further advance would have brought us into the crossfire between the Japanese and our own fire, but had we been able to continue we would have ended up behind the enemy defences and created major problems for them.

". . .We were brought to a halt and used as a solid flank for the Marines on Red 2 in their attempt to flush out the defending Japs. With us in force on the flank, the Japanese had nowhere to go but into the sea at their rear. There were still Japs in some of the larger bunkers, which were more than our force could handle as we had no suitable equipment for the task.

"The mixed-up bunch of Marines from all sorts of units banded together and made a concerted attempt to broaden our skimpy beachhead. Over the following hour or two we made our area virtually free of organised enemy forces; yes, there were still confined groups of Japs, but we were at least able to move about quite openly without fear of surprise attacks. The heaviest fighting seemed to be taking place on our left flank   - [we could hear] the sounds of deep explosions as pillboxes and bunkers were being dynamited with TNT and Bangalore torpedoes."[1]

---

[1] Tubular explosive charges intended for breaching deep obstacles, e.g. cutting wire entanglements; on Betio they were often pushed lengthways into the embrasures of Japanese emplacements.

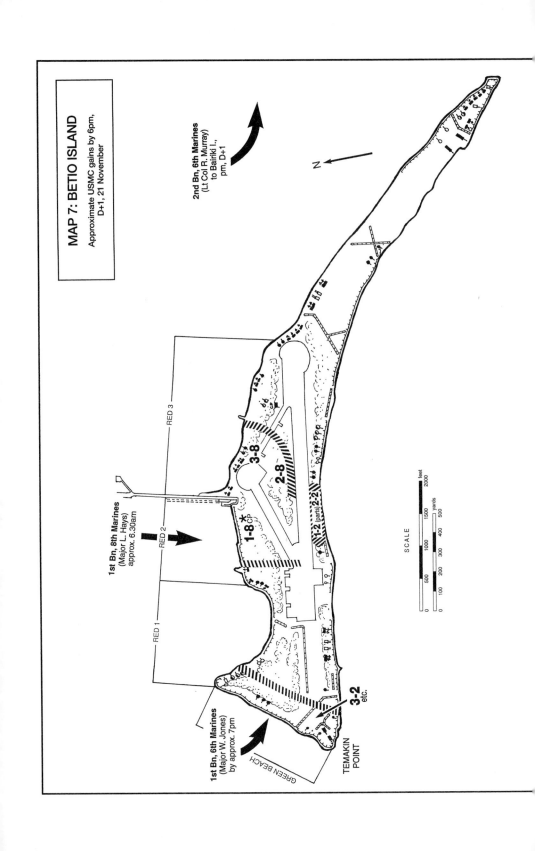

MAP 7: BETIO ISLAND
Approximate USMC gains by 6pm,
D+1, 21 November

2nd Bn, 6th Marines
(Lt Col R. Murray)
to Bairiki I.,
pm, D+1

N

RED 3

1st Bn, 8th Marines
(Major L. Hays)
approx. 6.30am

RED 2

RED 1

3-8

2-8

1-8 CP

1-2 (parts) 2-2

SCALE

feet
0   500   1000   1500   2000

yards
0   100   200 300   400   500

3-2
etc.

1st Bn, 6th Marines
(Major W. Jones)
by approx. 7pm

GREEN BEACH

TEMAKIN
POINT

When it seemed that Ryan's motley command had secured their area, Libby and his comrades did some exploring around the south-west of the island: "Standing on the southern beach we could look out over hundreds of yards of waterless reef; the Japs had expected us to make our assault from this direction, and we saw long stretches of barbed wire entanglements and many obstacles that appeared to be made of concrete or rock. Looking over to our left we saw a column of nine prisoners being herded along by several riflemen - someone told us later that they were Koreans, not Japs - and to our right was the remains of a large gun emplacement.

"...There were two emplacements each containing dual guns which looked like 90mm to me, both pointed out to sea. [Presumably these were the Type 89 twin 127mm guns, some hundreds of yards east of Temakin Point on the south shore.] We made a search of the area, and in doing so flushed out a very agitated looking Jap who, in his panic, ran towards us rather than away to his own lines. It made little difference, really, for he was doomed from the minute he saw us - our officer yelled for him to be taken alive, but he was too slow, as about five grenades followed him into the hole that he jumped into.

"Returning to the guns, we started fooling around, raising and lowering the barrels and pressing various buttons, and finally set off some kind of buzzer. Not knowing what we had done, we all made an undignified scramble for the nearest cover, but as nothing happened we eventually returned for another look. The emplacements were quite large and circular in shape with built-in revetments in the concrete walls.

"Looking inside one of them I came across a very dead Jap - there was not a mark on him and it was obvious that he had not been dead for very long. He was smartly dressed in his combat green uniform, wrap-around leggings and slot-toe shoes; to all purposes he looked as if he were sleeping. In his left hand was a live grenade, and alongside him was one of the old style bayonets, the type with the hook, which I knew were becoming pretty rare, so I decided to retrieve it. After carefully checking for booby traps I was able to slide my bayonet under his and lift it up without incident - I still have it in my collection.[1]

"At the rear of the emplacement a hatchway led into a sort of control room, a semi-blockhouse with slots dotted along the sides. Knowing the enemy's liking for hideaways we lobbed a hand grenade through one of the holes, and our suspicions proved to be correct as we were answered by a burst of machine gun fire - luckily no one was hurt. There was no way that we were going to tackle a blockhouse on our own, and someone went off in search of assistance. After what seemed to be an age he returned with two engineers complete with Bangalore torpedoes. They linked them up with detonators and stuffed them through one of the slots - a heavy muffled explosion followed, then silence.

"Moving to the other side of the bunker we found a flight of stairs with a door at the bottom; we tried to open it but it was either locked or barricaded from the

(1) Japanese *tabi* tropical boots, of canvas and rubber, had a separated big toe; the green drab 1938 model field uniform was worn with cross-gartered puttees; and the bayonet for the 1905 model Arisaka 6.5mm rifle had a single recurved quillon.

inside. We gathered together what grenades we had left between us and worked our way round, lobbing them into every slot and hole that we could find; we heard a number of shots from inside, and then silence. Nothing more was heard, and we assumed that the Japs who had survived had shot themselves, but we never found out for sure as we were relieved shortly afterwards and withdrew to our original position - only to find that a group of officers had moved into our little refuge, so we ended up the day trying to dig foxholes on the beach, a bit like spooning sugar out of a bowl.

". . . By nightfall we were comparatively safe in our little area (although we were not aware of this fact until later). . . .We had created a broad front safe enough for the 6th Marines to land safely on Green Beach behind us, and they passed through our holding line and became committed to action further along the island."

In Bob Libby's opinion Maj Ryan was not at all the glory-hunting type of officer so often depicted in wartime epics; he thought him a quiet, unassuming man who would work without panic and get results without a lot of fanfares. Libby thought it possible that Ryan's deceptively low key manner may have stood in the way of the full recognition that he deserved.

⋆   ⋆   ⋆

"Situation at 4pm: Our line runs generally from the Burns-Philp wharf across the east end of the triangle formed by the airfield to the south coast and along the coast intermittently to a place opposite the west end of the triangle; then from the revetments north of the west end of the main air strip on to the north; another line from most of the centre of Red 1 across the end of the island to the south coast west of the end of the main strip. Some troops in 227 [gunnery target area designation for eastern half of Red 1] dishing out hell and catching hell. Pack howitzers in position and registered for shooting on tail [of Betio]. Casualties many; percentage dead not known; combat efficiency - we are winning. Shoup".

So ran the message sent by the commander of the 2nd Marines combat team to Division on the late afternoon of D+1. General Julian Smith copied the message on to "Howling Mad" Smith, somewhere off the shore of Makin. On receiving it, the V Corps commander is said to have smiled at Adml Kelly Turner for the first time in weeks.

⋆   ⋆   ⋆

Although the situation in the centre of the island was more or less static, Ryan's successful advance down Green Beach allowed the 6th Marines a virtually undefended area in which to make their landing, in sharp contrast to the carnage that had taken place on the Red Beaches. In fact, the area was so secure that Maj Jones' 1st Bn, 6th Marines were given the unusual task of landing in rubber boats. LCRs (Landing Craft Rubber) had been used in river crossings in the past, but never for an amphibious landing (and, given the massive scale of future

Drawing by the author (top), and aerial photograph of Betio taken shortly after the battle. The viewpoint is from north-west to south-east: Green Beach is in the immediate foreground, Red Beaches 1 and 2 on the left shore this side of the long pier, Red 3 beyond the pier, the airfield runway central with its taxiways to the left. Note the pale, shallow water over the reef - cloud shadow hides this effect off Red 1 and 2 in the photograph. (US National Archives)

(Below) "Down the net - Tarawa": charcoal drawing by the war artist Kerr Eby, who accompanied the 2nd Marine Division ashore on Betio. (US Navy Art Collection)

(Right, above) Kerr Eby drawing of the view from inside a landing craft - "The wave breaks on the reef"; and (below) "The hard road to triumph". (US Navy Art Collection)

The first LVT to reach Red Beach 1 shortly after 9am on 20 November was No.49, "My Delores", driven by PFC Ed Moore; it reared up against the seawall at the extreme west of the beach, and he and his radioman Bob Thoreson narrowly escaped when the cab was riddled by machine gun fire coming through the underside. Repaired by a maintenance crew, "My Dolores" saw further use before finally coming to rest at the junction of Red 1 and Red 2 on D+3. Immediately above the muzzle of the horizontal .50cal in this photograph the turret roof of a "drowned" Sherman tank shows above the water.

Frontal armour plate, .50cal and .30cal guns were fitted to the LVT-1s of the 2nd Amphibian Tractor Bn. in New Zealand shortly before embarkation for Operation Galvanic. The armour was concentrated in the cab area, so amtracs which survived the landings and ferried wounded back to the transports normally reversed out over the reef to keep this minimal protection facing the Japanese guns. (USMC)

(Right, above) Kerr Eby's powerful drawing of a wading Marine tearing himself free from a wire obstacle - "Bullets and barbed wire". (Below) "Marines fall forward". Eby, a 54-year- old civilian, had been a war artist on the AEF front in France in 1918. (US Navy Art Collection)

(Above) Marines pinned down on the Red Beaches, 20 November. Many men were unable to get inland from the water's edge throughout the day; others made shallow advances, usually in small and unco-ordinated groups. (US National Archives)

(Right) Staff Sergeant William J. Bordelon, 1-18 Marines. One of only four survivors when his amtrac was hit off Red 2 on the morning of D Day, Bordelon continued to attack Japanese pillboxes with satchel charges after suffering serious wounds, but was killed knocking out the fourth. Awarded a posthumous Medal of Honor, this native of San Antonio, Texas, was finally brought home in November 1995, and lay in state at the Alamo before his reburial.
(USMC Historical Collection)

(Above) In the wreckage of a Japanese log-and-sandbag emplacement beside the bull-dozed sand hill protecting a larger shelter, one Marine throws a grenade while his buddy, grimacing in the heat, takes a drink - judging from the angle of his canteen it is almost empty. The landing force was desperately short of drinking water during the first two days' fighting in the furnace heat of the equatorial summer. (USMC)

(Right) While the exposure of this shot may exaggerate the effect slightly, the visibility of the Marines' printed camouflage utilities against pale sand is still very noticeable. Devised for use in jungle terrain, this clothing would never oust the old sage green uniform. (US National Archives)

(Left) Trying to identify the dead Marines who lie thickly at the edge of the water all along the Red Beaches. The flimsy timber catwalks and stilted sheds are Japanese latrines; it was from counting them on aerial reconnaissance photographs that David Shoup calculated the size of the garrison. (US Navy)

(Left, below) Abandoned amtracs and floating bodies at the log barricade which lined the water's edge right along Red 2. The viewpoint is roughly south-east to north-west, across the cove of Red 1 towards the point where Major Ryan's group got ashore. (US National Archives)

(Right) Colonel David Shoup, appointed to lead Combat Team 2 during the rehearsal phase, who commanded all the Marines ashore until the night of D+1. (USMC Historical Collection)

(Below) Shoup's makeshift command post beside a still-occupied Japanese bunker just behind Red 2. Shoup stands at centre, wearing green dungarees, uncovered helmet and mapcase; sitting slumped at his feet is Lt.Col.Evans Carlson, late of the 2nd Raider Battalion. Because of the radio failures Shoup sent him out to the USS *Maryland* on the afternoon of D Day to report the landing force's situation to Maj Gen Julian Smith; the trip took Carlson until almost midnight. (US National Archives)

(Left above & below) The dreadful flotsam on Red Beach 1 on the evening of D Day; the viewpoints are respectively to west and east from almost the same spot. The drowned-out Sherman has been identified elsewhere as "Cecilia", which was salvaged that night and brought back into action on D+1 in support of Maj Ryan's drive down Green Beach. (US National Archives, US Navy)

(Above) Marines, probably of 3-2, huddle under cover of a sand ridge on the western side of Red 1. The man at left is checking .30cal machine gun ammunition belts - dumped in the sand like this, they are vulnerable to grit and misalignment which may jam the gun. Losses off the beach left all the assault battalions dangerously short of support weapons. (US National Archives)

(Left, above left) 1st Lt William Deane Hawkins of the Scout Snipers, who cleared the long pier at the outset of the landings on D Day, and died of wounds suffered while attacking pillboxes on D+1; he was awarded a posthumous Medal of Honor. (USMC Historical Collection)

(Left, above right) Maj Michael Ryan, commander of L Company, 3-2, who assembled and led a motley force of Marines on the western point of Red 1 on D Day. His capture of Green Beach on D+1 would prove decisive, allowing the 6th Marines reserves to land over an uncontested beach. (USMC Historical Collection)

(Left, below) 75mm pack howitzer of the 10th Marines in action on Betio, probably on D+2. The section commander, standing at centre, is identified as Sgt Armstrong; note the entry and exit holes of a bullet or shell splinter in this lucky Marine's helmet. (USMC)

(Above) Men of a .30cal machine gun squad work their way inland from cover to cover, between a maze of Japanese positions. (US National Archives)

(Right) Two Marines - both wearing camouflage jackets and green trousers - escort a captured Japanese officer who has been stripped to his loincloth. On the morning of D+1 Bob Libby of 3-2 saw this picture being taken, behind the northern part of Green Beach. (US National Archives)

(Left, above) Marines dash across open ground on the airfield, probably on D+2. Japanese machine guns set up to enfilade the two taxiways made movement in and out of "the triangle", occupied by scattered groups from the 2nd and 8th Marines, especially perilous. A(US National Archives)

(Left, below) Marines take cover as they work their way across Betio, probably close to one of the heavy gun emplacements - note the searchlight, left. Veterans recall that the sand was unbearably hot to lie on. (US National Archives)

(Right) Col Merritt ("Red Mike") Edson, chief of staff of the 2nd Marine Division. (USMC Historical Collection)

(Below) Edson, second from right, arrived at Shoup's command post on the evening of D+1; here - with Evans Carlson, far right - he interrogates one of only 17 Japanese who were taken alive, on D+2 or D+3. (US National Archives)

Low level aerial photograph, probably taken
from a Navy Kingfisher, of bombardment
damage around one of the airfield taxiways;
this seems to show part of the ground where
the 8th Marines fought at the eastern end of
"the triangle". Note the huge bomb and
shell craters already flooding - the water
table was very shallow on Betio. The heavy
litter of palm fronds scattered all over the
island by the naval bombardment made it
even more difficult for infantry to spot concealed enemy positions. (US National
Archives)

The northern section of Green Beach, looking slightly west of due south. LCVPs lie off
the beach, and a few amtracs at the water's
edge. The large dark concentration, left centre, are some fifty of the rubber boats used -
with limited success - to land 1-6 on the late
afternoon of D+1. At right foreground a line
of concrete tetrahedron obstacles slants in
towards the shore. This view, looking right
across the south-west part of the island to
the reef beyond, emphasises the small size of
Betio - see Map 2. (US Navy)

(Left) 1st Lt Alexander Bonnyman, the engineer officer from 2-18 who won a posthumous Medal of Honor for his gallantry in close quarter fighting for the large concrete bunker which was holding up the 8th Marines' eastward advance inland from the Burns-Philp wharf on D+2. (USMC Historical Collection)

(Below) Marines, probably from "Jim" Crowe's mixed force of 2-8 and 3-8, atop the huge sand-covered concrete bunker behind Red Beach 3 which was neutralised thanks to Bonnyman's heroism. (US Navy)

Drawings by Kerr Eby of a Marine mortar crew in action from a captured weapon pit with log overhead cover. The mortar platoon of each battalion's weapons company had four 81mm tubes. (US Navy Art Collection)

(Left, above) Excellent aerial view of the eastern "tail" of Betio looking almost due south - the anti-tank ditches in foreground and background allow exact orientation with Map 2. This is the ground captured at a rush by 3-6 on the morning of D+3. Under the plough of naval and air bombardment the enemy positions have become hard to distinguish, but trenches (left foreground) and sea-wall (right) can be made out, as can various rectangular sand berms. Note also the deep holes beneath the shallows - it is hardly surprising that so many of the tanks bogged down off the other beaches. (US Navy)

(Left) Marines checking an enemy dug-out late in the battle; these men have dropped most of their "782 gear" and are probably relying on ammo clips and grenades carried in their pockets. Note a stretch of the palm log seawall in the background. (US National Archives)

(Above & right) As the fighting drew to a close many of the Special Naval Landing Force troops preferred suicide to the dishonour of being captured alive. Here, in the wreck of a concrete-roofed pillbox, one soldier lies dead with his toe still on the trigger of his rifle; and Marines stare at another who chose death in the open.

(Left, above) Part of Adml Shibasaki's large concrete command blockhouse between Red 3 and the eastern end of the runway. Abandoned outside it is one of the garrison's Type 95 *Ha-Go* light tanks. (USMC)

(Left) Marines examine another *Ha-Go*, this one in a camouflaged ground level emplacement of log construction. Prior reconnaissance reported fourteen static positions, but there seem only to have been seven actual tanks on Betio. Only one of them emerged from its hide to engage the Marine Shermans on D Day; they were outclassed by the M4A2 in both firepower and armour. (US Navy)

(Above) This appears to be another viewpoint of the highest concrete structure on Betio, the huge shelter whose summit was captured and held by Lt Bonnyman of 2-18. Massively banked with sand and coral, it rises nearly twenty feet. Many Japanese corpses lie at the foot of the slope on the left. (US National Archives)

(Right) V Amphibious Corps commander Maj Gen Holland ("Howling Mad") Smith, left, with 2nd Marine Division commander Maj Gen Julian Smith. (USMC)

(Left) Julian Smith briefs Adml Chester Nimitz, C-in-C Pacific Fleet, during his visit to Betio after the battle. (USMC Historical Collection)

(Below) Julian Smith, far right, leads Adml Nimitz, centre, and other visiting "brass" on a tour of Betio; the searchlight at left suggests that they are near a heavy gun emplacement. A couple of Marines in battle-worn green utilities, left and right of the admiral's entourage, present an immediate contrast with all this crisp khaki. (US Navy)

(Right) Burial detail somewhere on Betio. (USMC)

(Right, below) Kerr Eby's "March Macabre". (US Navy Art Collection)

(Left) After the battle: weary Marines rest in shallow scrapes in the churned-up sand, probably on Green Beach. (US National Archives)

(Left, below) On D+2, parking up with M3A1 Stuarts of the divisional light tank battalion, the scorched, battered, tireless, and apparently indestructible M4A2 Sherman "Colorado" from Company C, 1st Corps Tank Bn (Medium). This tank fought throughout the battle from D Day onward, and would be in at the kill with 3-6 on the eastern tail of Betio on D+3. Above the tank's name is painted the charging elephant insignia used at that date by this battalion. (USMC)

(Right) "He walks who can", and (below) "Long thoughts", by Kerr Eby. (US Navy Art Collection)

(OVERLEAF) Total war: a typical scene of carnage and destruction somewhere on Betio. It is not hard to understand the level of Marine casualties after getting ashore if one visualises having to skirmish forward over this kind of battlefield against a dug-in enemy. (US National Archives)

(Left) One of the 8in Vickers coastal defence guns at Temakin Point on the southern extremity of Green Beach, photographed shortly after the battle. (USMC)

(Left, below) November 1993: veterans examine one of the Vickers guns at Takarongo Point, still staring out over the vast reaches of the Pacific. (Jim Moran)

(Right) Local graffiti now cover a surviving Vickers gun at Temakin Point. (Jim Moran)

(Below) A rusting steel plate command post near Takarongo Point; originally this two-storey structure, made of two layers of plate with sand between, had a swivelling cupola on top. (Jim Moran)

(OVERLEAF, above) Kerr Eby drawing of wounded being brought aboard a transport ship for the voyage to Hawaii. (Below) Perhaps Eby's strongest image from this sequence of deeply felt charcoal drawings worked up from his on-the-spot sketches; he called it simply "Ebb Tide". (US Navy Art Collection)

operations on Saipan, Iwo Jima and Okinawa, would never be used for this purpose again).

The transport ship *Feland* closed to Green Beach at around 2pm on the 21st, and the disembarkation got under way; however, for some obscure reason the transport was ordered out to sea again, and the rubber boats had to be re-embarked with a great deal of confusion and delay. The *Feland* was finally given clearance to return to the beach and positioned herself 1,200 yards off shore, where the whole business of disembarkation started again.

Paddling the rubber craft in the choppy ocean proved to be very hard work, and in many cases they were linked up to Higgins boats in groups of six and towed in to shore. The southern part of Green Beach had been heavily mined by the Japanese; one LVT struck one of these mines and exploded in a spectacular fireball, only one of the crew surviving. Because of the delays, the landing of 1-6 was not completed until 7pm. Still more chaos attended the landing of B Co, 2nd Tank Bn - it was discovered that the M3A1 light tanks had been loaded onto the transport in the wrong sequence and were somewhere in the bowels of the ship. Huge amounts of equipment had to be moved to get at them, and when they were finally hoisted onto the landing craft and ferried to the beach it was nearly dark. Great difficulty was encountered in avoiding the numerous shell holes, mines and reef ledges; five tanks were flooded or bogged down; only one platoon was successful in getting onto the beach, the remainder being diverted to Red Beach 2, where they came ashore in total darkness. It had been hoped that an evening attack could be made from Green Beach, but because of the delays in landing the reinforcements and the failing light Col Shoup ordered 1-6 to consolidate their position and wait until dawn.

★   ★   ★

Some time during the afternoon an observer on one of the warships in the lagoon reported seeing Japanese troops moving from Betio to Bairiki, the next island in the chain. At low tide it was possible to wade or swim across the coral spit which connected the islands of the atoll. This confirmed Julian Smith's earlier fears, and vindicated his request for artillery on Bairiki during the initial landings. Raymond Murray's 2-6 Marines, who were to have supported Maj Jones' 1-6 on Green Beach, were now diverted to Bairiki to block these escape attempts - much to their disgust, as they were looking forward to taking part in the main sweep across Betio instead of being sidetracked into what they saw as a minor mopping-up operation.

★   ★   ★

As the second day of the battle drew to a close, the balance seemed to be tipping progressively in favour of the landing force. Having spent the previous night clinging precariously to the strip of beach along the sea wall and steeling themselves for what they expected would be an imminent *banzai* attack, the Marines now held a limited but apparently firm foothold on the south shore; a substantial northern beachhead stretching from half way across Red Beach 2 to the Burns-Philp Wharf, and inland almost to the main airfied runway; and the whole western end of the island to a depth of some 200 yards inland from Green Beach.

The supply situation was also beginning to improve, although the large and rather indiscriminate dumps on and near the long pier contributed little to the rifle companies' most desperate needs - water and ammunition. Working parties were sent to the pier to organise priority handling and movement of supplies.

During the daylight hours of D+1 Lt Col Rixey had been able to get all of his artillery ashore, using any means that he could lay hands on - amtracs, landing craft, rubber boats and rafts. The gun crews from 1-10 manhandled the short-barrelled howitzers onto the beach, and set them up to cover the enemy positions at the junction of Red 1 and 2 and beyond the Burns-Philp wharf. Murray's 2-6 had now landed on Bairiki and secured the island without difficulty; and the artillery of 2-10, under the command of the aptly named Col Shell, were boated over there to provide support for the final onslaught. On Betio, Lt Col Rixey said: "I thought up until 1 o'clock today that it was touch and go; then I knew we would win."

At around 5.50pm on 21 November the chief of staff of the 2nd Marine Division, Col Merritt Edson, left the *Maryland* at Julian Smith's request to take over command on Betio from the nearly exhausted David Shoup. He arrived at about 8.30pm after a tortuous journey via the long pier, and spent some time discussing the situation with Shoup and making plans for D+2 before officially taking command, leaving Shoup to get a little rest and concentrate on his own combat team.

Col David Shoup had borne the main responsibility for the conduct of the land battle for two days and a night, mostly cut off from communication with his divisional commander and other command elements by persistent radio problems. He had co-ordinated the movements of all the landing teams, most of whom were scattered and severely weakened in numbers and equipment from the moment of landing, and mixed haphazardly with other units. Despite these difficulties - and despite his own untreated and now infected leg wounds - he had succeeded in establishing a sound beachhead around Red 2 and 3 in the face of bitter enemy opposition from very well prepared positions. For his leadership he was to be awarded the Medal of Honor - the only one of the four Tarawa Marines awarded their country's highest decoration who survived to wear it. For the present he was content to have his wounds dressed and to find a patch of sand where he could stretch out for a while without someone stepping on him.

★   ★   ★

We may take it that Adml Shibasaki's boast that a million Americans would be unable to take Tarawa was mere rhetoric; but he had believed that reinforcements would be sent once the enemy landed in the Gilberts - had not Adml Koga said that a "hornet's nest for the Yankee" had been prepared? Unfortunately for Shibasaki and his naval infantrymen, events elsewhere in the Pacific had robbed Koga's words of meaning. The landings by the 3rd Marine Division on

Bougainville in the Solomons on 1 November had prevented Japanese troop reinforcements being sent to the Gilberts; and the massive American air strikes on the Japanese base and naval task force at Rabaul between 5 and 19 November had destroyed scores of aircraft and disabled many warships. Shibasaki and Tarawa had been abandoned; and over his still operative radio link to Tokyo he, or whoever was now exercising command in his stead, sent a last message: "Our weapons have been destroyed. From now on everyone is attempting a final charge. May Japan exist for ten thousand years!"

★   ★   ★

Some time around 2am on the morning of 22 November, D+2, a Japanese aircraft arrived over Betio and dropped a stick of bombs in the water about 50 yards from where Hawk Rader's group from 1-8 were set up. As the plane banked away the rear gunner strafed the area for good measure.

"Two men were lost to that attack," recalls Rader. "A guy named Mottershead from New Jersey, on his first invasion, was hit in the lower abdomen with a machine gun bullet and had to be evacuated. As far as I know he lived. Jesse Birdsong from Texas, a Guadalcanal veteran, was on watch at the time. . . . I thought he was wounded and tried to pick him up to carry him out. I talked to him before I took hold of him, but he didn't answer and I realised he was hurt very badly. As I picked him up, he just grunted and took his last breath in my arms. My hand had slipped up into a large hole just above his right kidney. The chunk of shrapnel that hit him must have been the size of a fist. I gently laid him down on the logs and knelt down beside him, and I was crying. Someone put their arm around my shoulder and said, 'Come on - Jesse is gone'."

Chapter 6:

The Day is Ours

> *"Oft have I struck those that I never saw - and struck them dead"*
>
> (William Shakespeare, *Henry VI*)

As the brief tropical evening fell over Betio on 21 November, "Red Mike" Edson and David Shoup laid their plans for the following day. There were still large numbers of Japanese troops in the eastern end of the island, and it was important that they be pinned down as thoroughly as possible while the Marines dealt with the western end and centre. A series of naval and air bombardments were requested, to start at 7am on the 22nd. The Navy was to pound the tail of the island with 14in and 16in shells, starting from a point about 500 yards beyond the outermost Marine positions; this was to be followed by a twenty-minute air attack from the supporting carriers; and the process was to be repeated at 8.30am, 9.30am and 10.30am. It was hoped that this repeated shelling and bombing would prevent the enemy from moving reinforcements westwards to where the main American effort was to be concentrated.

Edson and Shoup had decided on a three-front attack. Major W.K.Jones' 1-6 Marines, who had landed on Green Beach late the previous day, were to pass through Mike Ryan's men and attack eastwards between the southern edge of the airfield and the sea, to link up with those elements of 1-2 and 2-2 who had a foothold on the south shore and around the airfield triangle. At the same time Maj Hays' 1-8 were to move west from their positions on Red 2 in an attempt to reduce the stubborn pocket of enemy gun positions at the junction of Red 1 and 2. The third operation was to be an eastwards attack on the enemy positions inland of the Burns-Philp wharf by Col Elmer Hall's 2-8 and 3-8 Marines.

It was an ambitious plan, bearing in mind that only Jones' troops were fresh; the others had been fighting continuously for two days and two nights with little or no sleep, and under a relentless sun. Water continued to be a miserable problem. All of the water brought ashore from the transport ships was in five-gallon cans which had been filled in New Zealand; the water had reacted with the enamel lining in the cans, and tasted horrible.

In the meantime, Lt Col Kenneth McLeod with his 3-6 Marines had been kept bobbing around at the point of departure since 4pm the previous day by a series of contradictory instructions. He was finally ordered to land on Green Beach at 8am on the 22nd, much to the relief of his men. The Marines of 3-6 had been watching and listening to the battle raging some 1,000 yards away, and were wondering if they would ever become involved.

Major Jones' attack along the south shore was initially delayed because of radio problems. These failures had bedevilled the Marines from the onset of the battle, and were to continue. Now Edson and Shoup found that they were unable to contact Jones. Various attempts to raise him via signals to the USS *Maryland* were to no avail, and finally Edson had to send one of his staff, Maj Tompkins, through the largely Japanese-held west central area to give his orders verbally. At around 8.15am, after a further delay for tank refuelling, 1-6 got under way.

The area between the south of the main runway and the sea was only about 100 yards wide, so Jones was forced to attack with only his C Co "up", following about 50 yards behind the two leading tanks. The Japanese had a habit of dashing out of the undergrowth clutching magnetic mines in a suicidal bid to blow up a tank and its crew - the 1-6 Marines were determined that this was not going to happen here. Opposition was not as fierce as had been expected, although numerous pillboxes and trenches had to be stormed before Jones' men got into visual contact with the Marine enclave on the south shore at around 11am - their advance of about 1,000 yards in under three hours was quite sensational by the standards of the previous two days. In all around 250 of the enemy had been killed, and the way was open for reinforcements to flow through from Green Beach.

Meanwhile, on the south shore, Maj Wood Kyle's men from 1-2 were preparing to thrust eastward to clear the Japanese from the end of the airfield, and hopefully to link up with Jim Crowe's 8th Marines inland from Red Beach 3. It was a daunting task; the Japanese were gathered in considerable strength in this area, and the further east they were pushed the more concentrated they became. Kyle's men were nearing exhaustion, having fought non-stop since the 20th; supplies had not been getting through to them, as few Marines were able to cross the bullet-swept runway, and consequently ammunition was running short. Fortunately a Sherman tank was available to support them, although it was running short of main gun ammunition and would probably only be able to accompany the troops for a limited time.

Shortly after the Marines moved forward they came upon a complex of pillboxes and bunkers which stopped them in their tracks; only the tank's 75mm gun had any effect on this impenetrable barrier, but its meagre supply of shells was soon spent and it lumbered away in search of more. A naval air strike was called in; Hellcat fighters spent ten minutes raking the area with their .50cal machine guns, but to little avail. While the Marines cooled their heels, a destroyer which was deployed off the south coast was called in to send over some well-aimed 5in rounds. This gunfire support helped considerably; but after advancing about 200 yards in all the Marines could go no further without incurring heavy casualties. At around 11am Maj Jones' fresh 1-6 passed through Kyle's men with supporting tanks and cleared the entrenched Japanese, inflicting around 100 casualties.

★   ★   ★

Major Hays' 1-8 had been given the task of attacking to the west in an attempt to destroy "the Pocket", the formidable Japanese positions at the intersection of

Red Beaches 1 and 2, which had wreaked such havoc on the amtracs on D Day and which Shoup and Edson were determined to clear. Hays' three companies moved out at around 7am; B Co was nearest to the beach, A Co in the centre, and C Co as far inland as the revetments at the western end of the airfield (where the 2nd Marines Scout Sniper platoon would also fight that morning, clearing snipers and spotting for mortar fire). Three M3A1 light tanks from C Co, 2nd Tank Bn were sent along to support the assault; the company had perhaps twelve operational Stuarts ashore by now - although four of its LCMs had been sunk on D Day - and B Co had about the same number available. The Marines had only advanced a matter of 100 yards or so before they came across stiff opposition from a complex of pillboxes constructed of palm logs and covered in sand and coral, all with mutually supporting fire. The angular, old-fashioned-looking tanks rattled forward, in many cases to within yards of the Japanese positions, pointing their guns directly into pillbox embrasures; but the results were disappointing - the solid shot and high explosive rounds for the Stuart's little 37mm M6 gun, weighing less than 2lb, did not pack enough punch to destroy these tough positions. While the tanks kept the enemy busy, Marines moved forward with satchel charges and Bangalore torpedoes in desperate attempts to collapse individual strongpoints, but the casualty rate was so heavy that these attacks were soon called off.

At around 11.30am it was decided to withdraw the tanks, which were not serving any useful purpose - one had already been put out of action by a magnetic mine. They were replaced by two "SPMs" - 75mm guns mounted on M3 half-tracks, from the division's Special Weapons Bn - under the command of Maj Frederick Smith. The 75mm shells were more effective than the tanks' 37mm rounds; some Japanese positions were levelled by these guns, which got so close to the enemy that the explosions from the firing and the detonation were virtually simultaneous. The thinly armoured half-tracks were more vulnerable than the tanks, however, and one of them had to retire quite early when enemy fire damaged its radiator.

By the end of the afternoon A and C Cos of the 1-8 had made considerable inroads into the Japanese positions, but B Co, nearest to the beach, had been held up by vicious crossfire and had become bogged down quite early in the day. "The Pocket" had not been cleared as Shoup and Edson had hoped - in fact, this would be about the last point on the whole of Betio to fall to the Americans - but at least it had been contained and isolated.

★　　　★　　　★

During the morning of D+2, Julian Smith had decided that it was time to transfer his command from the USS *Maryland* to Betio. The old battleship had proved to be valuable as a relay centre for communications between elements on the island which were out of touch with one another; but now that a substantial foothold had been secured he felt that his place was ashore. Leaving Brig Gen Hermle to command the HQ element on the flagship, he boarded an amtrac with a ten-man command post group and, with Brig Gen Bourke of the 10th Marines and observer Brig Gen Underhill, he headed for Green Beach.

Landing at 11.55am, he made a brief inspection of the positions of Ryan's 3-2 and the recently arrived 3-6 of Lt Col McLeod. Deciding that he would get a better overall picture of the situation from Shoup and Edson, he reboarded his amtrac and headed for Red Beach 2 - an instructive voyage, as the Japanese gunners in the Pocket blasted the tractor as it rounded the north-west point, wounding the driver and disabling the vehicle. Smith and his party transferred to another amtrac, finally arriving on Red 2 at around 1.30pm to be briefed by Shoup and Edson on the latest situation.

One immediate impression was all too obvious to the party newly landed from the flagship: the appalling stench of death which was now inescapable anywhere on the island or its surrounding waters - or indeed, far off shore when the wind blew from Betio. Hundreds of bodies lay where they had fallen - blasted, torn, burned, swollen, they presented a grotesque contrast to what had once been almost an archetype of tropical beauty and tranquility. Out in the lagoon the corpses of men who had died on the first two days of the battle still bobbed back and forth with the tides and the swell, bloated with decomposition and riding obscenely high on the water.

Some attempts were made to clear away bodies from areas no longer under direct fire; bulldozers dug trenches for the Japanese dead, or their corpses were thrown into shell holes and unceremoniously levelled over. The Marines were temporarily buried in individual graves, for the most part at the place where they fell, and the traditional marker of a helmet on the butt of a jutting rifle spread like a melancholy crop all over the island. Robert Sherrod, the *Time Life* correspondent, wrote:

"Now they are bringing up the dead for burial near the command post. There are seven laid out about ten yards from where I sit. They are covered with green and brown ponchos, only their feet sticking out. I think: what big feet most American soldiers and Marines have - none of these looks smaller than a size eleven. The stench of the dead, as the burial detail brings them past and lines them up on the ground, is very heavy now. One Marine is brought in who has suffered the greatest indignity of all. His head has been blown off completely. His left arm is gone and only a few shreds of skin hang from his shoulders. I thought I had become inured to anything, but I am nauseated by this sight."

Ironically, on the third day the Marines who were near Red 2 and 3 beaches noticed that high tide was now up to the wooden sea wall and the water was deep enough for Higgins boats to come right up to the shore. More than one of them wondered - as those terrible corpses came nodding and wallowing in again with the rising water - why Operation Longsuit could not have been put off for two more days.

*　　　　*　　　　*

Major Crowe's composite unit of 2-8 and 3-8 survivors was to advance eastwards on the morning of D+2, pushing beyond the Burns-Philp wharf which had held them up so stubbornly, then south towards the end of the runway. Before any progress could be made there were three major enemy positions to be dealt with, and Jim Crowe was not looking forward to the task. To his left front, near the wharf, was a steel pillbox directly in front of the area occupied by F Co; the progress of K was blocked by a coconut log emplacement whose machine gun fire was pretty well pinning the company down; and the third and most daunting obstacle was a large concrete shelter a little way to the south of the steel pillbox. These three positions were mutually supporting - attack any one, and the Marines would immediately come under fire from the other two.

The 2nd and 3rd Bns, 8th Marines went into the attack at around 9.30am with a sustained mortar barrage, and their luck began to change almost at once: a mortar round landed among a heap of ammunition alongside the log emplacement, and the whole position erupted in flame, dirt and cartwheeling timbers. Company K rushed forward and overran the position; at the same time F, accompanied by the Sherman tank "*Colorado*", launched an attack on the steel pillbox. The tank clattered up to within feet of its firing aperture and blasted it with 75mm shells; the Marines of F Co then moved in with grenades and TNT charges, and this second obstacle was eliminated.

Crowe now regrouped his men in readiness for the assault on the concrete shelter, a formidable structure about 20 feet high and heaped with tons of sand and coral. He called in assault engineers from the 18th Marines armed with demolition charges and flame throwers and, under the cover of rifle fire, the attack began. For nearly an hour the Marines, under Lt Alexander Bonnyman, fought the Japanese troops to gain control of the top of the bunker, before Bonnyman finally reached the summit - the highest point on Betio. The enemy immediately launched a counter-attack from the other side, but Bonnyman held his ground, thwarting all attempts by the Japanese to regain the top of the shelter. Inevitably, he was hit; dropping to his knees to reload his carbine, he fired a final flurry of shots into the enemy struggling up the sandy ramp from the eastern side before he fell dead among the many bodies that littered the slopes. For his courageous stand Bonnyman became the fourth Tarawa recipient of the Medal of Honor, the third to be awarded posthumously.

His surviving engineers now dropped grenades down the vertical ventilator pipes which protruded from the top of the shelter, and this was enough to send swarms of Japanese pouring out of the two exits - straight into withering machine gun and rifle fire. As they fled eastwards a round of canister shot - a useful speciality unique to the Stuart tank's 37mm gun - killed at least twenty. Bulldozers were now moved forward to seal up the exits with walls of sand and coral, while Marines poured jerrycans of petrol down the vents and dropped lighted paper inside. In this ghastly inferno more than 150 Japanese perished.

With all the major obstacles eliminated Crowe's men surged forward towards the end of the runway, where they eventually halted. It was soon discovered that they were in the line of fire of Jones' 1-6 who had dug in on the south shore, so they moved back about 150 yards. The Marines now held a line from the eastern end of Red Beach 3 in the north to the end of the airfield on the south shore. There were still isolated pockets of undefeated Japanese troops throughout the island - most notably, the stronghold at the junction of Red 1 and 2 - but to all intents and purposes the Americans now held about two-thirds of Betio.

In comparison to the first two days D+2 had seen spectacular gains, with Jones advancing almost halfway down the south coast and Hays and Crowe making good progress westward and eastward from the central enclave. However, Julian Smith's 4pm situation report reflects a certain pessimism: "Situation not favourable for rapid clean up of Betio, heavy casualties among officers make leadership problems difficult. Progress slow and extremely costly. Complete occupation will take at least five more days."

★   ★   ★

By the end of that day the Marines were coming across significant numbers of Japanese who had obviously killed themselves; sensing that defeat was inevitable, they were returning to their bunkers and shooting themselves, the favoured method being to place the rifle muzzle under the chin and press the trigger with the big toe. One 2nd Marines veteran who saw action on several Pacific islands gives his impression of the quality of the opposition on Tarawa:

"The Special Naval Landing Force troops were of an entirely different calibre to the Japanese Army. They were well trained and disciplined, they knew what they were doing and usually did it well. When you think about it, they had the upper hand for some considerable time; the destruction of their communications system may have had a hand in their defeat. . . . When the landings began and the Japanese defenders threw everything that they had at us and mowed down dozens of Marines out on the reef, imagine what they must have been thinking when they saw us still on our feet and pressing on towards the beaches - they had always been told that we were soft and could not fight. They knew that the writing was on the wall, and that it wasn't going to take a million Americans a hundred years to take their island fortress.

"The difference between opposing forces really comes down to initiative - being able to think for yourself, and being unorthodox if necessary. The Japanese worked to a pattern and required constant direction and supervision in order to keep the battle going in their favour. We had the advantage in that Marine Corps training stressed self-reliance and the initiative to do what seemed best in any particular situation.

"Their battle practice of screaming and charging against the opposition to create panic may have worked against poorly trained Chinese forces, but against a disciplined Marine it meant nothing at all. They were cunning, and as patient as Job; perched high in a tree with a half-squeezed trigger, a sniper could remain motionless for hours on end and, using their smokeless ammunition, a shot would be heard and a casualty sustained, but from where nobody could find out.

"They were industrious, and had a penchant for cleanliness. Their Marines were well equipped, and would fight to the bitter end. The Japanese Army broke under pressure, but not their Marines - when we met head on it became like running into a brick wall, neither side gave an inch. They prided themselves in their overlapping style of defence - put one post out of action and you ran into another one covering the original position - but a considerable amount of pressure on their front or flank would usually find a weak spot to be explored.

"It was not in their nature to surrender, their military and religious doctrine deemed that it was preferable to die with honour for Emperor and country than to face the ignominy of capture; in the later stages of the fighting on Betio suicide was commonplace."

★   ★   ★

The 3rd Bn, 6th Marines under Lt Col Kenneth McLeod, who had made an uneventful landing over Green Beach earlier in the day, now moved along the south shore in the footsteps of Jones' 1-6 and took up supporting positions in their rear. The enemy were now in a desperate situation, compressed into the tail end of the island with their only escape route - to Bairiki - sealed by the 2-6. If ever they had contemplated a counter-attack, now was their last chance. For the Marines the day had gone better than Julian Smith's pessimistic forecast suggested. Progress had been excellent in comparison to the first two days; the reduction of well prepared and heavily fortified Japanese positions was of necessity a slow and dangerous operation, and perhaps some of the Marines could be excused if they felt that they could ease up a little now that the enemy were so obviously on their last legs.

Late in the afternoon of 22 November Col Maurice Holmes came ashore to establish a command post for the 6th Marines combat team, and was called to a meeting held by Julian Smith at Shoup's command post where the programme for the following day was discussed. On D+3 the 6th Marines were to continue their push along the south coast, passing McLeod's 3-6 through Jones' 1-6 to bring fresh troops to the front; all available tanks were to be provided, and artillery, naval gunfire and carrier aircraft were to act in close support.

As the searing heat of another tropical day gave way to a balmy night the light breeze could not hide the sickly-sweet stench of decay, but for those who had been on Betio since the beginning it was becoming almost unremarkable. The possibility of an enemy counter-attack was uppermost in the minds of many Marines as darkness fell, isolating them in their suddenly lonely foxholes and hiding the terrain to their front.

★   ★   ★

At some time around 7.30pm on the 22nd a group of about 50 Japanese quietly crept out of the undergrowth and moved forward, infiltrating a gap between Cos A and B of 1-6 in the southern sector of the line. This was an exploratory probe to try to determine the size and location of the American positions. Many of the Marines had fought on Guadalcanal and were familiar with this type of night prowling from their jungle days - they knew that however jumpy they felt it was essential not to open fire and reveal their positions.

Jones moved forward his battalion reserve - a small group from HQ Co and a mortar platoon from Co D - and a fierce hand-to-hand fight with knives and bayonets ensued. After about an hour the Japanese who were still alive were forced to retire to their own lines. The enemy soon mounted a second attack, however, and at this point Jones decided to call in support from Rixey's artillery. Using howitzers from Betio and Bairiki, Rixey directed a creeping barrage that came as close as 50 yards from the Marines' front line. Off shore destroyers were also engaged, firing first at the tail of the island and moving the fall of shot gradually north-west until they were hitting close to Jones' front. The enemy were badly mauled, and - thanks to the Marines' iron discipline - knew little more about the American positions than they had at the start of the attack.

At around 11pm yet another assault was mounted - a screaming wave of Japanese charged out of the brush, lobbing grenades and wildly firing their rifles in the general direction of the Marine positions; but this soon petered out, and a tense silence once again descended on the area. Nothing more happened for about four hours; then, shortly before 3am, a series of weird noises began to emerge from the Japanese lines: howling, monkey noises, and then calls in English - "Marines, you die!" and "Japanese drink Marine blood!". From wrecked trucks in front of Cos A and B enemy machine guns opened up; some were silenced by the Marines' .50cal guns, and others by volunteers who crept forward and lobbed hand grenades among the vehicles. Then the main attack erupted.

Several hundred howling Japanese came charging forward in a frenzied assault across the whole battalion front. The Marines replied with everything they had - machine guns, rifles, grenades and mortars - but some of the enemy managed to reach the line and hurl themelves into the foxholes. Then it was hand-to-hand again: a nightmare of stabbing and chopping at half-seen figures with bayonet, entrenching spade and rifle butt - even of desperate clawing with bare hands for the throat or wrist of a shockingly violent and almost invisible enemy who came hurtling and panting on top of you out of the dark. Artillery was again called in; the guns of the destroyers USS *Schroeder* and *Sigsbee* prevented any reinforcements from moving up from the end of Betio by blasting the area to the east of the airfield; and eventually the tide ebbed away.

Dawn showed the extent of the carnage. Immediately in front of 1-6's positions over 200 Japanese lay dead; and beyond them, in an area that had been pounded by the artillery and the Navy, a further 125 were counted. Jones' men had suffered 173 casualties - 45 dead, the remainder wounded. The enemy's last *banzai* charge had failed; for the Japanese now left on Betio there was no hope. PFC Joe Jordan of the 2-8, holding the northern sector of the line, vividly recalls the events of that night of 22-23 November:

"Early on the night was fairly quiet, but after a few hours we could hear *banzai* chants from our new unit's direction. This was followed by heavy firing, screams, cursing and you name it. The Japs had pulled a banzai with about 900 of their remaining troops and had hit the company front. Those guys had to hold, and they did. Any Japs that got through their front were handled with bayonets and K-Bars [combat knives] in the secondary line. Those Marines did an outstanding job that night. They were supported by land-based artillery and

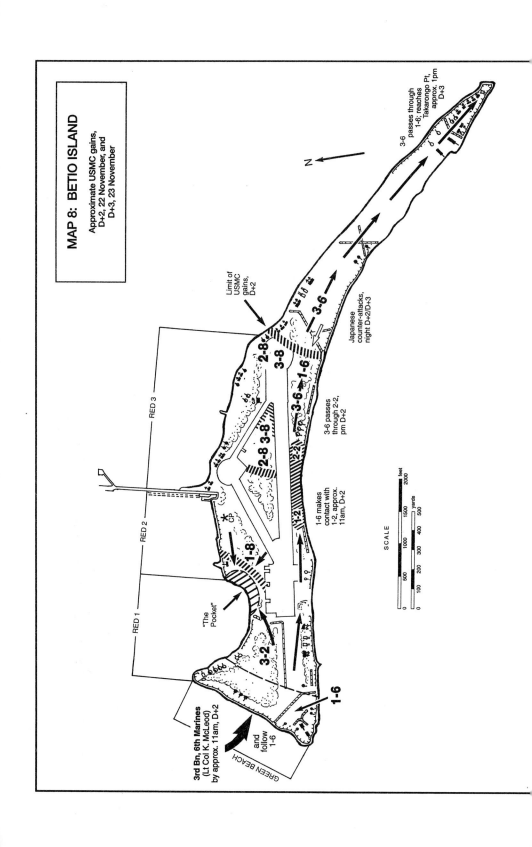

MAP 8: BETIO ISLAND

Approximate USMC gains,
D+2, 22 November, and
D+3, 23 November

N

3-6 passes through
1-6; reaches
Takarongo Pt,
approx. 1pm
D+3

3-6

Limit of
USMC
gains,
D+2

2-8
3-8
3-6 1-6

Japanese
counter-attacks,
night D+2/D+3

3-6

2-8 3-8

3-6 passes
through 2-2,
pm D+2

2-2

RED 3

1-2

1-6 makes
contact with
1-2, approx.
11am, D+2

CP

1-8

RED 2

"The
Pocket"

RED 1

3-2

GREEN BEACH

1-6

3rd Bn, 6th Marines
(Lt Col K. McLeod)
by approx. 11am, D+2

and
follow
1-6

SCALE

feet
0   500   1000   1500   2000

yards
0   100 200 300 400 500

naval guns also. This fight lasted a couple of hours . . .[before] everything again quietened down enough that we got some rest."

★   ★   ★

The Japanese high command had not abandoned Tarawa altogether. At around 3.40am on the 23rd enemy aircraft were picked up by the Navy radar watch coming in from the north-west. Four aircraft soon arrived over Betio, scattered their bombs at random and quickly withdrew.

Reports had also been forwarded to Adml Harry Hill that submarines were thought to be massing in the Tarawa area. At noon on the 22nd the USS *Gansevoort* made a contact to the west of the transport ship area, but a search showed nothing. Less than an hour later the USS *Meade* reported a contact in the same area, but lost it. Further contacts were made at 3.30pm and 4.27pm, and the two ships, joined by a third destroyer - the *Frazier* - dropped depth charges in a wide pattern in this area. This time they were lucky: the Japanese submarine *RC35* surfaced between the *Meade* and the *Frazier*, both destroyers immediately opened fire, and the *Frazier* swung round and rammed the submarine for good measure. Only three Japanese sailors were rescued; the *Frazier* received damage to her bow and was forced to reduce speed to avoid taking in too much water.

★   ★   ★

On Betio, 23 November dawned over a corpse-strewn landscape of scorched and shell-pocked sand, shredded coconut palms and smashed pillboxes. Some hollow-eyed boys were facing their fourth day of battle on this grotesquely dangerous scrap of coral; but the vanguard would be the fresh Marines of Kenneth McLeod's 3-6.

McLeod received his orders from Col Holmes, commander of the 6th Marines combat team: he was to pass through Jones' battalion and the grisly debris of the failed nighttime *banzai* charges, and press forward down the tail of the island until all enemy resistance had been eliminated. Carrier aircraft had softened up the area from 7am to 7.30am, and the guns of the destroyers lying off the southern shore had added their weight with a fifteen-minute barrage.

Spreading his force across the 300-yard width of the island, with Co L on the left and Co I on the right, McLeod moved out at around 8am. The riflemen were supported by two Sherman tanks - "*Cecilia*", and the apparently indestructible "*Colorado*" - and by seven Stuarts bringing up the rear. Ahead of them lay a maze of dug-outs, blockhouses and log emplacements, where an estimated 500 of the enemy were preparing to sell their lives dearly.

There was little resistance until the Marines were beyond the anti-tank ditch that stretched most of the way across the island about 100 yards past the end of the airfield runway; but here they were halted by a complex of pillboxes and dug-outs, all with excellent fields of fire. Not wishing to lose the impetus of the advance, Lt Col McLeod decided to bypass this area with Co L and leave the mopping up to Co I and some of the tanks. Moving against the pillboxes with flame throwers and charges, the men of Co I were surprised to see the occupants of the largest of the blockhouses come charging out en masse. *"Colorado"* was only yards away; swinging the turret around, the Sherman gunner fired a 75mm high explosive round point blank into the seething crowd. The tank crew later estimated that they had killed between 50 and 75 enemy with that single shot; this seems optimistic, but whatever the actual number this slaughter signalled the end of resistance in that area, and Co I were able to move forward.

All that now lay in McLeod's path were an assortment of individual emplacements, and the battery of coastal defence guns at Takarongo Point on the very tip of the island. Company L called for naval gunfire at 12.50pm, and the final advance was completed in just fifteen minutes. McLeod had lost only nine men killed and 25 wounded - the Japanese, 475 killed and 14 prisoners (mostly Korean labourers). At 1pm a tired, sweaty Marine stepped into the water lapping over the sand spit at the far tip of Betio, and swilled the dust from his face in the tepid water. The whole eastern half of the island was in American hands.

★   ★   ★

While McLeod and his 3-6 were clearing the end of the island there remained the stronghold at the intersection of Red Beaches 1 and 2 - "the Pocket". This most damaging of all the Japanese positions on Tarawa was now to receive the Marines' undivided attention.

From the east side, Lawrence Hays' 1-8 attacked in a semi-circular line, supported by flame throwers and demolition crews from Co C of the 18th Marines. Two half-track 75mm guns with infantry support under Maj Hewitt Adams moved right out onto the reef and attacked from close range, eliminating some of the enemy positions. From the west side, Maj Schoettel's 3-2 swung around the rear of the Pocket as far as the revetments of the airfield, and made contact with 1-8 at around 10am. The position was now completely encircled, and it was just a matter of time before the contracting American lines finally blasted and burned out the remaining Japanese, who steadfastly refused to surrender.

Now in a much more optimistic mood than on the previous afternoon, Julian Smith send a message to Adml Harry Hill at 11.50am: "Decisive defeat of enemy counter attack last night destroyed bulk of hostile resistance. Expect complete annihilation of enemy on Betio this date. Strongly recommend that you and your chief of staff come ashore this date to get information about the type of hostile resistance which will be encountered in future operations."

During the whole of the battle every attempt had been made to avoid causing damage to the main runway of the airfield, and as early as D+1 the Seabees had been working with bulldozers and levellers - often under fire - to repair the craters caused by the occasional misplaced shell. At noon on D+3 a Navy Hellcat fighter landed in a rolling cloud of dust; the neatly dressed and clean-shaven pilot stepped down among the filthy Marines and asked, "Is it over?" At 1pm on D+3 - Tuesday 23 November - Maj Gen Smith finally signalled that Betio was secure.

All over the island - an area of just over one square mile - more than 5,000 bodies were by now putrefying under the equatorial sun. The first priority was to dispose of them, as much to prevent disease as from any considerations of decency. This ghastly aspect of Tarawa was central to the experience and the memories of the men who fought there, and to pass over it too lightly would be deeply dishonest.

Many Japanese corpses had already been tipped into bomb craters and shellholes and bulldozed over. Now that the island was relatively quiet, hundreds of Japanese bodies were moved to the south shore and taken out to sea, where they were unceremoniously dumped overboard for the sharks to take care of - in those waters it would be a rapid process. (The pilot of one of the Kingfisher spotters which flew over the island during the battle had reported seeing sharks feeding on the bodies of "dead Japanese" out in the lagoon, but as so few of the enemy were killed during the landings it is almost certain that what he saw were Marines.)

Needless to say, the dead of the US Marines were treated with more dignity than the enemy. A collection point was established at the end of the main pier where identifications were made and personal possessions gathered together by the Grave Registration crews. In many cases identification was virtually impossible - an added misery for the many Marines who came to the pier looking for friends, not knowing who had survived the battle. Eventually a cemetery would be laid out in the area behind Red Beach 2 (now known as the Memorial Garden), with row after row of neat white crosses surrounded by a low wall of palm logs - the best that the Seabees could manage with the available resources. In time, some of the Marines would be returned to America at the request of their families to be laid to rest in their home towns; others would be remembered at the huge war memorial in Hawaii.

PFC Hugh Adams recalls: "I will never forget the day that our ship got under way for Hawaii after Tarawa was secured. I was standing at the rail and watching several small boats working their way among the bodies of Marines floating about. The bodies were so bloated that the Navy men used bayonets to puncture them, and then weighed them down with chains so they would sink. This was sea burial for some, and probably there was no other choice. [After a] few days at sea. . .we conducted more proper sea burials for those Marines who died aboard ship from wounds."

★　　　★　　　★

Of this immediate aftermath of battle Bob Libby of 3-2 wrote: "On the northwestern corner of Betio, according to the map [of the] defences, is shown a 140mm weapon. . . when things got to the stage of being able to move about a bit easier, I entered this gun emplacement.

"From memory, the gun itself had been blown out of existence and I don't recall seeing any sign of it. Entering the emplacement, I noted the stench of the place, plus the fact that my combat boots seemingly weighed more than usual. Looking at the soles of the boots, I found that I had tracked through something in the sandy soil: it turned out that I was walking about in the remains of those Japanese who manned that particular gun. Getting to hell out of there, I removed my leggings and promptly discarded them; cleaning my boots was a different matter, even wading in the sea didn't clean them properly. Right up to the time that I stepped on the deck of the ship to leave the island I had to put up with my unwanted footwear - once aboard I sixed them over the side, glad to be rid of them."

★   ★   ★

Joe Jordan was among the Marines with the unenviable job of disposing of the dead: "One detail was left, and that was to clean the dead out of the area and place them in the mass grave. Corpses were everywhere and had been burned almost black in the sun. We worked to identify the folks from our unit, and placed them in the trench covered by their ponchos. For a good friend we scraped a shallow hole for him to lie in. The burial ceremonies were very solemn and lasted about thirty minutes. Then bulldozers pushed sand in on top of the bodies. Someone also had to get the dead off the barbed wire barricades on the reef, and any that were left in the water. They had been dead at least two or three days and this was almost the centre of the hottest area of the earth. Guess who drew this detail from my squad?. . . Finally we got them all into a trench; and were told that the company was going to move to the next island for the night, but that the clean-up detail would stay on Helen [Betio] until morning. We would then be evacuated and go to a rear area for regrouping and retraining."

★   ★   ★

Robert Sherrod had returned to one of the transports to clean up and start writing his story. When he heard that it was all over, he went back - something that he had hoped that he would never have to do - to survey the scene:
"The smell of the dead is unbelievable. The ruptured and twisted bodies which expose their rotting inner organs are inexpressibly repellent. Betio would be more habitable if the Marines could leave for a few days and send a million buzzards in. The fire from a burning pile of rubble had reached six nearby Jap bodies, which sizzle and pop as the flames consume flesh and gases. Fifteen more are scattered around a food dump, and two others are blown to a hundred pieces - a hand here, a head there, a hobnailed boot further on."

★   ★   ★

Although Julian Smith had declared Betio "secure", this did not mean that all fighting was over. Throughout the island there were enemy troops holed up in hidden positions, ready to attack any Marines who came within range. Mopping up continued for many days, with fanatical Japanese having to be blasted or burned out of their dug-outs. The report on the activities of the 2nd Marines

Scout Sniper Ptn mentions that some Japanese opened fire at about 4.30pm on D+3 from positions previously thought cleared near the regimental command post, and were dealt with using TNT and Bangalore torpedoes; and that at 5.30pm they were ordered to report to Maj Kyle of 1-2, by then on Green Beach, to assist that battalion's C Co in eliminating several pillboxes.

Joe Jordan of 2-8 was relieved that he had come through the battle unharmed, and gave way to exhaustion:

"After three nights of very little sleep and four days of very tiring work everyone was just worn out. By dark we had found places to stretch out and were sound asleep. We knew that there were a few stragglers left and we should have posted a watch, but that is from hindsight. I was sleeping with my back to a coconut stump and was rudely awakened by someone crawling over me. Then my left shoulder was on fire. One of the stragglers had crawled into our area and was doing a job on my back with a bamboo-handled knife with about a 6in blade [which hit] the bone of the left shoulder blade and slid several inches through the flesh.

"Needless to say, I let out a scream which probably woke the guys on watch in the battleships; it also woke a couple of the guys close to me, and they killed the Jap. Again, the wonderful corpsmen were there almost immediately and proceeded to render first aid. [I] went to the aid station immediately, and slept the rest of the night in a cot with a blanket. [I was] evacuated the next morning and went to a hospital ship; then to Pearl Harbor Navy hospital; then to the States, for repair to the bone that had been damaged."

At dusk on the 23rd a Marine came across an underground emplacement and, hearing Japanese voices, threw a grenade into what turned out to be a magazine for 5in shells: the eastern end of Betio erupted into a display of pyrotechnics that lasted for the rest of the night.

Colonel Hall moved the survivors of 2-8 and 3-8 over to the island of Bairiki, and set about making a roll call to determine how many of his men had survived. It became clear that some units had suffered much higher casualties than others; in the 8th Marines, as in the 2nd, more than one man in three had been killed or wounded.

★   ★   ★

Hawk Rader of the 1-8 recalls: "I started back over to the beach, and someone who recognised me asked if I had seen Sgt Maj Musing, our battalion Sergeant Major. I said no and asked him why - he informed me that he was missing. To some he may have been lost, but he knew what he was doing. He had jumped into a large crater to escape from some small arms fire and saw the cap of a beer bottle sticking out of the sand. He started to dig, and realised that he had come across a beer store - a thousand pound bomb had dropped very close and covered it up. We spotted the Sergeant Major coming out of the crater with seven or eight bottles of Triple X lager beer under his arms - the rush was on! We jumped into the crater and started digging; many of the guys got a bottle, but I wasn't one of the lucky ones. I did share a bottle, and it was quite cool, having been buried for a few days under the sand - the beer was very good."

Later the same day Hawk's group began their evacuation of the island, but even that was not altogether uneventful: "We milled around the island for another hour or two, then we reboarded the same ship - the USS *Sheridan* - from which we had landed. We had barely gotten aboard when we received news over the loudspeaker system that a large number of Japanese aircraft were heading for Tarawa. This happened so suddenly that some of the Amphibious Attack Transports did not have time to retrieve their small landing boats. The little boats started following us to sea, still hoping to be taken aboard, but they were waved off. They were told over the loudspeaker to report back to the beach. The look of despair was awful on the faces of those coxswains [as] we sailed without them.

"The ship was not as heavily laden now as it was before we landed, and we could hear the bow slap the water and hear the screws grinding away when the aft of the ship would rise out of the water. This went on for three days, with the troops being strapped to their bunks most of the time. This was a hell of a bad experience in itself, but nothing like what we had just gone through - Tarawa was behind us!"

★   ★   ★

At noon on D+4, Wednesday 24 November, there was a formal flag-raising ceremony a little to the rear of Shoup's old command post inland from Red 2. Two defoliated palm trees were used as flagpoles, and the Stars and Stripes - together with a small Union Jack to acknowledge that Tarawa was a British colony - were raised to the accompaniment of a bugler sounding "To the Colours". The bugle was heard throughout most of the tiny island; men straightened to attention, and saluted.

Earlier that day Maj Gen Holland Smith had arrived to inspect the island and to see exactly what his Marines had been up against; the V Corps commander would be only the first of many members of the "brass" to visit Betio. Admiral Nimitz himself would arrive, accompanied by a train of admirals and generals including Adml Spruance, who disembarked for the first time from the *Indianapolis*.

Spruance was anxious to get back to Hawaii: not only had he to write his action report for Nimitz and King, but the next battle in the "island-hopping" programme - Kwajalein in the Marshalls group - was only two months away, and there was little enough time to discuss and apply the lessons learned at Tarawa.

Chapter 7:

Other Islands

As the battle raged on Betio on D+1, Herbert Deighton, a private first class with the Intelligence section of the 2nd Bn, 6th Marines, was having a very uncomfortable trip to Bairiki. Herbert, who had seen action at Guadalcanal and was later to serve on Saipan and Tinian, had watched the initial attack on Betio from the troopship *J.Franklin Bell*, and was under the impression that he was part of the reserve force to be landed on Green Beach. Plans had changed immediately Japanese troops had been seen crossing the sand spit to Bairiki. As their landing craft wallowed across the two miles of choppy ocean the Marines of the 2-6 were desperately trying to keep down their 11am lunch of spaghetti - many were unsuccessful, and Herbert's most vivid recollection of the trip was of strands of spaghetti hanging all over the sides of the boat.

As the LCVP turned for the approach to the island a machine gun opened up, and the deadly sound of bullets clanging against the ramp shook the Marines out of their lethargy. "As I cautiously looked over the side of the LCVP, I could see one of our planes drop a bomb that landed right at the back of the entrance to the bunker, and it was enveloped in a huge ball of flame - no more machine gun there.We found out later that the Japanese had placed a five-gallon drum of gasoline at the bunker back entrance."

No other resistance was encountereed, and after a search it was found that there were no more enemy troops on the island. Lieutenant Colonel Murray had mortars and machine guns set up opposite the eastern tip of Betio, and his Marines dug in for the night. "It was almost dark when a Jap ran past us," says Deighton; "everyone was surprised, [and] all we could do was holler at him to halt, but he ran into the night across the sand towards the next island."

★   ★   ★

Living on one of the smaller islands of the atoll was a Sgt Joseph, a native of Tarawa who had served in the New Zealand Army during the First World War. Division Intelligence, aboard the *Maryland*, thought that any information which a man of his background could supply might be valuable; so three platoons from D (Scout) Co, 2nd Tank Bn were given the task of finding Sgt Joseph and bringing him back to the flagship. The transport *Doyen* was detached, and steamed as far into the lagoon as was thought safe. Three Higgins boats, carrying the scouts and their rubber rafts, sailed to within 100 yards of the designated beaches, and the ten-man crews paddled ashore.

They were not certain whether they had landed exactly where they were supposed to; navigation had proved difficult on this moonless night, although the explosions and flashes of tracer from nearby Betio helped to some extent. They were under instructions to avoid contact with the enemy if at all possible. The rubber boats were hidden in the undergrowth and one man was detailed to guard them, while the remainder split into three parties: one group headed south, one north and the other directly eastward. The easterly squad soon came upon a well worn path; turning south, they arrived at a small village where an English-speaking native welcomed them.

They were told that Sgt Joseph lived two islands to the north, and some villagers volunteered to go and collect him. Lieutenant Drake, commanding 2nd Ptn, radioed the other parties to return and to avoid the path, which the natives said was frequently used by the Japanese. After some two and a half hours Sgt Joseph appeared, and readily agreed to return with the Marines to offer what assistance he could. They all made their way back to the beach and headed out into the lagoon to rendezvous with the waiting Higgins boats.

It was at this point that someone realised that the Marine who was supposed to have been guarding the inflatables was missing. After an arduous paddle back to the island Sgt Weaver's squad found the missing Marine asleep in the shrubbery; his fate on return to the troopship was unrecorded, but presumably unenviable. Dawn was not far away, but Sgt Joseph was delivered to the *Maryland* without further incident.

★   ★   ★

Theodore Stueber was with the 1st Ptn of D Co, who landed on an island further north than Lt Drake's group. Having established a defensive position from which they could observe the path running from island to island, they tried to obtain information about the size and movements of any Japanese force present:

"Our platoon spent the night of 22 November in two-man foxholes, one hour on watch and one hour off, just waiting and watching. I no longer have any idea of what time it might have been, but I was awakened by my foxhole buddy, Doyle, who suggested that I make the people in the next foxhole aware of noises that indicated possible movement near our position. With knife in hand (we didn't want to shoot to betray our position) I started to crawl to the next foxhole - and stopped immediately! Two fully armed Japanese soldiers stepped from the water, walked away from the path and stopped no more than ten feet away from our foxhole. They talked and gestured, I listened and prayed, then thank God they moved south. I can still see the bayonets on their rifles silhouetted against the starlit sky.

"These two men may have been the vanguard of the enemy survivors moving towards the northernmost island in the atoll. During the remainder of that night, in three large groups, some 250-300 men passed by our observation point; fortunately we were not discovered". After the enemy had passed the platoon commander sent a scout to try to locate the other two platoons; the wisdom of this precaution seemed confirmed when they saw natives evacuating a village, who told them that the Japanese intended to destroy their meagre force that night.

"Fully aware of the situation on Betio after the first two days of battle, and not certain when help would arrive, we moved our position," recalls Steuber. "We set up in an area where any attacking force would be required to cross an open stretch of water before reaching our lines. Although we had confidence in our fields of fire, we were apprehensive when we considered our supply of ammunition and hand grenades compared to the enemy force. We spent another almost sleepless night, and will never know why the enemy did not choose to attack - we fully expected a *banzai* attack. During that night we thought we observed some movement on the other side of the water, but since we could not establish [whether it was] the natives or the enemy, not a shot was fired."

The next morning reinforcements arrived; and, after accompanying the 2-6 Marines north over the next two islands, the Scout Company was withdrawn. They would land in their rubber boats on other atolls in the Gilbert Islands to seek out and destroy enemy radio installations.

★   ★   ★

When the war broke out in 1939, the New Zealand government believed that their army would be called upon to serve in Europe as they had during the 1914-1918 war; but they were uneasy about the potential threat from the Japanese Empire. With this in mind they set up a chain of "coast watchers" throughout the British and New Zealand mandated islands of the South Pacific. These radio operators were to report on any Japanese landings, naval movements, troop dispositions, in fact anything that would be of use to the Allies in the event of war. It was a perilous duty; they were unarmed - a decision which later would be bitterly questioned - and if war did come they would be stranded on whatever island they had been assigned, in constant danger of capture by a ruthless enemy, for however long the war might last. In July 1941 radio operators from the Postal & Telegraph Department, together with personnel drawn from the New Zealand forces, left Fiji for their allotted islands.

Two days after the attack on Pearl Harbor the Japanese landed in the northern atolls of the Gilbert Islands, and seven of the coast watchers were captured. Morale remained high among those in the south, and fresh supplies were sent to them from Fiji in February 1942; but seven months later the Japanese occupied the remainder of the Gilberts. On 25 September 1942 the last message was received in Wellington: "Japanese coming - regards to all".

Three watchers were taken the next day on Nonouti, and over the following weeks more were captured, many of them betrayed by islanders threatened with Japanese reprisals. From among these prisoners seventeen New Zealanders, together with the Rev A.D.Sadd and Capt I.R.Handley - a blind, 73-year-old retired sea captain - were taken to Betio.

When the Americans took Betio in November 1943 there was no sign of any coast watchers; but local natives were able to give some information which led to an inquiry by the High Commission for the Western Pacific in February 1944. It was reported that during their first few days as prisoners on Betio they had all been tied to coconut trees with telegraph wire, eating only what food courageous islanders were able to smuggle to them when the Japanese were inattentive. After some days they were taken to a compound near the local hospital, and during daytime they were put to menial work under the supervision of Korean labourers who worked for the Japanese.

On 15 October 1942 an American warship shelled Betio and US aircraft bombed two ships lying in the lagoon to the north of the island. The Catholic bishop, Octave Terrienne, recalled that after the attack a group of Koreans armed with axes and shovels ran around the island looking for Europeans who they claimed had escaped - the bishop later saw one of them with a bloodstained sword. A cook from the hospital said that later the same day he saw all the

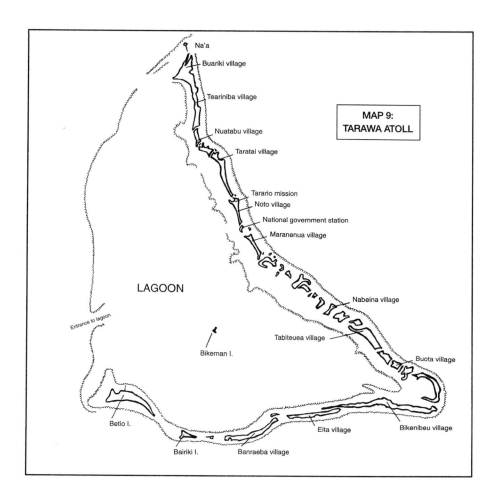

MAP 9:
TARAWA ATOLL

Europeans sitting in a line near a house; a Japanese stepped forward and cut off the head of the first in the line, then the second, before the cook fainted. An islander and a local constable both testified to the commission that they had seen headless, partly burned bodies lying in a pit. Sister Mary Oliva of the Sacred Heart Mission on Tarawa reported being told that when the warship shelled the island one of the prisoners escaped and ran down to the beach, and that during the shelling the prisoners had clapped their hands. The bodies were never found - unsurprisingly, after the massive destruction of November 1943; but to this day there remains a simple memorial in the Protestant cemetery to these brave New Zealanders.

*   *   *

Raymond Murray's 2-6 Marines had been given the job of clearing the remaining islands of Tarawa Atoll, but some preliminary reconnaissance work had already been carried out apart from the nighttime raid to collect Sgt Joseph. Also on 21 November, other elements of D (Scout) Co of the light tank battalion under Capt John Nelson had landed on the islands of Eita and Buota at the eastern end of the atoll - over 100 Japanese were thought to be on Buota, where a radio station was located. Another element landed near Tabiteuea village, about a quarter of the way up the eastern chain of islands from Buota to Na'a - the extreme northern end of Tarawa. Two days later, while the 3-10 were setting up their howitzers on Eita to support the infantry on Betio, the Japanese on Buota escaped to the north.

Murray's battalion embarked in boats from Betio at 5am on 24 November en route to Buota to start their long trek around the atoll. Herbert Deighton of 2-6 remembers loading aboard a landing craft at the end of the pier; they could not board from the beach because the tide was still out, and men were unwilling to wade out amid the floating corpses:

"We went across the lagoon in the landing craft to the island of Buota (about the fifth island up the chain from Betio). We landed and started our march from island to island. . . .We did not make contact with the Japs, but the natives told us in every village we went through that the Japs were just ahead of us. The natives were happy to see us, as they had been forced to work for the Japs in building bunkers on Betio and only paid with a handful of rice a day; they were used to fishing and raising their root crops, and with the Japs they had no time for that. Besides, the Japs made them cut down their beloved coconut trees to make the bunkers. . .

"We were always thirsty and short of water; we were ordered not to drink from the wells we found in the native villages - they were afraid that the wells had been poisoned. Advancing at dawn the next day, myself and another man from the second section were sent out to make a reconnaissance of a village. As we went through the village hut by hut we came across a church with a steeple and typical architecture of a normal church except that it was unpainted and of rough wood. Jim and I were about to enter the church when from around the side came a voice, 'Would you gentlemen like a drink of water?' - and who appeared but an English nun in full habit. We got our drink of water and. . .the information. . .that the Japs had passed through the village the night before and were gone - much to our relief. The nun was one of two who had stayed on when the rest of the non-native whites had fled earlier in the year.

"At low tide you could walk from island to island, but between tides the depth of water varies and in most places is impassable at high tide. We walked between some islands and came close to swimming between the others. We set up a defensive line halfway up the atoll that night; still no contact with the Japs - reports that they are just ahead of us. We jumped off early next day, island to island; we all had young native boys carrying our packs, and when we stopped for a break they climbed the coconut trees and picked the coconuts for us. We chased the Japs on up the atoll until by afternoon we were on the last but one island" [this was Buariki].

The battalion commander sent out a fighting patrol from E Co while the rest of 2-6 dug in for the night. Moving through thick undergrowth, the Marines clashed briefly with a Japanese patrol, killing three of them before breaking contact. As soon as there was daylight on 26 November Murray moved the rest of his battalion forward. A fierce engagement followed, in which 175 of the Japanese were killed; Marine losses were also heavy - 32 dead and 59 wounded. Herbert Deighton recalls:

"As soon as the firing began we made it to the front, going from coconut tree to coconut tree. I dived behind a coconut log lying on the ground thinking it would give me some protection; as soon as machine gun bursts hit the log I realised it was an old rotten log and I might as well stand up and take off for better cover. E Company was badly hit, so Murray sent F through E Company. By late afternoon it was all over; our battalion had three officers and 29 enlisted men killed and 59 wounded - we killed 175 Japs. Our two sections came through well - one enlisted man wounded (Ray was shot through the neck, he recovered and was reunited with 2 Section in Hawaii in February). We spent the rest of the day going over the Jap bodies for intelligence information - I never did like this part of the job, lots of blood and guts. We dug in for the night expecting another firefight on the last island, Na'a - at least, Col Murray asked for and received an OK for aircraft strafing runs and destroyer fire support tomorrow."

On the morning of 27 November Lt Col Murray sent a patrol over to Na'a, the very last island on the atoll, after the Navy aircraft and destroyers had pounded it for around twenty minutes. They found nothing but torn-up buildings. Its mission completed, the battalion returned to Eita for rest and reorganisation.

Raymond Murray recalls two entirely non-military impressions from that march: discovering from a chance aside that his native guide was a fully qualified surgeon educated at the British medical school in Fiji; and that on the night before the battle on Buariki, "a group of young girls from a nearby village came to my command post and wanted to sing for my Marines. They sang several songs the missionaries had taught them; the only one of which I remember is 'You are my sunshine'."

Although the seizure of Tarawa was the key to Operation Galvanic, mention must be made of the two other atolls in the Gilberts which formed part of the operation - Makin and Apamama.

The northern Task Force 50, off Makin, was of similar size to that at Tarawa; but they also had Task Group 50-1 under Adml "Baldy" Pownell - the fleet carriers USS *Lexington* and *Yorktown* and the light carrier *Cowpens*, three battleships and six destroyers - standing by to counter any Japanese force that might venture from the naval base at Truk. Task Group 50-2 - the fleet carrier *Enterprise* and the light carriers *Belleau Wood*, *Liscomb Bay* and *Monterey*, the battleships *Pennsylvania*, *North Carolina* and *Indiana*, and six destroyers - was the main component of the Makin force; and the preliminary bombardment of Butaritari, the main island of the atoll, was of a similar ferocity to that at Betio.

The plan was for two battalions of the 165th Infantry from the US Army's 27th Division to attack the western end of the six-mile-long island from the ocean side, and for a third battalion to land later the same day - 20 November - from the lagoon side. This was an Army operation under Maj Gen Ralph Smith - something that the Marine general, Holland Smith, viewed with some scepticism; but that was how Spruance had planned it, so he was stuck with it. The fact that 6,500 soldiers would be attacking a Japanese garrison of around 800 suggested to the V Corps commander that Makin should take about one day to secure.

In stark contrast to Betio, the amtracs that came ashore on Makin around 8.30am on 20 November faced no opposition; the Japanese were dug in two miles inland, and stayed there. Apart from some sporadic sniper fire the assault battalions landed unopposed; they soon secured the western end of the island, and within an hour and a half they had a firm beachhead and were advancing eastwards toward the enemy. The third battalion landed from the lagoon side at around 10.40am; again, there was no opposition, and the troops were able to wade the 300 yards to shore unharmed. The three battalions reached the Japanese defence lines; and from then on it was stalemate.

Untried in combat, the 165th Infantry had spent too long on garrison duty in Hawaii. Their training had instilled the doctrine of advancing cautiously to minimise casualties and to ensure that no enemy remained to threaten their rear - unlike that of the Marines, which emphasised fast forward movement at almost any cost, because their seaborne support was exposed for every extra hour that they had to wait offshore for an island to be secured. Holland Smith, rapidly losing what little patience he had, came ashore to see what was going on. He found light tanks standing idle, the crews refusing to move without orders from their own commanding officer - who was elsewhere on the island. One infantry company were firing so indiscriminately that other troops had to dive for cover; when asked what they were firing at they replied that they were clearing out snipers; when told that there were no Japanese anywhere in that area, they said they were just following orders. When he arrived at Ralph Smith's headquarters "Howling Mad" - by now a living caricature of his nickname - was told that there was heavy fighting in the north of the island. Commandeering a jeep, he drove to the scene of the supposed battle, and reported it as being "as quiet as Wall Street on a Sunday." It took over three days to secure Makin, a performance which Holland Smith described as "infuriatingly slow." The American casualties amounted to 64 dead and 154 wounded; only one of the 800 Japanese on the island survived to be captured.

∗   ∗   ∗

By far the heaviest casualties in the northern phase of the operation were sustained by the Navy with the sinking of the light carrier USS *Liscomb Bay*. This occurred on 24 November; had the island been taken in one day as Holland Smith had confidently anticipated, the *Liscomb Bay* would have been well on her way back to Hawaii. The Japanese submarine *I-175* had been in the area for some time and had been shadowing the carrier, hoping for a clear shot. The submarine captain's chance came at around 6am when the *Liscomb Bay* came to general quarters and turned north-west to launch aircraft for an early morning strike. The turn brought the carrier directly across *I-175's* bow, and the captain unleashed three "Long Lance" torpedoes. The result was horrific: one or more of the torpedoes struck the bomb storage compartment and every bomb exploded simultaneously, blowing off the whole stern of the carrier. The inferno exploded the carrier's fuel storage tanks; the battleship USS *New Mexico*, sailing almost a mile behind the *Liscomb Bay*, was showered with debris, plating, and a ghastly assortment of clothing and human flesh. The *Liscomb Bay* sank in less than 23 minutes with the loss of 644 lives including that of Rear Adml Henry Mullinex - a loss more than ten times as great as the Army fatalities on Makin. The *I-175* escaped detection by the escorting destroyers, and returned to Kwajalein.

∗   ∗   ∗

In total contrast, the taking of the third atoll in Operation Galvanic - Apamama, 75 miles south-east of Tarawa - reads like the libretto of a slightly macabre Gilbert and Sullivan opera. To probe its defences a party of 78 US Marines from V Amphibious Corps Scout Co under Capt James Jones were embarked at Hawaii aboard the USS *Nautilus* - one of the submarines which had taken Carlson's Raiders to Makin fifteen months earlier. The *Nautilus* was tasked first to observe any enemy shipping movements off Tarawa; but while sailing on the surface around the atoll she was attacked by an American destroyer - the magnificent *Ringgold* - which had not been informed that a US submarine was in the area. The *Nautilus* was struck on the conning tower by a 5in shell, and left the area at best speed. After making repairs to the damage, she arrived off Apamama. This island had once been the home of the writer Robert Louis Stevenson, who described its "superb ocean climate, days of blinding sun and bracing winds, and nights of heavenly brightness." More to the immediate point, the lagoon - twelve miles long and five miles across - was ideal for a forward naval base.

The Marines landed in rubber boats and advanced along the six islands that make up the atoll, killing one of a three-man Japanese patrol on the way. The local natives told them that there were 25 Japanese on the next island; so the *Nautilus* provided a bombardment with her deck gun to soften up the enemy. By the morning of 25 November all was silent on the island; and a native told the Marines that all of the Japanese were dead. It transpired that the Japanese commander, while addressing his assembled men with a pistol in one hand and a sword in the other, had accidentally shot himself in the head. The distraught troops, unable to make any decisions without their commander, had dug their own graves and then killed themselves - all that the Marines had to do was come along and fill them in.

Chapter 8:
Semper Fidelis

"If the Army and the Navy ever gaze on Heaven's scenes,
They will find the streets are guarded by United States Marines"
(The Marines' Hymn, 1880)

Some of the transports remained at Tarawa for two weeks, unloading supplies for the troops who would occupy the island and try to create some order out of the carnage and chaos. While the 2nd and 8th Marines began shipping out on D+4, the relatively less mauled 6th Marines stayed on for two more months to provide an infantry garrison. On 4 December command of the atoll was formally turned over to the Navy.

The 2,000-mile voyage to Hawaii was a depressing experience for the Marines. Every day there were burials at sea as casualties died from their wounds. There were no new Marine uniforms available, and the survivors could do little to rid themselves of the terrible smell of corruption which clung to their clothing. Bob Libby remembers:

"Gathering up our gear, we trudged through the rubble towards where we were to board landing craft and be transported out to the waiting ships. . . . [Feeling] surprise and disbelief over surviving the nightmare experience, we left the island behind us. . . .Away from the stench of death and destruction, we welcomed the cleaner air and light sea breezes. Wallowing in the swell, our landing craft swung in alongside the ship we were going to board; the cargo net dangling down and trailing in the water was made secure to our landing craft. Looking up the side of the ship, I recall the feeling of not having the strength to haul myself up to the deck above - I surmise those around me felt the same. It took us longer than usual to finally feel the steel deck beneath our feet. . . . A sudden bustling around took place; the crew burst into action, racing to their battle stations; the loading of troops was hastened, landing craft were hoisted aboard even as the ship was [getting] under way - the reason was a submarine alert. Without looking back towards the last four days of hell, we went below to our troop compartments and flung our combat gear onto any convenient bunk. . . .

"We were a filthy looking lot; the ship's crew stared at us as though they had never seen such a sight before - and maybe they hadn't. Apparently our appearance and the aroma of death that we brought aboard was too much for the captain - he wanted us cleaned up and into clean clothes. Getting cleaned up was no problem, but the only clothes we had were those we stood in. The captain ordered his quartermaster to issue each of us with new seaman's working gear; our battle clothes were to be destroyed. . . ."

The thought of Hawaii cheered many, who had wild fantasies of grass-skirted girls on Waikiki Beach and nights in the bars of Honolulu; but it was not to be. One veteran recalls: "Once I was on the troopship a kind of numbness set in; I looked at that stinking little slaughterhouse of an island for a while, but nothing registered in my head. To the sailors I must have had a zombie-like appearance; it was significant that nobody spoke to us much, they seemed to sense that we had been through something that put us apart from other people - for a while, anyway. There were a number of burials at sea as some of the wounded died a few days out, and this all added to the gloom; but gradually we all seemed to return to some form of normality - I even saw a smile or two and heard a few jokes, but they struck me as being a bit forced, with a hint of hysteria behind them.

"After what seemed like an age we all crowded to the side as we entered Pearl Harbor on Oahu island; someone had done a fine job of clearing up the mess, but there were still some big warships lying at pretty funny angles. . . . We all assumed that this was going to be the end of the line and we would be getting off here. Not so: we had only put in at Pearl so that the wounded could be taken off, once that was done we upped anchor and off we went again. Where now?, we asked each other. . . We docked once more, this time on Hawaii Island, the biggest of the chain, at the docks at Hilo. From the ship we transferred to a fleet of trucks. We had practically no equipment - our small arms and the uniforms that we stood up in - in fact some of us didn't even have that, the Navy brass had made some of us dump our stinking uniforms over the side, so a whole heap of the guys were wandering around in Navy denims.

"The trucks took us to the interior to an area called the Parker Ranch; I remember it was near to two extinct volcanoes called Mauna Loa and Mauna Kea, and it looked a pretty inhospitable spot, certainly not what I had imagined Hawaii to be like. The camp was still being constructed where I was - the Seabees were doing a fine job as usual. Most of the accommodation was made up of tents. . . .This didn't bother me, until it got dark. We soon realised that Camp Tarawa (as it came to be called) was around 3,000 feet above sea level. . . It may seem crazy saying that it was cold in Hawaii, but after Tarawa that is exact-ly what it was.

"On Tarawa you would be gasping for breath after running 20 yards from one sandpile to another; when you threw yourself down on the ground the heat burned through your flimsy clothing and you wanted to jump up again - but daren't. The end of your nose went bright red and started to peel, and your lips dried up and then cracked, and you didn't have enough spit left to wet them as your water had most likely run out hours ago. At Camp Tarawa you really noticed the difference, and of course there was a shortage of blankets. We heard that General Julian was doing his best with the Army to get us some, and as the weeks passed the blankets, along with the uniforms and equipment, began to slowly work through the pipeline. The guys gradually settled at Camp Tarawa and we soon started training for the next big one - that was to be Saipan; but that's another story."

Since the raising of the Corps during the Revolutionary War in 1775 the US Marines had distinguished themselves on many battlefields, but Tarawa had added a whole new dimension. "Guadalcanal was something; but I never saw anything like this", declared the redoubtable Col Evans Carlson. The losses at Tarawa were three times those suffered by a far larger force during the North African landings of November 1942, twice as many as in the Sicilian landings of July 1943, and only some 500 less than in the fierce two-week battle for Salerno, Italy, that September. As the war progressed the losses would mount, and the butcher's bill for Iwo Jima and Okinawa would eclipse Tarawa; but for concentrated, bloody, close-quarter fighting there were few battles to compare with those four days on Betio.

This type of fighting only occurs when the combatants have no room to manoeuvre, when there are no flanks to turn and the only way to advance is straight ahead. The achievements of the 2nd Marine Division on Betio removed any lingering doubts - and there had been many in Washington - as to the feasibility of amphibious landings against heavily defended Pacific islands. Mistakes were made, plans went awry, equipment proved unsuitable or inadequate - all the shortcomings of any pioneering military enterprise were present at Tarawa; and yet the island was taken in 76 hours, largely through the determination and aggressiveness of the Marines.

Some of them were veterans of Guadalcanal; but many of them were little more than boys, facing battle for the first time. It was not unusual to find, among the laden Marines struggling towards the beaches in the teeth of a murderous fire, youths of less than eighteen, who six months earlier had taken the first train ride of their lives from the peace of some Mid-West corn belt town to the harsh awakening of Parris Island or San Diego.

★   ★   ★

There was feverish activity in the offices of the Navy and Marine planning staffs in Hawaii over the weeks following Operation Galvanic. The invasion of the Marshall Islands was set for the first days of February 1944, and the mistakes of Tarawa had to be learned and rectified in a matter of weeks. Officers, from company commanders upward, were interviewed about anything that they thought could be improved. The 2nd Division were not backward in letting Spruance and his team know what they considered to be the shortcomings of Galvanic; and high on the list was communications.

There was universal condemnation of the use of warships as communications centres. The first salvo from the 16in guns on the USS *Maryland* had virtually wrecked the ship-to-shore radio links, and technicians spent the whole of the remainder of the battle attempting to maintain lines of communication. The converted transport ships, bristling with antennae, that soon became the communications centres for subsequent invasion fleets throughout the Pacific (and even as far away as the Normandy beaches) owed their origins to lessons learned at Tarawa.

The portable man-pack radios which the Marines carried ashore had fared no better. The equipment was basically sound, but lacked any effective waterproofing; when the Marines were compelled to wade in through water up to chest deep the radio packs became saturated and most of them failed.

The amtrac had come into its own at Tarawa. Had there been more of them most of the terrible casualties of the first day could have been avoided. After Tarawa, no assault landing took place in the Pacific without wave upon wave of amtracs leading the way - better armed and armoured, and with more powerful engines. Their enormously improved successors are still the key to the USMC's amphibious assault capability today.

There was much criticism of the naval bombardment of Betio. It was the most powerful yet seen in the war, but the Marines still had to face dozens of undamaged pillboxes, bunkers and emplacements that had shrugged off the best that the Navy could throw at them. The admirals had assumed that saturating the island from end to end with heavy gunfire would automatically silence the Japanese defences, but it just did not work that way. All the warships were operating from fairly close range, which meant that the shells had a low trajectory. Admiral Harry Hill stated:

"We had to work from scratch. There had never been a landing made upon such heavily defended beaches, and while we knew pretty well the location of the strong points to be knocked out, we could only guess at the structural strength of these installations and what type of bombardment was required to destroy them. Our cruisers and battleships were provided with high capacity projectiles with a very sensitive impact fuse. If penetration was required, an appreciable angle of fall had to be provided for the armour piercing projectiles, which if fired at too flat trajectories would ricochet without explosion. This presented a problem for the destruction of the beach dug-out defences, for most of the heavy calibre fire on them would be from relatively close range."

The Japanese emplacements were all dug into the ground and covered, some with layers of treetrunks and some with concrete, on top of which mounds of sand and coral had been piled up. Unless there was a direct hit the shells were ineffectual, many of them bouncing off the earthworks and landing in the sea off the southern shore. Probably the greatest contribution that the naval bombardment made was to disrupt the Japanese communications system - though as already discussed, what part this actually played in preventing an effective counter-attack must remain speculative. In later operations the Navy concentrated more on pinpointing individual targets, and where a blanket barrage was called for it was delivered from well off shore to achieve a more plunging fire.

★   ★   ★

In the early stages of the planning of the battle there had been much discussion about the best site for the initial landing on Betio. Admiral Hill had some interesting recollections of these meetings:

"The south shore had a flat coral shelf extending offshore about 700 yards, where the seaward edge dropped off abruptly to deep water. Near the outer edge a barbed wire barricade extended along the entire reef, and toward the western end of the reef there was a similar barrier close inshore. But as we got pictures at low tide, the shelf proved to be so flat that even at high tide no landing craft could have gotten closer than 100 yards or so from the beach. There were many beach defences of similar construction to these on the north shore, but these could have been definitely demolished by frontal gunfire before landing. A few months later, with plenty of LSTs and LVTs available. . . I'm sure this beach would have been favoured, and the landing would have been effected with considerably less casualties, as troops would have been transported in LVTs, and both LVTs and trucks embarked in LSTs could have solved the emergency supply problem. Lacking these, my staff and Julian Smith's staff independently rejected this plan.

"Western Beach [Green Beach]: initially from the naval point of view this seemed the ideal landing point, as the reef gradient provided good access to shore in any tide, even for the heaviest LCMs. Closer examination of the low water pictures, however, disclosed a row of several large V-shaped coral fish traps, not awash at low tide, but probably shallow enough so that the boat lanes would have to be bent around them. As previously stated, this beach had 8in gun turrets at each corner, with other emplaced mounts covering it; and a few of the beach pillboxes, but these also could have been destroyed by frontal pre-landing bombardment at close range."

★   ★   ★

The question of tides has always held the key to Tarawa. The only nautical maps available to the planners at this time dated back to the turn of the century and contained many inaccuracies. The members of the advisory group of pre-war mariners and inhabitants of the Gilbert Islands - the "Foreign Legion" - were divided in their estimates of the depth of water over the reefs on 20 November, although Maj Frank Holland surely deserved to have more notice taken of his predictions of an extremely low dodging tide. Julian Smith was very concerned by Holland's predictions, and raised the matter with "Howling Mad" Smith during one of their preliminary conferences. The upshot was the request for more amtracs which resulted in the hasty despatch of the LVT-2s from San Diego. But evidence suggests that fears about the possibility of a dodging tide which might hang landing craft up on the reefs hundreds of yards from the shore were subordinated to the need to execute Operation Galvanic to the pre-arranged schedule.

When recalling these events many years later, Julian Smith said: "Well, I consulted this old man Major Holland, who had been on the island, and . . . had kept the tide records on Tarawa for the British Government. And when I saw him he said 'General, I never said you could land there on a neap tide .'" Admiral Hill seems to have been more concerned about the operation going to schedule than about the dangers of a very low tide. "After the amtracs, succeeding waves were to be embarked in LCVPs which according to the tidal data would negotiate the reef and land their troops on all three beaches. High tide was scheduled for 11.15am with a height of five feet. Low tide was at 5am with a height of 0.9 feet. One of the requirements for amphibious landings is that it [sic] should be on a rising tide, preferably about two hours before high tide. Had D Day been postponed, the next day with suitable tide conditions as just outlined would be 5 December, which was also a neap tide period."

In giving priority to the pre-arranged timetable over Maj Holland's repeated warnings the planners made their major blunder of the battle. Admiral Hill recalled a meeting on 12 October with Julian Smith, Holland Smith, Nimitz, Spruance and Kelly Turner - all the major protagonists in the planning and execution of the battle: "All phases of it were thoroughly discussed, particularly the decision to land on the lagoon side - all were approved without any modification in any important detail. The question of tides was discussed in some detail at this presentation, but I can recall no concern on anyone's part regarding the chances of severe consequences from a dodging tide . . . there was no useable spring tide until January 1944, so it was obvious that the landings must go as planned."

★   ★   ★

The inquest into the Tarawa landings made a number of recommendations regarding equipment. In a circular dated 8 January 1944 Julian Smith questioned the amount of equipment that his Marines were required to carry when landing on enemy-held shores: "It is the consensus among assault troops that this amount of equipment is neither necessary nor desirable in an operation of this type. In particular it was remarked that the gas mask (Army type) was an encumbrance, the pack was unnecessary, and all the rations carried were not consumed. It was realised that it was necessary to carry a gas mask, but a great many were ruined by immersion in salt water when men waded ashore, and in nearly every case as soon as men reached the beach and found that there was no evidence of gas and became involved in close combat they discarded their masks." It was suggested that the Army assault gas mask - a lightweight affair that could be carried in a small waterproof case slung on the chest, shoulder or hip - should be used, as more likely to withstand the rigours of a seaborne attack.

The widespread use of the reversible camouflage uniform was also recommended in preference to the standard utilities, as there had been some confusion on Tarawa when it was discovered that some Japanese wore a two-piece suit of green drab which could be mistaken for Marine dungarees. (Nevertheless, as already remarked, photographic evidence shows that this recommendation was to a large extent ignored by battle-proven troops; as the war progressed their use of the camouflage suit for beach landings became less, not more common.)

On a more grisly note, it was also suggested that the Marines be issued with two sets of identification "dog tags", one around the neck and the other in the form of a wrist bracelet. Many bodies had been found at Tarawa with heads completely blown off, and according to the coldly practical view expressed by 2nd Division medical officers, "identification of dead would be speedier and more accurate were one identification tag worn on the wrist and one around the neck." (It has since become common to wear dog tags at both the neck and the ankle.)

The question was asked, was the 2nd Division sufficiently prepared and trained to mount an operation on this scale?

It was not until July 1943 that Adml Nimitz received his orders from the Joint Chiefs of Staff to mount the invasion of the Gilbert Islands; and it was August before Adml Spruance was to meet with Julian Smith, Edson and Shoup at the Windsor Hotel in Wellington to brief them on the details of Operation Galvanic. At that meeting Spruance was under the impression that the beachhead landings would be made by conventional LCVP Higgins boats. It is well known that Julian Smith raised the question of the shortage of amtracs with Holland Smith, who in turn confronted Kelly Turner with his ultimatum - "more amtracs, or we don't go". The last-minute rendezvous with the LVT-2s from San Diego, and the jury-rigging of improvised armour there and in New Zealand, could have left no one in any doubt that suitable landing craft were in short supply.

The training of the Marines in embarkation and disembarkation before the division's departure for Tarawa was also less than adequate, although some preliminary training had been carried out earlier in the year. On the way to Tarawa the invasion fleet put in at Efate for amphibious landing rehearsals, but circumstances did not allow for realistic simulations. There were no carriers in attendance, so there was no opportunity to practice ground support co-ordination, nor was there time to land tanks or artillery; and the naval gunfire was directed at beaches miles away from those used in the practice landings.

The use of rubber boats (nicknamed the "Condom Navy") in the landings on Green Beach on D+1 was also questionable; in the event some Marines had difficulty in making headway while others drifted away, and various vessels had to be sent to tow them to shore. They were never again to be used in a large scale operation during the war, and it is fortunate that Japanese opposition on Green Beach had been virtually eliminated by Mike Ryan and his men.

Experience on Betio also led to the appointment of beachmasters to control the flow and priority of supplies. More training was given in the use of flame throwers and bazookas, which had proved so useful in clearing pillboxes and emplacements, but which had been delivered so late that the Marines had no chance to practice their tactical integration with the rifle squads. The co-ordination of air support was also greatly improved for future operations. Aerial reconnaissance, and the use made of its results, emerges well from the postmortem on Tarawa[1].

A less quantifiable but still fundamental lesson of Tarawa which was undoubtedly absorbed by the American military was the sharp reminder it provided of that ancient, simple imperative: never underestimate your enemy.

★   ★   ★

Tarawa was one of the best documented battles of World War II. Early in the war the Marine Corps had created a Photographic Section for the purpose of documenting its battles across the Pacific. The 2nd Division unit was under the command of Capt Louis Hayward (a former Hollywood actor well known at the time for his starring roles in such films as "*The Man in the Iron Mask*"). The unit land-

---

(1) See Appendix 10 for passages from the Intelligence Annex to the Special Action Report of January 1944.

ed with the combat troops on the first day, and recorded most of the important sequences of the battle, using 16mm Kodachrome colour film for some of the footage - something of a novelty in combat photography at the time. In all 900 stills, 2,500 feet of black-and-white and 5,000 feet of colour film were shot by the Marines, in addition to material shot by the numerous press correspondents who also covered the battle. Staff Sergeant Hatch and Cpl Newcomb between them shot a sequence of the four-hour siege of the Japanese bunker where Lt Bonnyman earned his Medal of Honor; this can still be seen on video, along with many other aspects of the operation, while the National Archives in Washington hold hundreds of still photographs of the battle.

As well as the work of the courageous Marine photographers and cameramen and the war correspondents, some remarkable images of Tarawa would be created by Kerr Eby, an accredited artist-correspondent. A veteran of the Western Front in World War I, Eby made dozens of rapid sketches which were later developed into a series of superb charcoal drawings, of a poignancy and impact seldom equalled by war artists. This 54-year-old civilian went from Tarawa to other Marine battlefields on Bougainville, and later on New Britain.[1]

With the battle over, the war correspondents were eager to get their stories back to America. This had been the first of what were going to be many amphibious landings in the drive toward the Japanese homeland, and they were determined to be the first with their accounts. What they had to say came as a profound shock to the American public. The sombre photographs of bodies floating in the lagoon, strewn around wrecked amtracs on the beaches or hanging in the barbed wire sent a wave of shock through the civilian population. The authorities initially had strong reservations about allowing these grim images to be released, fearing that the public could not accept the stark realities of the battlefield; but - perhaps surprisingly - a more robust common sense prevailed, and for a while the dead of Tarawa dominated the American print media and newsreels.

The folks at home had come to look upon the war as something that happened to other people; sons, husbands and brothers went away to war, and some of them did not return, but for many people life remained to all intents and purposes much as it had been before Pearl Harbor. There was a mild form of petrol rationing and some commodities were in short supply; but the privations which were commonplace to, for instance, the British public after four years of war - tens of thousands of civilians killed during the bombing of cities, severe rationing of food, fuel and most other necessities, the burden to morale of repeated and costly setbacks - were still more or less unimaginable in the American heartland. There was no widely shared civilian experience of personal hardship in this war, and most were innocent of the physical currency of battle. With no personal frame of reference, the news that over a thousand Marines had died in 76 hours to secure an island two-and-a-half miles long by half a mile wide appalled them. "You have murdered my son", wrote one distraught mother to Adml Nimitz; and there were calls for a government inquiry.

(1) See Appendix 11

Robert Sherrod recalled a conversation that he had with President Roosevelt after a news conference in Washington a few weeks after the battle. FDR asked Sherrod, "'Have you seen those bloody films of the Tarawa battle?'; I said I had seen the rough, unedited prints. 'I hear they are gruesome', he said. 'Gruesome, yes, Mr President; but that's the way war is out there, and I think the people are going to have to get used to that idea.'"

Much of the blame for the public's unrealistic expectations lay with the media. Since the outbreak of war Hollywood had been churning out a continuous stream of war movies in which the Japanese were depicted as myopic, bandy-legged midgets with buck teeth whose principle occupation was shooting unarmed civilians and raping young women, and who fled in terror at the appearance of a Marine uniform. The news that the Japanese had first class troops, well equipped, skillful and determined, who considered death preferable to capture, was not what people wanted to hear. Inevitably, as the war progressed and casualties mounted, the dreadful reality of total war began to sink in; but the shock of Tarawa, though short-lived, was profound. Robert Sherrod wrote: "Why did so many Americans throw up their hands at the heavy losses at Tarawa? I reasoned that many Americans had never been led to expect anything but an easy war. Our communiqués gave the impression that we were bowling over the enemy every time a handful of bombers dropped a few pitiful tons of bombs from 30,000 feet. The stories accompanying the communiqués also gave the impression that any American could lick any twenty Japs."

★   ★   ★

And what of the impact on the Marines themselves? Evans Carlson would remark that even some battalion commanders in the division had underestimated the enemy, and the ordeal which faced them. No one who was at Tarawa now had the remotest illusions about the island war, nor about the length of the road to Tokyo Bay.

Private David Spencer wrote home to his parents from Hawaii on 28 December: "That's about the size of it - to the people in the States, Tarawa and the other islands might be another glorified chapter in the history of America, but I have a different version of it."

Bob Libby's recollections of his feelings during those momentous days, and afterwards, can probably stand for those of a great many of the veterans:

"I had no illusions about being a hero, in fact while I was still chin deep in the waters of the lagoon I asked myself what the hell I was doing here. . .how alone I felt, and how unreal the whole situation was. Here I was being shot at, shit at and being abused in general, but I couldn't do a thing about it. There were no patriotic thoughts going through my head; I had been deposited on an unfriendly reef surrounding a useless bit of real estate with only one way to go, or die where I stood. Survival became the most important thing.

"Remember that the greatest stories to be told about the battle for Tarawa - from those who were there - can never be told: those who could have told them were those who remained behind after the battle was over. We, the survivors, did not encounter what those who died there had seen or done in their last moments on earth. Whole outfits disappeared in the flash of a direct hit, others. . . disappeared beneath the surface, their silent death unseen. . . .

"The mouth dried out through fear, and the taste of metal in the mouth attested to that. . . . Each was left to his own devices as to whether he lived or died; no one was in a position to assist another at this stage - orders had been given not to try and help those in the water if they should be wounded. The priority was to get ashore as fast as possible; under the circumstances the wounded were left to fend for themselves - some never made it ashore, or to the boats collecting the wounded. If they did, their safety was not assured as enemy fire destroyed many of them. . . .

"Prior to the landing some men had already sensed that their time in life was ending - these men had already written their final letters and given them to those they felt would survive. Others did not feel this way - I was in the latter category, even though there were numerous moments when the chances of survival looked very bleak indeed. . . .

"Today I can look back with a sense of pride in the fact of having been a part, however small, of that epic battle and to have been tested as few have experienced and lived to tell the tale. True, I received no physical wound at Tarawa (although I made up for that oversight on Saipan); but I think that I can say that the mental side had a terrific effect which has lived with me since.

"As a result of Tarawa we all became older than our years. I lived to fight another day, and by the time I was 21 I suppose that I could call myself a veteran, having fought on four Japanese-held islands - and by the following year I would have another two to add to the tally. The greatest blessing of all was coming through virtually unscathed; I was travelling under a lucky star, it seemed - but looking at the world today I sometimes wonder what the hell I was fighting for."

★　　　★　　　★

Julian Smith faced an impossible choice when deciding who to recommend for decoration for gallantry during the battle; there had been so many acts of heroism that one wag suggested that every Marine in the division should be given a medal, and in a way that was what did happen - the 2nd Marine Division would receive a collective Presidential Unit Citation "for outstanding performance in combat" and "heroic fortitude under punishing fire."

The Medal of Honor (popularly called the Congressional Medal of Honor) is America's highest military decoration for valour. It was awarded posthumously to Lts Hawkins and Bonnyman, but Staff Sgt Bordelon's Medal was held up for three years until a persistent Navy Department forced it through. David Shoup was the only surviving Medal of Honor recipient; his great contribution to the battle was never questioned, but some of his fellow Marines are reported to have disagreed with the supreme award, given his actual role. Many other nominations were approved, including a posthumous Navy Cross for Maj Henry Drewes, the amtrac battalion commander, and another for Lt Col Herbert Amey, the commanding officer of 2-2 killed leading his men ashore on Red

Beach 2 on D Day. Navy Crosses went to Maj "Jim" Crowe for his leadership on Red Beach 3, and to Navy Lt Heimberger (Eddie Albert) for the rescue of dozens of Marines from the fire-swept reefs off Red Beach 1.

Major Mike Ryan also received the Navy Cross, in recognition of his gathering the survivors of the horrendous landings on Red Beach 1 on D Day and leading them to secure Green Beach on D+1, thus allowing the 6th Marines to land safely and advance along the whole south side of Betio. With hindsight, the capture of Green Beach was the single factor that turned the tide irrevocably in favour of the Americans.

★   ★   ★

Tarawa blazed into the headlines for a brief moment, and then drifted out as the media followed the rapidly developing campaign to other islands on the road to Japan. From the Gilberts the Nimitz juggernaut moved on to the Marshalls, where the lessons learned at Tarawa were put into effect during the assault on Kwajalein in February 1944. Diving parties surveyed the beaches beforehand to determine the extent of underwater obstacles; and the preparatory bombardment was concentrated on individual targets. A line of the new armoured "amtanks", mounting a 37mm gun and three .50cal machine guns, preceded the first wave of amtracs to the beach, providing some direct fire support until the tanks could land. And this time there was to be no miscalculation of the depth of water over the reef - at Kwajalein no Marine would face the appalling prospect of wading 500 yards in the face of annihilating enemy fire.

Equipment and tactics for the island-hopping war evolved steadily during a series of often terribly punishing battles. After Kwajalein and Eniwetok in the Marshall Islands came Saipan, Tinian and Guam in the Marianas. Saipan - where 700 amtracs were available, with two battalions of amtanks including LVT(A)-4s mounting 75mm howitzers - cost the Marines and Army 14,000 dead and wounded during three weeks' fighting in June-July 1944. On Guam they suffered some 7,000 casualties to re-take an island that had been under American occupation since the Spanish-American War (the last enemy soldier came down from the hills in 1972, to be greeted as a national hero in Japan).

Japanese tactics were now evolving, too; rather than defend the high water mark they were building their fortifications inland in the most suitable terrain. On 15 September 1944 (against the advice of Adml "Bull" Halsey, who favoured Leyte in the Philippines), Nimitz ordered the landing on Peleliu in the Palau group of the Caroline Islands. The commander of the 1st Marine Division predicted that the assault would be "rough but fast - we'll be through in three days". The problem of a 500-yard surrounding reef was overcome by running the assault waves as far in as possible on LSTs, then transhipping to amtracs for the last leg. In one of the most horrible battles of attrition in the Pacific War the Americans suffered over 10,000 casualties in fighting that dragged on until 25 November (although the US Army 81st Infantry Division took over from the Marines in mid-October).

The Japanese 14th Division, some 11,000 strong, occupied sophisticated interconnecting bunkers dug and concreted into rocky ridges well inland, which were largely proof against the naval gunfire - some were six storeys deep. The plentiful amtracs and amtanks were obstructed on the beaches by the massive destruction caused by the bombardment, and it was the Shermans of the 1st Marine Tank Bn which really secured the beachhead on D Day, fighting off a Japanese tank charge. During the subsequent battle the Japanese launched many determined *banzai* counter-attacks from their maze of mutually supporting emplacements. Individual Marine battalions suffered casualties of the same order as those at Tarawa.

The assaults on both Iwo Jima and Okinawa were authorised by the Joint Chiefs in October 1944; the former was important, the second critical to the plans for moving US strategic air power close enough to the Home Islands to prepare for and support their eventual invasion. After massive bombardments six regiments of the 4th and 5th Marine Divisions got ashore on the black volcanic sands of Iwo Jima on 19 February 1945, using some 480 amtracs, and the 3rd Marine Division followed; each now had a battalion of nearly 70 M4 tanks, so the thinly armoured LVT(A)s were able to stand off and deliver the indirect fire support for which they were more suited while the Shermans advanced with the riflemen.

Although the actual landing was not seriously opposed, once ashore the Marines came under relentless fire from Gen Kuribayashi's determined garrison of some 21,000 men, well fortified in dominating terrain. The tactics of "corkscrew and blowtorch" - satchel charge or tank shell, accompanied by flame thrower - were now the well-practised norm; but it still took the three divisions until late March to overrun the island, and isolated resistance continued into June. Iwo Jima was the Marines' greatest battle of the war; American casualties totalled nearly 7,000 dead and 18,000 wounded. Just over 1,000 Japanese were taken alive.

The last great landing operation, on Okinawa in the Ryukus on 1 April 1945, faced Gen Oshima's 80,000-strong 32nd Army. The 1st and 6th Marine Divisions were committed under 10th Army alongside strong US Army forces, from an invasion fleet which came under frenzied *kamikaze* attacks. The landings were unopposed; but the subsequent battle, which lasted until 22 June, cost 10th Army some 40,000 casualties (in addition to nearly 10,000 suffered by the Navy). Its character was that of conventional positional warfare - a grinding advance against strong defensive positions by infantry supported by artillery, tanks and air support. The amphibious aspect of the campaign was essentially irrelevant to this battle, apart from the ability to turn the enemy's defensive lines by a secondary landing behind their flank - and apart from the Marines' relatively light scale of equipment, dictated by their amphibious insertion but inadequate for this sort of fighting.

★   ★   ★

General Holland Smith maintained for the rest of his life that the Gilberts should have been bypassed so that the first main attack could be directed toward

Kwajalein in the Marshall Islands. He also pointed out that Tarawa offered no worthwhile harbour, and that the airfield was too small to be anything other than a staging post. There is much merit in his argument; but there remains the question of what kind of casualties would have been suffered at Kwajalein had the lessons of Tarawa not been applied. General Mike Ryan is of the opinion that Tarawa was the inevitable choice to start the island-hopping campaign:

"Some people have been highly critical of the selection of the Gilberts as the initial objective of the attack on Japanese atoll defences. The fact is that the enemy defence line had to be breached, and if it were not the Gilberts the Marshalls would have been the most logical choice. In my opinion, if Kwajalein in the Marshalls had been chosen, American casualties would have been much heavier than on Tarawa.

"Learning from Tarawa, the naval preparation for the landing in the Marshalls was expanded. Instead of five or six hours of bombardment, naval forces took several days. First the heavy ships knocked out the coastal defence guns, then ships moved in to heavily bombard the beach defences, taking several days to ensure that they were completely destroyed. Landings then were made with relatively light casualties. The operation at Kwajalein was so successful that the floating reserve was sent west to take Eniwetok, which then became a fleet anchorage. This essentially completed the atoll campaign in the Central Pacific.

"After the atoll fighting the Japanese did not base their island defences on stopping a landing at the water's edge. They knew that the overwhelming naval superiority of the Americans made such a defence futile. Then, too, the islands attacked later were larger, with varied terrain. The defence ashore on these islands was largely entrusted to the Japanese Army rather than Special Naval Landing Forces. As operations moved west and north in the Pacific, the Japanese settled down to making any further American conquests as costly as possible. They did not contest landings on the beach, but withdrew to hill positions on Okinawa or cave positions on Iwo Jima. By then they could not have expected their Navy to come in and drive us away.

"But the defensive efforts of the troops ashore were just as fierce, just as dedicated as the actions of those who made the final charge on Saipan. Without hope of support or relief, they would fight to the last with the aim of causing the maximum American casualties, perhaps to inspire other Japanese to emulate their efforts in future battles. They gave full meaning to our own slogan: Duty, Honor, Country."

★   ★   ★

On 20 November 1993 - fifty years to the day after D Day at Betio - a group of Marine veterans returned to the island. For almost all of them it was the first, and probably the last visit since the battle. They were to find a very different island from the reeking, shattered moonscape that they left in 1943. The profusion of greenery provided the initial shock; they all remembered the blasted and uprooted trees which had allowed coast to coast visibility in all directions. The second surprise was the teeming population of Betio: there are now almost as many people on the island as there were at the height of the battle, yet living among the trappings of modern civilisation - hotels, bars, shops and a cinema. But there still remain some rusting relics of the Marines' days of horror and glory. On Temakin Point two 8in Vickers guns still stand defiantly pointing out over the vast stretches of the Pacific. Walking along the coastline the visitor still encounters concrete bunkers, pyramid-shaped steel command posts, tetrahedrons and the crumbling remains of amtracs as reminders of those savage 76 hours half a century ago.

Although instantly recognisable to the veterans as their aircraft flew into Tarawa, the island of Betio has changed in many ways over the years. The airfield that dominated the island has long gone - only a small area remains at the west end of the island for use as a football ground. The cove which formed Red Beach 1 has been largely filled in; and the infamous wooden "long pier", the scene of Lt Hawkins' famous charge, is little more than a few rotting stumps, replaced by a longer and wider concrete structure to the east.

Ironically, the Japanese influence remains strong on Betio. The cluster of buildings at the end of the pier is dominated by a Japanese-owned frozen fish plant - in fact the economy of Kiribati is largely supported by Japanese investment in the fishing industry. A photograph published in a Los Angeles newspaper some years ago, showing the 2nd Marine Division war memorial being unceremoniously lifted to one side by a Japanese mobile crane to make way for the building of their fish plant, no doubt raised a few cynical eyebrows among Pacific veterans.

★   ★   ★

After the catalogue of setbacks throughout the Pacific which lasted until 1943, the exploits of the 2nd Marine Division at Tarawa uplifted the spirits of the American people. In the blazing words of one national magazine: "Last week some 2,000 or 3,000 United States Marines, many of them now dead or wounded, gave the nation a name to stand beside those of Concord Bridge, the Bon Homme Richard, the Alamo, Little Big Horn and Belleau Wood - that name is Tarawa". From Tarawa onward the war in the Pacific would only be going one way; although terrible battles had still to be fought by land and sea, never again would anyone have cause to say "Issue in doubt".

On the new generations who have been sheltered from the horrors of world war, there surely still rests an obligation to recognise and honour what yesterday's generation did for their country; and never to forget those who made the ultimate sacrifice.

Appendix 1

Japanese Garrison & Defences

(A) Garrison

Tarawa atoll was the responsibility of the 4th Fleet. All the naval troops listed below were deployed to Betio island, less small detachments on Bairiki and Buota islands, the latter subsequently withdrawing to Buariki island. Further detached elements of these units also defended Butaritati island, Makin atoll.

Gilbert Islands Garrison Force HQ (Betio)	
3rd Special Base Force (formerly 6th	
Yokosuka Special Naval Landing Force)	- 1,122 men
7th Sasebo Special Naval Landing Force	- 1,497 men
111th Construction Unit	- 1,247 men
(Detachment) 4th Fleet Construction Dept.	- 970 men
Total	- 4,836 men

(B) Japanese weapon emplacements reported on Betio

Type	USMC estimate 15 Aug. 1943	Emplacements actually found, Nov. 1943	Size
Coast defence:	4	4	8in
	4	4	14cm
	6	6	80mm
Anti-aircraft	4	4	127mm (twin)
(dual purpose):	8	8	7cm (twin)
Anti-aircraft:	12	27	13mm
	4	4	13mm (twin)
Beach defence &	6	10	75mm Type 94
anti-boat:	5	6	70mm Type 92
	6	9	37mm Type 94
	16	31	13mm (single & twin AA/DP)
	17	-?-	7.7mm
(for tanks)	14	14	37mm

(C) Japanese defences on Betio

After the battle a detailed study was carried out by Marine Corps, Army and Navy Intelligence officers into the defences of Betio island. It was immediately apparent that the Japanese had organised their defences with the primary object of preventing the enemy from reaching the beaches. Fourteen heavy coastal defence guns were emplaced at strategic points; 40 to 50 medium and light field pieces and dual-purpose anti-aircraft guns, and more than 30 single- and twin-mounted heavy machine guns were located all round the edges of the island in well prepared emplacements constructed of palm trunk logs, concrete and heaped sand and coral, sited to cover palm log and concrete obstacles, log perimeter barricades, barbed wire entanglements, anti-tank ditches and mine fields.

The defences further inshore were generally of a much lower standard, and once the beach defences were abandoned the Japanese were largely compelled to rely on personnel shelters, anti-tank ditches and dug-outs for cover.

Offshore obstacles
Up to the time of the invasion the Japanese had been working continuously on a series of pyramid-shaped reinforced concrete obstacles - "tetrahedrons" - at various locations on the reefs surrounding the island; these were usually around four feet wide on the base, the height being determined by the depth of water at their location. They were spaced anything from six to 20 feet apart depending upon location, and just cleared the water at high tide; they were designed to obstruct landing craft or to force them into pre-determined channels which were covered by fields of fire. At the time of the invasion only about half of the planned total of these obstacles were in place. Other stretches of the reef were defended with wire barricades, mines and piles of rock.

Anti-boat defences
The Japanese constructed a barricade of palm logs just off the southern shore, approximately ten feet high, and in the shape of a wide, shallow V with one leg some 700 yards long and the other 300 yards long. This was intended to direct landing boats away from the centre of the island and into the fields of fire of the gun emplacements at the east and west ends of the beach. A log *perimeter barricade*, of varying heights, was constructed around almost the entire circumference of the island, liberally covered by rifle pits and machine gun emplacements; this is usually referred to in contemporary accounts as "the sea wall".

Mines
A profusion of mines was discovered both on land and along the beaches. Magnetic mines (Model 99) were intended to disable tanks and other vehicles, while anti-personnel mines (Model 93) were usually arranged in patterns 30ins apart. Anti-boat mines were found on the south and west coasts (Green Beach) and were usually sited about 20 yards apart, both underwater and on the edges of the beach.

Tank traps
The anti-tank ditches on Betio were fairly shallow, around five to six feet deep, because of the high water table on the island; depending upon location they were anything from eight to 14 feet in width. Enfilading machine gun positions were often located at the ends of the ditches.

Pillboxes
Many pillboxes protruded in front of the barricades to provide enfilading fire; the walls and roofs were usually made of 14in thick concrete reinforced with ½in steel rods. They were connected to the barricades by tunnels. There were also a few bolted steel plate pillboxes, tapering hexagonal in shape, about 15 feet high by 12 feet at the base, with a revolving turret on top.

Machine gun emplacements
There were a variety of machine gun posts for both single and twin-mounted 13mm Type 93 guns (heavy MGs equivalent to the US Browning M2 .50cal gun). For the single mounts, the position was usually around four feet deep with the gun pedestal only 12ins to 18ins above ground level; the emplacement was about ten feet in diameter and was constructed of logs with sandbags on the parapets. Others were placed above ground level with two-foot-thick walls of sand or sandbags contained by corrugated iron sheets. A few

simple sandbagged positions were installed on top of buildings.

The twin-mount MG posts differed in a number of ways. Some were tapered from around ten feet wide across one end to six feet at the other, with floors sloping to the front; the sides were of sandbag construction, about three feet thick, reinforced with heaped sand and coral. Other posts were around ten feet square, banked to a height of two feet with sandbags, sand and coral.

Guns and emplacements

The numbers of guns, and their exact types and calibres, vary between the several sources. This is particularly true of the intermediate pieces in the range 70mm-76mm; and the numbers, categories and exact locations shown on the map reproduced on page 20 - copied from a declassified joint services report on *The Defenses of Betio* - should be regarded with some caution in such cases. The Marines were not concerned with technical niceties at the time; e.g. one report refers to the 140mm coastal defence guns simply as "5in (approx) single mount naval guns", and the recollections of various veterans quoted in this book are often difficult to reconcile in such fine matters of detail. The picture is further confused by the fact that the battle reduced many emplacements and their contents to scrap; and it is also reported that some guns were dragged out of their prepared emplacements during the battle and re-sited to face the unexpected threat from the north.

At the time of the battle the term "anti-boat gun" was widely used in US reports; technically speaking no such piece of ordnance exists, and the term was used simply to describe the intended use on Betio of various guns which would normally be termed field pieces, howitzers, anti-aircraft guns, etc.

Three types of field gun were found on Betio: 75mm mountain howitzers Type 94, 70mm infantry battalion howitzers Type 92, and 37mm Type 94 - obsolete anti-tank guns now issued with HE and shrapnel as well as AP for general infantry support work. These totalled about 33 pieces, all primarily intended as anti-boat defence weapons. The emplacements were all similar, broad at the rear and tapering to a narrower firing port; all walls were of log construction with vertical retaining posts, the joints being secured by steel fasteners; most positions had log roofs covered with up to three feet of sand, and were partly masked by additional frontal anti-blast walls constructed of logs.

Anti-aircraft/dual purpose guns

Four anti-aircraft/dual purpose guns are shown as sited on the point at the western end of the Red beaches, two close to the Japanese command post, three midway along the south shore, and two on the north coast at the eastern "tail" of the island. These eleven pieces are referred to variously in the sources as 70mm, 75mm, 3in "or similar". The pair at the "tail" of Betio are described as "resembling the 75mm M1922 with a five-armed split trail . . .in sunken octagonal coconut log emplacements immediately behind the sea wall and heavily buttressed with sand." The emplacements were dug about five feet below sea level, the sides revetted with oil drums and faced with 1in boards held in position by vertical logs. Ammunition storage bunkers were built into the side walls, and communication passages connected the sites with nearby bombproof shelters. Each gun was complete with range finder, sound locator (with four horns) and searchlights of either 90cm or 150cm.

More formidable still were four twin-mounted Type 89 dual purpose 127mm guns, two reported on the south shore about 500 yards east of Temakin Point, and two on the north shore of the eastern "tail". Traversed and elevated electrically, with automatic ramming and fuse setting, the Type 89 could fire twelve 50lb shells per barrel per minute. The circular concrete emplacements were about 40 feet across and 15 feet high, and "in all respects equipped the same as 8in batteries with CP, magazine, searchlights and bombproofs. Several Nambu LMGs were mounted on the edge of each emplacement."

Coastal defence guns

The major coastal defence pieces were six 80mm, four 140mm and four 8in naval guns. The 80mm guns were in two batteries of three guns each, one in the centre of Green Beach and the others at the eastern end of the south shore. Emplacements were six-sided, of the usual log and sand construction, and were open at the top with a rear entrance. Concrete ammunition bunkers were built into the rear walls, capable of holding 36 rounds. Each battery had its own bombproof shelter and a 15-foot-high observation tower.

Two 140mm guns were located at the northern end of Green Beach and two more at Takarongo Point, the end of the south-east "tail" of Betio. They were housed in open-backed steel turrets on low concrete emplacements sited at ground level about 60 yards apart. Each pair of guns had its own fire control system with an 80-foot-high observation tower and an electricity supply.

There were four 8in naval-type guns on the island, two at the southern end of Green Beach (Temakin Point) and two on the south-east coast about 300 yards short of Takarongo Point. These were the so-called "Singapore guns", mistakenly thought to have been captured from the British at Singapore and transported to Tarawa. (During a visit in 1974 William H.Bartsch, a UN Labour Office Advisor to the government of Fiji, recorded information stamped on the guns; the manufacturers, Vickers, were able to confirm that the guns were part of a consignment supplied to a then-friendly Japan in 1905.) The 8in gun installations included a bombproof ammunition shelter with a narrow gauge railway track for hand-drawn wagons, a plotting room at a lower level than the gun, and a 70-foot-high observation tower. The guns were in open steel turrets on circular concrete emplacements, ten feet above sea level.

Tanks

There were reportedly seven light tanks on Betio; these lightly armoured Model 1935 (Type 95 *Ha-Go*) vehicles were dug into static positions, and camouflaged with sand and palm leaves. The ten-ton *Ha-Go* normally had a crew of three and mounted a 37mm gun and two machine guns.

Command posts

The rifle pits and machine gun posts around the island were controlled from pyramid-like command posts situated at 300-yard intervals. These were constructed of two layers of ¼ in steel plate with the space between filled with sand. Inside were upper and lower compartments, the upper for an observer and the lower, which had two gun ports, capable of housing a machine gun.

Shelters

Two types of shelter were observed on Betio. One type, located at barracks or HQ positions, was designed solely to protect personnel during shelling or bombing raids, and was constructed of layers of logs and sand to a thickness of seven feet, incorporating ventilators. The others were near the coastal gun emplacements and were designed for gun crews waiting to man their positions; these were smaller than the inland shelters, some being made of reinforced concrete up to 16ins thick, others of logs and sand.

Appendix 2

Command & Staff, V Amphibious Corps & 2nd Marine Division, 20 November 1943

V Amphibious Corps
Commanding General: Maj Gen Holland M.Smith
          Chief of Staff: Brig Gen G.B.Erskine
G1: Lt Col Albert F.Metze   G2: Lt Col St.Julien R.Marshall
G3: Col Peter P.Schrider   G4: Col Raymond E.Knapp

2nd Marine Division
Commanding General: Maj Gen Julian C.Smith
Asst.Div.Commander: Brig Gen Leo D.Hermle
          Chief of Staff: Col Merritt A.Edson
D1: Lt Col C.P.Van Ness   D2: Lt Col T.J.Colley
D3: Lt Col J.P.Risely   D4: Lt Col Jesse S.Cook

2nd Marines
Commanding Officer: Col David M.Shoup
      Executive Officer: Lt Col Dixon Goen
R1: Capt James E.Herbold   R2: Capt John L.Schwabe
R3: Maj Thomas A.Culhane Jr R4: Capt Vernon L.Bartram

1st Battalion, 2nd Marines
Commanding Officer: Maj Wood B.Kyle
      Executive Officer: Maj William S.Vasconcellos
                BN3:   Capt Harold R.Thorpe

2nd Battalion, 2nd Marines
Commanding Officer: Lt Col Herbert R.Amey (k.i.a.)
      Executive Officer: Maj Howard J.Rice
                BN3:   Capt Benjamin T.Owens

3rd Battalion, 2nd Marines
Commanding Officer: Maj John F.Schoettel
      Executive Officer: Maj Samuel D.Mandeville
                BN3:   Capt Richard Phillippi

6th Marines
Commanding Officer: Col Maurice G.Holmes
      Executive Officer: Lt Col Russell Lloyd
R1: First Lt P.J.Costello   R2: Capt Donald Jackson
R3: Maj Loren E.Haffner   R4: Maj Cyril C.Sheehan

1st Battalion, 6th Marines
Commanding Officer: Maj W.R.Jones
      Executive Officer: Maj John E.Semmes Jr
                BN3:   Capt Charles H.Triplett

2nd Battalion, 6th Marines
Commanding Officer: Lt Col Raymond L.Murray
Executive Officer: Maj Richard C. Nutting
BN3:   Capt Joseph E.Rowland

3rd Battalion, 6th Marines
Commanding Officer: Lt Col Kenneth F.McLeod
Executive Officer: Maj John E.Rentsch
BN3:   Capt William W.McKinley

8th Marines
Commanding Officer: Col Elmer E.Hall
Executive Officer: Lt Col Paul D.Sherman
R1: Capt Cleland E.Early   R2: Capt Wilmot J.Spires
R3: Maj Jewitt D.Adams   R4: Capt Alfred E.Holland

1st Battalion, 8th Marines
Commanding Officer: Maj Lawrence C.Hays Jr
Executive Officer: Maj Robert J Oddy
BN3:   Capt Daniel V.McWethy Jr

2nd Battalion, 8th Marines
Commanding Officer: Maj Henry P.Crowe
Executive Officer: Maj W.C.Chamberlin
BN3:   First Lt K.C.Fagan

3rd Battalion, 8th Marines
Commanding Officer: Maj Robert H.Ruud
Executive Officer: Maj Stanley E.Larsen
BN3:   Capt Scott S.Corbett

10th Marines
Commanding General: Brig Gen T.E.Bourke
Executive Officer: Lt Col Ralph E.Forsyth
R1: Capt Ralph D.Pillsbury   R2: First Lt David J.Lubin
R3: Lt Marvin H.Floom   R4: Capt Marshall R.Breedlove

1st Battalion, 10th Marines
Commanding Officer: Lt Col Presley M.Rixey
Executive Officer: Maj James E.Mills
BN3:   Maj Wendell H.Best

2nd Battalion, 10th Marines
Commanding Officer: Lt Col George R.E.Shell
Executive Officer: Maj Richard B.Church
BN3   Maj Kenneth C.Houston

3rd Battalion, 10th Marines
Commanding Officer: Lt Col Manly L.Curry
Executive Officer: Maj Gen N.Schraeder
BN3:   Maj Earl J.Rowse

4th Battalion, 10th Marines
Commanding Officer: Lt Col Kenneth A.Jorgensen
Executive Officer: Maj Harry N.Shea
BN3:   Maj James O.Appleyard

5th Battalion, 10th Marines
Commanding Officer: Maj Howard V.Hiett
Executive Officer: Maj William L.Crouch
BN3:   Maj Wade H.Hitt

18th Marines
Commanding Officer: Col Cyril W.Martyr
Executive Officer: Lt Col Ewart S.Lave
R1: First Lt Haldon E.Lindfelt   R2: Maj James F.Geary
R3: Lt Col Kenneth P.Corson   R4: Capt Robert F.Ruan

1st Battalion, 18th Marines
Commanding Officer: Maj George L.H.Cooper
Executive Officer: Maj Joseph S.Reynaud
BN3:   (unknown)

2nd Battalion, 18th Marines
Commanding Officer: Lt Col Chester J.Salazar
Executive Officer: Maj Robert L.Smith
BN3:   Capt Jerome R.Walters

3rd Battalion, 18th Marines
Commanding Officer: Cdr Lawrence E.Tull USN
Executive Officer: Lt Cdr Edwin E.Gibson USN
BN3:   Lt Robert Cleghorn USN

2nd Amphibian Tractor Battalion
Commanding Officer: Maj Henry C.Drewes (k.i.a.)
Executive Officer: Capt Henry G.Lawrence
BN3:   Capt William H.Houseman

2nd Tank Battalion
Commanding Officer: Lt Col Alexander B.Swenceski
Executive Officer: Maj Charles W.McCoy
BN3:   First Lt Edward C.Hennessey (k.i.a.)

Appendix 3

Ground Unit Campaign Participation

Gilbert Islands Operation, Operation Galvanic,
13 November-8 December 1943

This operation included Operation Longsuit, the Tarawa atoll assault (20 November-4 December 1943) with the main effort on Betio island (20-23 November); and the landings on Apamama atoll (21-26 November) and Makin atoll (20-23 November), the latter conducted by the 165th Infantry Regiment (Reinforced), 27th Infantry Division, US Army.

Betio	H-Hour/D-Day	0845hrs, 20 November 1943
	Secured	1321hrs, 23 November 1943
Makin	H-Hour/D-Day	0832hrs, 20 November 1943
	Secured	1130hrs, 23 November 1943
Apamama	H-Hour/D-Day	0445hrs, 21 November 1943
	Secured	am, 24 November 1943

Operation Galvanic was preceded by the unopposed Ellice Islands occupation, south of the Gilberts, which took place between August and October 1943. Their occupation provided supporting air bases for the Tarawa, Apamama and Makin landings. The units involved also received credit for the Gilbert Islands operation. This preliminary phase to Operation Galvanic was launched by Defense Force, Samoa Group:

2nd Airdrome Battalion(1)	21 Aug-8 Dec 1943
5th Defense Battalion (Reinforced)	
(Defense Force, Funafuti)(2):	2 Oct 1942-8 Dec 1943
Provisional Cos.X & Y, 3rd Marines	
1st Separate Medical Co.	
7th Defense Battalion(3)	20 Nov-8 Dec 1943
V Amphibious Corps:	13 Nov-8 Dec 1943
V AC HQ & Service Bn.	20-25 Nov 1943
V AC Reconnaissance Co.(4)	18 Nov-3 Dec 1943
2nd Defense Bn.	24 Nov-8 Dec 1943
8th Defense Bn.	28 Nov-8 Dec 1943
25th Replacement Bn.	13 Nov-8 Dec 1943
2nd Marine Division (Reinforced)	
(Southern Landing Force):	20 Nov-4 Dec 1943
Division HQ	20 Nov-4 Dec 1943
Div.HQ & Service Bn.	20 Nov-4 Dec 1943
Div.Special & Service Troops	20-24 Nov 1943
2nd Amphibian Tractor Bn.(Reinforced)(5)	20 Nov-5 Dec 1943
2nd Medical Bn.	20-24 Nov 1943
2nd Service Bn.	20-24 Nov 1943
2nd Special Weapons Bn.	20-24 Nov 1943
2nd Light Tank Bn.(Reinforced)	20-24 Nov 1943
Co.C, 1st Corps Tank Bn.(Medium)	20-24 Nov 1943
2nd Marines	20-24 Nov 1943
6th Marines(6)	20 Nov-8 Dec 1943

8th Marines	20-24 Nov 1943
10th Marines (Artillery)	20 Nov-1 Dec 1943
18th Marines (Engineer)	20-24 Nov 1943
16th Naval Construction Bn.	21-23 Nov 1943

Notes:
(1) Nukufetau Atoll, Ellice Islands occupation, 27 Aug 1943, with elements of the 16th Naval Construction Bn.; elements detached to Tarawa with the 2nd Defense Battalion.
(2) Funafuti Atoll, Ellice Islands occupation, 2 Oct 1942, with elements of the 2nd Naval Construction Bn.; Cos. X and Y were redesignated 26th and 27th Provisional Marine Cos. on 15 Dec 1942. The occupation was not publicly announced until after the Japanese discovered it in April 1943. Japanese air attacks were conducted from the Gilberts from April to Nov 1943.
(3) Nanomea Atoll, Ellice Islands occupation, 5 Sept 1943, with elements of the 16th Naval Construction Battalion.
(4) The company secured Apamama atoll, 21-26 Nov; 4th Platoon participated in the Makin atoll landings with the 165th Infantry Regt., 20 Nov 1943.
(5) Equipped with LVT(1)s. A provisional company was formed and equipped with LVT(2)s with retrofitted armour plating.
(6) Initial V AC reserve, released to 2nd Marine Division on D-Day afternoon.

Remarks:
Once Betio island was secured, Co.D (Scout), 2nd Light Tank Bn. and 2nd Bn., 6th Marines secured the remaining, mostly unoccupied islands of Tarawa atoll between 21 and 28 Nov 1943. The former reconnoitered the unoccupied Abaiang, Marakei and Maiana atolls between 29 Nov and 1 Dec 1943.

The 2nd Anti-tank Battalion is officially listed as participating in the operation from 20 to 30 Nov, but no reference could be found in the 2nd Marine Division operation order, after action reports, or the unit history.

Courtesy Gordon L. Rottman

Appendix 4

Task organisation, 2nd Marine Division (Reinforced), Operation Longsuit, Betio Island, 20-23 November 1943

Combat Team/Regimental Landing Team 2
2nd Marines (Reinforced)
Landing Team 2/8
1st Battalion, 10th Marines (artillery)
  Battery O, 5th Bn, 10th Marines
Special Weapons Group, 2nd Defense Bn
Company C, 1st Corps Tank Bn (Medium)
Co.A, 1st Bn (Engineer), 18th Marines
Co.D, 2nd Bn (Pioneer), 18th Marines
2nd Amphibian Tractor Bn (-)
Co.A, 2nd Medical Bn

Combat Team/Regimental Landing Team 6
6th Marines (Reinforced)
2nd Bn, 10th Marines (artillery)
5th Bn (- Bty O), 10th Marines
Bty.A, 2nd Special Weapons Bn
Co.B, 2nd Light Tank Bn
Co.B, 1st Bn (Engineer), 18th Marines
Co.E, 2nd Bn (Pioneer), 18th Marines
Co.B, 2nd Amphibian Tractor Bn
Co.B, 2nd Medical Bn

Combat Team/Regimental Landing Team 8
8th Marines (Reinforced)
3rd Bn, 10th Marines (artillery)
Co.C, 2nd Light Tank Battalion
Co.C, 1st Bn (Engineer), 18th Marines
Co.F, 2nd Bn (Pioneer), 18th Marines
Co.C, 2nd Amphibian Tractor Bn
Co.C, 2nd Medical Bn

Support Group
10th Marines (artillery) (-)
  HQ & Service Bty., 10th Marines
  4th Bn, 10th Marines
18th Marines (engineer) (-)
  HQ & Service Co., 18th Marines
  Cos.H & I, 3rd Bn (Naval Construction),
  18th Marines
Special Troops (-)
  HQ, 2nd Marine Division
  2nd Signal Co.
  2nd Military Police Co.
  HQ & Service Co., 2nd Light Tank Bn
  Co.D (Scout), 2nd Light Tank Bn
Service Troops (-)
  HQ & Service Co., 2nd Medical Bn
  Co.A, 2nd Motor Transport Bn
  Co.E, 2nd Medical Bn

Note:
This listing does not include a number of small sub-units and detachments of various kinds, which were attached to each of the Combat Teams and the Support Group.

Courtesy Gordon L. Rottman

Appendix 5 Message from Maj Gen Julian C.Smith to officers and men of 2nd Marine Division, read to all hands on 19 November 1943:

A great offensive to destroy the enemy in the central Pacific has begun. American air, sea and land forces, of which this division is a part, initiated this offensive by seizing Japanese-held atolls in the Gilbert Islands, which will be used as bases for future operations. The task assigned to us is to capture the atolls of Tarawa and Apamama. Army units of our Fifth Amphibious Corps are simultaneously attacking Makin, 150 miles north of Tarawa. For the past three days, Army, Navy and Marine Corps aircraft have been carrying out bombardment attacks on our objectives. They are neutralising, and will continue to neutralise, other Japanese air bases adjacent to the Gilbert Islands.

Early this morning combatant ships of our Navy bombarded Tarawa. Our Navy screens our operations and will support our attack tomorrow morning with the greatest concentration of aerial bombardment and naval gunfire in the history of warfare. It will remain with us until our objective is secured and our defences are established. Garrison forces are already en route to relieve us as soon as we have completed our job of clearing our objective of Japanese forces. The division was especially chosen by the high command for the assault on Tarawa because of its battle experience and its combat efficiency. Their confidence will not be betrayed.

We are the first American troops to attack a defended atoll. What we do here will set a standard for all future operations in the central Pacific area. Observers from other Marine divisions and from other branches of our armed services, as well as those of our allies, have been detailed to witness our operations. Representatives of the press are present. Our people back home are eagerly awaiting news of our victories. I know that you are well trained and fit for the tasks assigned to you. You will quickly overrun the Japanese forces; you will decisively defeat and destroy the treacherous enemies of our country; your success will add new laurels to the glorious tradition of our Corps.

Good luck and God bless you all.

Appendix 6 Message from Maj Henry P.("Jim") Crowe to the 2nd Battalion, 8th Marines prior to landing:

November 15 1943

The following are "do's" and "don'ts" for all personnel landing on Red Beach 3 and must be followed to the letter.

On D-1 Day
Carefully check all arms and equipment, especially first aid packs and gas masks.
Be sure you have your ammunition, two full canteens and rations. Remember this may be all the ammunition, water and rations you will have for 24 to 48 hours. Do not waste it.
Do not load weapons until ordered to do so.
All packs and rolls must be made up.
Clean all troop spaces thoroughly so there will be very little cleaning necessary on D Day.
Be sure to have a good pair of shoes to wear ashore.

D Day
Again check all arms and equipment.
Do not load weapons until ordered to do so.
Carry your four hand grenades in your pockets - and remember your hand grenades are Mark 2 with a three (3) second fuse - after releasing the safety lever get rid of the grenade.

148

Be prompt in carrying out all orders - remember the time elements have been carefully figured, and one man doping off may be the cause of serious delay or even unnecessary casualties.

After getting in amphibious tractors or boats all hands except the boat group commander, crew chief or coxswain must stay down - this includes boat gunners until needed. Do not load weapons or fix bayonets until ordered.

After leaving line of departure, weapons will be loaded and bayonets fixed on orders of boat group commander. Remember the M1 rifle is automatically loaded when the clip is inserted - be careful - lock all weapons, we must not have casualties due to carelessness. Boat gunners will open fire only on orders of boat group commander.

Boat gunners must not waste ammunition, it may be needed after landing.

Boat group commanders and crew chief must be on the alert - it is your job to keep your amphibious tractor in position - Do not dope off - to hell with watching the ships and aircraft. They'll do their jobs, you pay strict attention to yours.

Do not discard your gas mask on landing, gas may be encountered at any time and without your gas mask you are helpless, but if you have it and use it properly it will furnish all the protection required. After landing be aggressive but not foolish - when you shoot, have something to shoot at and be sure to hit it, whether it be a Jap, position or vehicle.

Remember to help your leaders maintain control by controlling yourself.

Bear in mind at all times that we are here to kill, not to hunt souvenirs. When you stop to pick up a Jap sword or anything else your guard is down and if a Jap doesn't kill you, a booby trap will. Your Regimental Commander, Regimental Exec, Battalion Commander, Battalion Exec do not want souvenirs and after our mission is completed, you can have all the souvenirs except those of value to intelligence units.

Remember the natives are friendly. Treat them accordingly.

Do not drink any water except that which you take ashore.

Our mission is to seize and hold Helen Island. The plans to carry out that mission are carefully thought out and made by others, but you are the ones who have to execute those plans. All the help possible has been furnished you prior to your landing. After landing you are the ones who take over. It is your show from here to the South beach. Make it a good show by being a MARINE.

H. P. Crowe
Major USMC Commanding

Appendix 7

Casualties

The Casualty Division of the Headquarters of the US Marine Corps issued the following list in 1947:

US Marine casualties:	Officers	Enlisted
Killed in action	47	790
Wounded - killed	2	32
Died of wounds	8	82
Missing, presumed dead	0	27
Wounded - missing dead	0	2
Wounded in action	110	2,186
Combat fatigue	1	14
	168	3,133

Japanese casualties:	
Garrison strength, Tarawa	4,836
Total killed on Tarawa	4,690
Prisoners (Japanese)	17
Prisoners (Korean labourers)	129
Garrison strength, Apamama	23
Total killed, Apamama	23

Approximately 100 Japanese were killed on Bairiki island on 21 November; and another 175, plus two taken prisoner, on Buariki on 26 November by 2nd Battalion, 6th Marines.

The Japanese on Tarawa and Apamama lost 4,713 killed out of a total of 4,859, while the US Marines lost 990 dead. This bald figure does not convey the dramatic losses that some units suffered during the battle. For example, the 2nd and 8th Marine Regiments sustained casualty rates of 35% - more than one in three killed or wounded. The 2nd Amphibian Tractor Battalion suffered 325 casualties from an original strength of 661; and two-thirds of the Marines who were equipped with flame throwers were killed. About half of the US Marine dead were killed in the water while attempting to reach the beachheads; and of the 125 amtracs, 72 were destroyed or disabled before reaching or on the beaches.

As a comparison, at Guadalcanal some 1,600 men had been killed and 4,700 wounded in six months; 25,851 would subsequently be killed and wounded in four weeks on Iwo Jima, and 49,151 (including US Navy) in less than three months on and around Okinawa. One is left in little doubt that had it not been for the dropping of the atomic bombs on Hiroshima and Nagasaki, American and British Commonwealth casualties during the planned assault on the Japanese mainland would have been counted in some hundreds of thousands.

Finally, it should be added that the deaths suffered by the US Navy during the whole of Operation Galvanic were not greatly fewer than those suffered by the Marines on Betio. The sinking of the carrier USS *Liscomb Bay* by a Japanese submarine off Makin cost 650 lives; an explosion in one of the battleship *Mississippi's* 16in gun turrets killed another 43; and there were numerous losses among the crews of the small landing and supply craft.

Appendix 8
Medal of Honor Awards

Staff Sergeant William J. Bordelon

Staff Sgt Bordelon of the 1st Battalion, 18th Marines (Engineers), hailed from San Antonio in Texas. He was promoted to sergeant after only six months in the Marines, and served on Guadalcanal. Of his action on D Day the report of the Commanding Officer of the 18th Marines, dated 22 December 1943, states:

"Staff Sgt Bordelon and Sgt Beers with the other squad attached to F Company, landed as planned on Red Beach 2 about 125 yards west of the pier. Their LVT had stopped 15 yards short of a 40mm gun and a heavy calibre machine gun, suffering heavy casualties. Capt Norris, Staff Sgt Bordelon, Sgt Beers and Pte Ashworth reached the beach, after which Sgt Beers was wounded. Bordelon was hit four times, along with having a blasting cap detonate prematurely in his hand. He refused aid and succeeded in neutralizing four enemy positions. He was killed while destroying the fourth position."

In 1995 the Bordelon family had his remains transferred from the National Memorial Cemetery of the Pacific in Honolulu to Fort Sam Houston National Cemetery, and were afforded the singular honour of having his flag-draped casket, surrounded by a Marine Corps honour guard, lie in state at the Alamo in San Antonio from 6pm to 10pm on 19 November 1995, prior to his burial the following day on the anniversary of his death. More than 2,500 people passed by his bier in honour of the occasion.

Citation

Staff Sergeant William J. Bordelon, United States Marine Corps

For valorous and gallant conduct above and beyond the call of duty as a member of an Assault Engineer Platoon of the First Battalion, Eighteenth Marines, tactically attached to the Second Marines, Second Marine Division, in action against the Japanese held Atoll of Tarawa in the Gilbert Islands on 20 November 1943. Landing in the assault waves under withering enemy fire which killed all but four of the men in his tractor, Staff Sergeant Bordelon hurriedly made demolition charges and personally put two pill boxes out of action. Hit by enemy machine gun fire just as a charge exploded in his hand while assaulting a third position, he courageously remained in action and, although out of demolition charges, provided himself with a rifle and furnished fire cover for a group of men scaling the sea wall. Disregarding his own serious condition, he unhesitatingly went to the aid of one of his demolition men, wounded and calling for help in the water, rescuing this man and another who had been hit by enemy fire while attempting to make the rescue. Still refusing first aid for himself, he again made up demolition charges and single-handedly assaulted a fourth Japanese machine gun position but was instantly killed when caught in a final burst of fire from the enemy. Staff Sergeant Bordelon's great personal valour during a critical phase of securing the limited beachhead was a contributing factor in the ultimate occupation of the island and his heroic determination reflects the highest credit upon the United States Naval Service. He gallantly gave his life for his country.

Lieutenant Alexander Bonnyman

Close to the Burns-Philp wharf a sand-covered concrete blockhouse, defended by up to 200 Japanese troops, was holding up the progress of the Marines as they pushed towards the eastern end of Betio. From the top, perhaps 20 feet above sea level, the enemy held a commanding view of the surrounding terrain, and the only way that the Marines were going to take it was by frontal assault. Infantrymen and engineers led by Lt Bonnyman -

the second in command of the 2nd Platoon, 18th Marines, and a Guadalcanal veteran - charged up the western side of the shelter with demolition charges and flame throwers, killing the crew of an enemy machine gun post and exploding TNT charges at the two entrances. The Japanese immediately counter-attacked from the opposite side, but Bonnyman remained at point blank range, preventing them from reaching the summit until he fell dead. Bonnyman, a graduate of Princeton, had enlisted in the Marine Corps as a private at the age of 30, although he could have avoided service as he was a married man with three children and owned and ran a copper mine at Santa Fe, New Mexico - a reserved occupation in the national war effort.

Citation
First Lieutenant Alexander Bonnyman Jr, United States Marine Corps Reserve
For conspicuous gallantry and intrepidity at the risk of his life above and beyond the call of duty as Executive Officer of the Second Battalion Shore Party, Eighteenth Marines, Second Marine Division, during the assault against enemy Japanese held Tarawa in the Gilbert Islands, from 20 to 22 November 1943. Acting on his own initiative when assault troops were pinned down at the far end of Betio Pier by the overwhelming fire of Japanese shore batteries, First Lieutenant Bonnyman repeatedly defied the blasting fury of the enemy bombardment to organise and lead the besieged men over the long, open pier to the beaches and then, voluntarily obtaining flame throwers and demolitions, organising his pioneer shore party into assault demolitions and directed the blowing of several hostile installations before the close of D Day. Determined to effect an opening in the enemy's strongly organised defence line the following day, he voluntarily crawled approximately forty yards forward of our lines and placed demolitions in the entrance of a large Japanese emplacement as the initial move in his planned attack against the heavily garrisoned, bombproof installation which was stubbornly resisting despite the destruction earlier in the action of a large number of Japanese who had been inflicting heavy casualties on our forces and holding up our advance. Withdrawing only to replenish his ammunition, he led his men in a renewed assault, fearlessly exposing himself to the merciless slash of hostile fire as he stormed the formidable bastion, directed the placement of demolition charges in both entrances and seized the top of the bombproof position, flushing more than one hundred of the enemy who were instantly cut down and effecting the annihilation of approximately 150 troops inside the emplacement. Assailed by additional Japanese after he had gained his objective, he made a heroic stand on the edge of the structure, defending his strategic position with indomitable determination in the face of the desperate charge and killing three of the enemy before he fell, mortally wounded. By his dauntless fighting spirit, unrelenting aggressiveness and forceful leadership throughout three days of unremitting, violent battle, First Lieutenant Bonnyman had inspired his men to heroic effort, enabling them to beat off the counter-attack and break the back of hostile resistance in the sector for an immediate gain of four hundred yards with no further casualties to our forces in this zone. He gallantly gave his life for his country.

First Lieutenant William Deane Hawkins
Although he was born in Kansas, Hawkins grew up and spent most of his life in El Paso, Texas. At the start of the war he attempted to join both the Army and the Army Air Corps, but was rejected because of severe scarring on his body caused by a childhood accident. He succeeded in being accepted for the Marine Corps in 1941, and a series of rapid promotions culminated in a field commission on Guadalcanal. During the battle he commanded a 36-strong Scout Sniper Platoon, whose first assignment was to land ahead of the first wave of amtracs on D Day and dislodge the enemy from the long pier between Red Beaches 1 and 2. This was achieved successfully; and upon instructions from Col Shoup, he went on to lead his platoon in a series of assaults against Japanese strongpoints,

and into the revetments of the airfield to clear out troublesome snipers.

It was during these attacks that he was wounded in the hand when a mortar bomb landed among his men, killing three of them. Although he was offered medical treatment he refused, saying "I came here to kill Japs, not to be evacuated." Later in the day, when leading a hand grenade attack on enemy positions at the base of a sandy hill, he was hit in the shoulder and chest by a burst of machine gun fire. Bleeding profusely, he was carried to a field hospital where the surgeon did what he could for him, but he died before dawn on the following day. Upon the instructions of Adml Nimitz, the airfield on Betio was named Hawkins Field in his honour.

Citation
First Lieutenant William D. Hawkins, United States Marine Corps Reserve
For valorous and gallant conduct above and beyond the call of duty as Commanding Officer of a Scout Sniper Platoon attached to the Second Marines, Second Marine Division, in action against Japanese held Tarawa in the Gilbert Islands, November 20 and 21, 1943. The first to disembark from the jeep lighter, First Lieutenant Hawkins unhesitatingly moved forward under heavy enemy fire at the end of the Betio pier, neutralizing emplacements in coverage of troops assaulting the main beach positions. Fearlessly leading his men on to join the forces fighting desperately to gain a beachhead, he repeatedly risked his life throughout the day and night to direct and lead attacks on pill boxes and installations with grenades and demolitions. At dawn on the following day, First Lieutenant Hawkins returned to the dangerous mission of clearing the limited beachhead of Japanese resistance, personally initiating an assault on a hostile position fortified by five enemy machine guns and, crawling forward in the face of withering fire, boldly fired point blank into the loopholes and completed the destruction with grenades. Refusing to withdraw after being seriously wounded in the chest during this skirmish, First Lieutenant Hawkins steadfastly carried the fight to the enemy, destroying three more pill boxes before he was caught in a burst of Japanese shell fire and mortally wounded. His relentless fighting spirit in the face of formidable opposition and his exceptionally daring tactics were an inspiration to his comrades during the most crucial phase of the battle and reflect the highest credit upon the United States Naval Service. He gallantly gave his life for his country.

Colonel David M. Shoup
David Shoup, born in 1905 in Battleground, Indiana, was the only one of the four Medal of Honor recipients who lived to receive his award. As Operations Officer of the 2nd Marine Division he had planned a great part of Operation Longsuit and, as we have seen, upon the indisposition of the assigned commander of Combat Team 2, Col William Marshall, he found himself implementing his own plans. Coming ashore on D Day, he set up his command post on Red Beach 2 within feet of the enemy and, although wounded in the leg, continued to organise and direct operations until relieved by Col Edson, the divisional chief of staff, at about 8.30pm on 21 November. He remained at the command post with Edson throughout almost the entire battle, assisting with the planning and implementation of the operation. David Shoup had a long and distinguished career, being selected by President Eisenhower as Commandant of the Marine Corps in 1959 before retiring in 1963 as a four-star general. He died in 1983 at the age of 78, and is buried in Arlington National Cemetery. Contrary to appearances this short, fiery, bull-necked, and often profane fighting man was also something of a poet, moved to write touching verses by his first hand experience of battle - among them, these lines in memory of a fellow officer:

"Drag from my sight this blear-eyed thing that was my friend.
Return all to mother earth, except that ring to prove his end on Tarawa".

Citation

Colonel David M. Shoup, United States Marine Corps

For conspicuous gallantry and intrepidity at the risk of his life above and beyond the call of duty as Commanding Officer of all Marine Corps troops in action against enemy Japanese forces on Betio Island, Tarawa Atoll, Gilbert Islands from November 20 to 22 1943. Although severely shocked by an exploding enemy shell soon after landing at the pier and suffering from a serious, painful leg wound which had become infected, Colonel Shoup fearlessly exposed himself to the terrific, relentless artillery, machine gun and rifle fire from hostile shore emplacements and, rallying his hesitant troops by his own inspiring heroism, gallantly led them across the fringing reefs to charge the heavily fortified island and reinforce our hard pressed, thinly held lines. Upon arrival on shore, he assumed command of all landed troops and, working without rest under constant, withering enemy fire during the next two days, conducted smashing attacks against unbelievably strong and fanatically defended Japanese positions despite innumerable obstacles and heavy casualties. By his brilliant leadership, daring tactics and selfless devotion to duty, Colonel Shoup was largely responsible for the final, decisive defeat of the enemy and his indomitable fighting spirit reflects great credit upon the United States Naval Service.

Appendix 9
Presidential Unit Citation, 2nd Marine Division

The Secretary of the Navy
Washington

The President of the United States takes pleasure in presenting the Presidential Unit Citation to the Second Marine Division (Reinforced)

Consisting of Divisional Headquarters, Special Troops (including Company C, 1st Corps Medium Tank Battalion), Service Troops, 2nd, 6th, 8th, 10th & 18th Marine Regiments in the Battle of Tarawa as set forth in the following.

Citation

For outstanding performance in combat during the seizure and occupation of the Japanese-held Atoll of Tarawa, Gilbert Islands, November 20 to 24, 1943. Forced by treacherous coral reefs to disembark from their landing craft hundreds of yards off the beach, the Second Marine Division (Reinforced) became a highly vulnerable target for devastating Japanese fire.

Dauntlessly advancing in spite of rapidly mounting losses, the Marines fought a gallant battle against crushing odds, clearing the limited beachheads of snipers and machine guns, reducing powerfully fortified enemy positions and completely annihilating the fanatically determined and strongly entrenched Japanese forces. By the successful occupation of Tarawa, the Second Marine Division (Reinforced) has provided our forces with highly strategic and important air and land bases from which to continue future operations against the enemy; by the valiant fighting spirit of these men, their heroic fortitude under punishing fire and their relentless perseverance in waging this epic battle in the Central Pacific, they have upheld the finest traditions of the United States Naval Service.

For the President

James Forrestal
Acting Secretary of the Navy

Appendix 10
Reconnaissance & Intelligence

Aerial photography had played an important role during the planning phase, and during the battle itself. B24 Liberator bombers flying from Funafuti had carried out preliminary reconnaissance and bombing misions over Tarawa since the beginning of 1943, when the airfield was discovered. This led to the damaging raids on Betio from Adml "Baldy" Pownell's *Lexington, Princeton* and *Belleau Wood* that September, which destroyed many enemy aircraft and, more significantly, obtained up-to-date photographs of the island's defences.

Throughout the fighting, Vought OS-2U Kingfishers - two-seat monoplanes with a distinctive single float - repeatedly flew over Betio at between 1,000 and 1,500 feet, and between 12.29pm and 2.10pm on D Day took a series of photographs with an overprinted clock recording the second that each exposure was made; these can be tied up with the stills taken by the Marine photographers to help establish the sequence of events during the fighting.

The Kingfishers, which were launched from catapults on battleships and could therefore work independently of the aircraft carriers, were invaluable in spotting for naval gunfire support. They also led the minesweepers to the various shoals in the lagoon which would have been hazardous to the destroyers operating in close support; the USS *Pursuit* was able to mark each shoal with smoke pots which burned for several hours on D Day.

Beginning in September, the submarine USS *Nautilus* had spent nearly three weeks cruising the waters around Tarawa taking over 2,000 water level photographs of the coastline. As it was the end of October before she got back to Pearl Harbor there was frenzied activity at the Joint Intelligence Center as technicians worked day and night to process and print dozens of copies of the photos of the atoll which gave a composite picture of the intended target.

*   *   *

In January 1944 an Intelligence Annex to a Special Action Report carried a host of observations relating to the battle. The passages relating to reconnaissance are interesting.

On ground reconnaissance, the report stated (fairly obviously) that it was not practical to put scouts ashore on Betio without arousing suspicion because of the small size of the island and the large number of enemy troops. There was a little more on the air reconnaissance background:

"Visual reconnaissance before D Day was confined to such observations as could be made by members of bombardment crews from carrier groups and AAF units involved in preliminary bombing. Reports from these were fragmentary and only stated the apparent damage caused by the strike and the amount of anti-aircraft fire met."

The outstanding part played by the Kingfisher pilots, Lt Cdr Robert A.MacPherson and LtWhaley, is emphasised: "During the assault, observation flights were flown by scout planes of support group BBs [battleships]. In the case of BB46 [USS *Maryland*] these flights, carrying as they did certain Divisional Staff officers as observers, provided considerable battle information on our own and the enemy troops. In the future it is planned to utilise trained air observers for this purpose."

The report continues: "Aerial photography in this operation was excellent, providing by far the greatest share of the information on the enemy installations on Betio. The first aerial photographs received by this headquarters were two sorties of verticals of Tarawa, taken in January and February 1943; these showed the early stages of development of the Betio defences, the preliminary work on the airfield and provided mosaics from which maps and overlays were made [previously the only maps of Tarawa available were enlargements from hydrographic charts, which were found to be very inaccurate].

"The next occasion on which photographs were received was 28 September, when complete coverage of Tarawa in verticals was provided by the carrier groups involved in the 18 September raid, as well as certain obliques of Betio, which showed clearly the barricade beach defences and in conjunction with the verticals, made possible a most thorough interpretation showing the Betio defences nearly as complete as they were on D Day."

The report then details the size and distribution of maps for the operation, including the issue of 1in to 1 nautical mile maps of Tarawa Atoll and Betio Island. An operational map of Betio on the scale 1/3150 was also issued to small units for their tactical planning; this was later overlaid in red with the enemy positions and became the D-2 situation map. Because of the time element and the distance from the rear base at Hawaii, it was not possible to supply aerial photographs in sufficient quantities for distribution to units below Division.

The 18th Marines made a relief model of Betio to the scale of 1/1000, which was considered to be outstanding - two more were provided for distribution to the headquarters of the assault regiments. All regimental and battalion staff planning was done on these two models in Wellington prior to embarkation; one was taken along to the rehearsal area, where it was again used by staff and for familiarisation of naval gunfire and air liaison personnel. Every officer concerned said that these models were of the highest value in helping them visualise the landing area.

The report then makes a note about enemy morale, whose final sentence seems entirely at odds with the eyewitness testimony of many Marines on D+2 and D+3: "The garrison occupying Tarawa exhibited high morale. For the most part, the defenders continued to resist to the end. Only a relatively small number committed suicide when faced with imminent defeat."

The very few Japanese who were captured alive (the official USMC report gives a figure of 17 from a garrison of 4,836) were interrogated briefly on the spot - the enemy's situation was so obvious that little further information of the type available to junior ranks was required. After the battle all Japanese and Korean prisoners were evacuated to Hawaii aboard the troopship *Monrovia* for systematic interrogation by Japanese-speaking officers of the division. Marines involved in the attack on Betio had previously been briefed about the importance of enemy documents, and a large number of papers and drawings arrived at divisional and regimental HQs during and after the battle. Among the items found were hydrographic charts of the Marshall Islands, and dozens of blueprints and engineer's drawings of defence structures.

The report concluded with a note about signal communications security. About 98% of the landing force's radio messages were transmitted in the clear throughout the first four days of the operation, security being deliberately sacrificed in the interests of speed. "Identity of naval forces was repeatedly disclosed both on landing forces and naval circuits. This was due simply to the widespread failure to use assigned code names; voice circuits offended most often. The single reported instance of attempted enemy deception (naval circuit) failed because the radio operator was alert to the absence of authentication." This highlights the experimental nature of the Tarawa operations; along with a great many other systems, the security of radio transmissions would be examined and tightened up for the many forthcoming amphibious operations.

Appendix 11 Kerr Eby, War Artist

The drawings of war artist Kerr Eby remained in storage and virtually unknown until the 1950s, when the book *Life's Picture Book of World War II* brought them to the attention of the American public. Born in 1889 in Japan, where his father was a Methodist mission- ary, Eby was taken to Canada when he was two years old; he subsequently studied at the Art Students League in New York and the Pratt Institute in Brooklyn. His first experience as a war artist came in World War I; attached to the US Army's 40th Engineers in France, he completed a series of drawings of the battles at Belleau Wood, Chateau Thierry, Saint Mihiel, and the Meuse-Argonne campaign. These were featured in a book entitled *War* which was published in 1936.

By 1943 Eby was working for Abbott Laboratories as an accredited artist/correspondent; and that November, at the age of 54, he accompanied the Marines during the attack on Tarawa. Little is known of his activities during the battle; the famous *Time Life* corre- spondent Robert Sherrod recalled that Eby only appeared once in his notebook, on 25 November at the end of the battle. He stayed on the atoll a few days longer than Sherrod, probably to complete his drawings. From Tarawa he proceeded to Bougainville, where the 3rd Marine Division were fighting. In the Abbott Laboratories catalogue *Marines in Action* Maj Gen Julian Smith wrote: "His finished paintings and drawings are richly successful, they have caught the dramatic intensity and the spirit of men at war." In October 1945 Gen Smith accepted the Eby drawings on behalf of the US Navy at a ceremony held at the University of Southern California in Los Angeles. Kerr Eby died in November 1946 at his Connecticut home; but his paintings and drawings are held by the Navy Art Collection in Washington, DC.

Select Bibliography

Alexander, Joseph H., *Across the Reef, The Marine Assault of Tarawa*, Marine Corps History Center, Washington (1993)

Gregg, Charles T., *Tarawa*, Stein & Day, New York (1984)

Hoyt, Edwin P., *Storm over the Gilberts*, Mason/Charter, New York (1978)

Hammel, Eric & Lane J.E., *76 Hours - the Invasion of Tarawa*, Pacific Press, California (1985)

Rottman, Gordon L., *US Marine Corps World War II Order of Battle, 1939-49: Ground and Air Units in the Pacific War*, Naval Institute Press, Annapolis, Maryland (1997)

Rottman, Gordon L., *US Marine Corps 1941-45 (Elite series No. 59)*, Osprey Publishing, London (1995)

Russ, Martin, *Line of Departure - Tarawa*, Doubleday, New York (1975)

Shaw, Henry I., *Tarawa - a Legend is Born*, Purnell's History of WWII (1968)

Sherrod, Robert, *Tarawa, the Story of a Battle*, Pocket Books (1944), reprinted The Admiral Nimitz Foundation, Fredericksburg, Texas (1973)

Stockman, James R., *The Battle for Tarawa*, official US Marine Corps History (1947), reprinted The Battery Press, Nashville, Tennessee

Zaloga, Steven J., *Armour of the Pacific War (Vanguard series No. 35)*, Osprey Publishing, London (1983)

Zaloga, Steven J., *Amtracs: US Amphibious Assault Vehicles (Vanguard series No. 45)*, Osprey Publishing, London (1987)

Index

Note: Names and units which do not appear in the body of the text but only in the tables in Appendices 2, 3 and 4 are not duplicated in this index. Only basic entries have been included for Tarawa atoll and Betio island, the location of virtually all events described from page 40 onwards.

Adams, Maj Hewitt, 110
Adams, PFC Hugh, 111
Albert, Eddie, see Heimberger, Lt Edward A
Alexander, Col Joseph, 81
American Samoa, 30, 31
Amey, Lt Col Herbert, 47-48, 59, 134
Apamama atoll, 24, 81, 121-123, 145, 150
Ashworth, Pte, 151

Bairiki island, 28, 31, 97, 107, 113, 115, 150
Bartsch, William H, 141
Bataan, 15
Beers, Sgt, 151
Betio island ("Helen"), fortification and garrison of, 19-22, 138-141; planning of USMC assault on, 28, 40; Operation Longsuit begins, 40; thereafter *passim;* in 1993, 136-137
Birdsong, Pte Jesse, 99
Bismarck Islands, 27
Blakeman, Pte George, 85
Bonin Islands, 9
Bonnyman, Lt Alexander, 104, 131, 133, 151-152
Bordelon, SSgt William, 59-60, 133, 151
Bougainville, 99, 157
Bourke, Gen T E, 102
Brukardt, Lt Herman, 86
Buariki island, 119-120, 150
Buota island, 119
Burma, 12, 15
Butler, Ralph, 40, 49-50

Camp Tarawa, 75, 125
Carlson, Lt Col Evans, 18, 67, 73, 82, 126, 132
"Carlson's Raiders", 18, 19
Caroline Islands, 10, 12, 134
Casablanca, 16
Celebes, 27
Chiang Kai-shek, Gen, 11
China, 9-12, 15
Churchill, Prime Minister Winston, 15, 24
Coral Sea, Battle of
Corregidor, 15
Crowe, Maj Henry "Jim", 48, 57-58, 62, 65, 69, 71, 73, 75, 79-80, 85, 90-91, 104-105, 134, 148-149

Deighton, PFC Herbert, 115, 119-120
Drake, Lt, 116
Drewes, Maj Harry, 30, 134
Dutch East Indies, 11-12, 15

Eby, Kerr, 131, 157
Edson, Col Merritt, 33, 40, 47, 98, 100, 101, 103, 130
Edwards, Capt Aubrey, 48
Efate, 38
Eisenhower, Gen Dwight, 17, 24
Eita island, 119, 120
Ellice Islands, 24, 145
Eniwetok atoll, 134, 136

Fiji, 117, 121
Fletcher, Adml, 15-16
Fletcher, Lt John, 86
Forbes, Lt, RNZN, 44
Formosa, 9
French Indo-China, 11
Funafuti, 24, 31, 40, 155

Gavutu, 32, 57
Gilbert Islands, 8, 18-19, 24, 25-27, 98, 117
Greene, Lt Thomas, 91-92
Guadalcanal, 16, 25, 29, 32, 57, 79, 126, 150
Guam, 8, 10, 15, 22, 38, 134

Hall, Col Elmer, 65, 81, 82, 86, 100, 113
Halsey, Adml William F, 23, 134
Handley, Capt I R, 117
Hatch, SSgt, 131
Hawaii, 30-31, 121, 122, 124-126
Hawke Bay, 33, 35
Hawkins, Lt William D, 48-49, 69-70, 87, 133, 137, 152-153
Hays, Maj Lawrence, 67, 78, 81, 82, 84, 85, 87, 100-102, 105
Hayward, Capt Louis, 131
Heimberger, Lt Edward A ("Eddie Albert"), 86, 134
Hermle, Gen Leo, 33, 67, 81-82, 102
Higgins, Andrew Jackson, 25
Hill, Adml Harry W, 24, 38, 43, 44, 46, 82, 110, 127-129
Hilo, 125
Hirohito, Emperor, 11
Hiroshima, 8
Holland, Maj Frank, 28, 29, 37, 47, 128
Holmes, Col Maurice G, 106, 109
Hong Kong, 15
Hooper, Gny Sgt, 48, 69
Horner, Capt R D, 30

Iceland, 31-32
Inchon, 9
Iwo Jima, 8, 16, 25, 135, 136, 150

Japan, expanding power of, 9-12

Japanese formations and units:
2nd Fleet, 26
3rd Fleet, 27
3rd Special Base Force, 19, 138
4th Fleet, 138
4th Fleet Construction Department, 19, 138
6th (Yokosuka) Special Naval Landing Force, 19, 22, 138
7th (Sasebo) Special Naval Landing Force, 19, 22, 138
14th Division, 135
22nd Air Flotilla, 27
25th Army, 15
32nd Army, 135
111th Construction Unit, 19, 138

Japanese ships:
Akagi, 13, 16
Hiryu, 13, 16
Kaga, 13, 16
Musashi, 11
Niminoa, 50, 83-86
Shoho, 16
Shokaku, 13
Soryu, 13, 16
Yamato, 11
Zuikaku, 13
I-175, 122
RC-35, 109

Johnson, Capt, USN, 76
Jones, Capt James, 122

Jones, Maj W R, 96, 100-101, 105, 106
Jordan, PFC Joe, 58, 71, 79, 89, 107, 112, 113
Jordan, Lt Col Walter, 59, 62, 77, 80, 85, 87, 90
Joseph, Sgt, 115-116

King, Adml Ernest, 16, 24, 25, 114
Knight, Sgt Raymond, 37, 64-65
Koga, Adml, 98
Kondo, Adml, 26
Korea, 9
Kuribayashi, Gen, 135
Kurile Islands, 9
Kusaka, Adml, 26
Kwajalein atoll, 8, 114, 134, 136
Kyle, Maj Wood, 62, 70, 77, 90, 101, 113

Lamon Bay, 15
Leslie, Lt, 48
Leyte, 38, 134
Libby, PFC Bob, 38, 55-57, 68-69, 71, 79-80, 84, 92-93, 95-96, 111-112, 124, 132-133
Lingayen Gulf, 15
Luzon, 15

MacArthur, Gen Douglas, 16-17
MacPherson, Lt Cdr Robert, 45-47, 64, 155
Makin island, 18, 24, 25, 26, 38, 44, 121-122, 145
Malaya, 12, 15
Manchuria, 9-11
Mariana Islands, 10, 12, 25, 27, 134
Marshall, Col William, 38
Marshall Islands, 10, 12, 24, 27, 79, 126, 134, 155
Mary Oliva, Sister, 119
McLeod, Lt Col Kenneth F, 100, 106, 109
Mele Bay, 38
Meiji, Emperor, 9
Midway island, 13, Battle of, 16, 17
Montgomery, Adml A E, 26
Morgan, Sgt, 69-70
Moore, PFC Edward, 49
Mullinex, Adml Henry, 122
Mukden (Shen-yang), 9
Murakami, Lt, 19, 21
Murray, Lt Col Raymond L, 97, 115
Musing, Sgt Maj, 113

Na'a island, 119-120
Nagasaki, 8
Nagumo, Adml, 13
Nanking, 11
Nauru island, 24
Nelson, Capt John, 119
Newcomb, Cpl, 131
New Georgia, 25
New Guinea, 15, 16
New Hebrides, 38
New Zealand, 27, 32-33, 35-37
Nimitz, Adml Chester W, 16-17, 23, 114, 129, 132
Nonouti island, 117
Norris, Capt, 151

Okinawa, 8, 9, 16, 23, 25, 135, 136, 150
Oshima, Gen, 135

Pango Point, 38
Pearl Harbor, 11-13, 23, 125, 155
Peleliu island, 8, 134-135
Perry, Cdre Matthew, 9
Philippines, 10, 12, 15, 16
Port Arthur (Lu-shun), 9
Port Moresby, 15-16
Pownell, Adml C A, 26, 121, 155
HMS Prince of Wales, 12, 15

Rabaul, 27, 32, 99

Rader, Pte Hawk, 83-84, 88-89, 99, 113-114
Radford, Adml A W, 26
HMS Repulse, 13, 15
Rixey, Lt Col Presley, 66, 85, 98, 107
Roebling, Donald, 25, 29
Roosevelt, Maj James, 18
Roosevelt, President Franklin D, 15, 17, 132
Roosevelt, President Theodore, 10
Royal Navy, 12, 15
Russia, 9, 11
Ruud, Maj Robert, 63-65, 71, 72-73
Ryan, Maj Michael, 51-55, 61, 62, 70, 78, 80, 91-92, 134, 136
Ryuku Islands, 135

Sadd, Rev A D, 117
Saipan, 8, 10, 25, 57, 134
San Diego, 30, 130
Schoettel, Maj John, 47, 61-62
"Seabees" (Naval Construction Bns), 33, 110, 125; see also 3-18 Marines
Shanks, Pte Clarence, 89
Shaw, Artie, 33
Shell, Lt Col George R, 98
Sherman, Adml F C, 26, 27
Sherrod, Robert, 40, 58, 75, 77, 88, 103, 112, 132, 157
Shibasaki, Adml, 8, 21, 44, 48, 80-81, 98-99
Shoup, Col David M, 28, 29, 35, 38, 40, 53, 60-65 , 67, 69, 73, 78, 80, 82, 84-85, 90, 92, 96, 98, 100, 103, 130, 133, 153-154
Singapore, 10, 15
Smith, Gen Holland M, 8, 24, 30, 31, 44, 63, 67, 96, 114, 121-122, 128-129, 135
Smith, Gen Julian C, 26, 29, 31, 35, 44, 46, 61, 63, 67, 73, 78, 80-82, 85, 96, 98, 102, 105, 106, 110, 125, 128-130, 133, 148, 157
Smith, Gen Ralph, 26, 121
Solomon Islands, 16, 22, 27, 32
Spencer, PFC David, 73, 75, 132
Spruance, Adml Raymond L, 16, 23, 24, 26, 38, 44, 46, 63, 114, 129, 130
Stimson, Henry, 24
Strange, PFC Adrian, 77
Stueber, Pte Theodore, 116-117
Swango, Pte Melvin, 66-67, 69
Swenceski, Lt Col Alexander, 69

Takarongo Point, 131
Taranto, 12
Tarawa atoll, pre-war history of, 18-19; Japanese occupation of, 18, 19; USMC assault on Betio island (qv), 40 and thereafter *passim;* USMC landings on other islands of, 115-121; in 1993, 136-137
Temakin Point, 43, 91, 137, 141
Terrienne, Bishop Octave, 118
Tinian island, 57, 134
Tojo, Gen Hideki, 11
Tompkins, Maj, 101
Truk, 12, 24, 26, 27
Tsushima, 10, 12
Tulagi, 32, 33
Turner, Adml Richmond Kelly, 24-25, 26, 30, 44, 96, 129, 130

United States formations and units:
1st Corps Tank Bn (Medium), C Co, 33, 35, 66-67, 69, 77, 135
1st Marine Brigade, 25
1st Marine Division, 32, 134, 135

2nd Amphibian Tractor Battalion, 30, 33, 150
2nd Defense Bn (Special Weapons Group), 32, 102
2nd (Light) Tank Bn, 32, 33, 35, 97, 102; D (Scout) Co, 35 115-117, 119
2nd Marine Raider Bn, 18

2nd Marine Division (Reinforced), 26; pre-Tarawa service of, 31-32; component units and equipment of, 33-35; personal equipment of troops, 41-43; thereafter *passim*; 133, 154

2nd Marine Regiment, 31, 32, 38, 113, 124, 150
1st Bn, 2nd Marines (1-2), 62, 70, 77, 90, 100-101, 113
2nd Bn, 2nd Marines (2-2), 40, 47, 58-59, 61, 70, 73, 77, 87, 90, 100
3rd Bn, 2nd Marines (3-2), 38, 41, 47, 49-57, 61, 68, 70, 103, 110
2nd Marines Scout Sniper Ptn, 48-49, 69-70, 87, 112-113, 153

6th Marine Regiment, 31, 32, 38, 62, 67, 124
1st Bn, 6th Marines (1-6), 96-97, 100-101, 104, 106-107
2nd Bn, 6th Marines (2-6), 97-98, 106, 115, 117, 119-120, 150
3rd Bn, 6th Marines (3-6), 100, 103, 106, 109-110

8th Marine Regiment, 31, 32, 38, 113, 124, 150
1st Bn, 8th Marines (1-8), 62, 67, 78, 81, 82-85, 88-89, 101-102, 110, 113
2nd Bn, 8th Marines (2-8), 38, 48, 57-58, 73, 79, 89, 100, 103-104, 113
3rd Bn, 8th Marines (3-8), 37, 62-65, 71, 73, 100, 103-104, 113

10th Marine Regiment, 31, 32, 35
1st Bn, 10th Marines (1-10), 77, 85, 98
2nd Bn, 10th Marines (2-10), 98
3rd Bn, 10th Marines (3-10), 119

18th Marine Regiment, 32, 35, 104, 156
1st Bn, 18th Marines (1-18), 48, 59, 110, 151
2nd Bn, 18th Marines (2-18), 152
3rd Bn, 18th Marines (3-18), 72

3rd Marine Division, 99, 135, 157
4th Marine Division, 135
5th Marine Division, 135
V Amphibious Corps, 8, 25, 35, 67,
V Amphibious Corps Scout Co, 122
6th Marine Division, 135
7th Air Force, 40
10th Army, 135
27th Infantry Division, 26, 38, 121
81st Infantry Division, 134
165th Infantry Regiment, 121

5th Fleet (Central Pacific Force), 23
Task Force 17, 15
Task Force 50, 26, 121
Task Force 52, 24
Task Force 53, 24
Task Force 54, 24
Task Group 50-1, 26, 121
Task Group 50-2, 26, 121
Task Group 50-3, 26, 76
Task Group 50-4, 26, 27
Task Group 53-1, 38
Task Group 53-4, 38
Transport Division 4, 38
Transport Division 6, 38
Transport Division 18, 38

United States Navy warships & transports:
Anderson, 38
Argonaut, 18
Arizona, 13
Arthur Middleton, 38, 41, 50
Ashland, 38, 61,
Bailey, 38
Bellatrix, 38
Belleau Wood, 26, 121, 155

Biddle, 38
Birmingham, 38, 76
Bunker Hill, 26, 45, 76
California, 13
Colorado, 38, 76, 85
Cowpens, 26, 121
Dashiell, 38, 40, 47, 57, 81
Doyen, 38, 115
Enterprise, 13, 26, 121
Essex, 26, 45, 76
Feland, 38, 97
Frazier, 38, 109
Gansevoort, 38, 109
Hale, 76
Harris, 38, 43
Heywood, 38
Independence, 26, 45, 76-77
Indiana, 121
Indianapolis, 38, 44, 46, 76
J Franklin Bell, 38, 115
Lasalle, 38, 43
Lee, 38
Lexington, 13, 16, 26, 155
Liscomb Bay, 26, 121, 122, 150
Maryland, 38, 43, 45, 46, 61, 67, 76, 79, 82, 85, 98, 102, 115, 116, 126, 155
Meade, 38, 109
Mississippi, 150
Mobile, 38, 76
Monrovia, 38, 65, 82
Monterey, 26, 121
Nautilus, 18, 122-123, 155
New Mexico, 122
North Carolina, 121
Oklahoma, 13
Ormsby, 38
Pennsylvania, 13, 121
Portland, 38, 76
Princeton, 26, 27, 155
Pursuit, 40, 44, 45, 46, 81-82, 155
Requisite, 40, 44
Ringgold, 38, 40, 45, 47, 57, 79, 81, 82, 123
Russell, 38
Santa Fe, 38, 76
Saratoga, 13, 26, 27
Schroeder, 38, 107
Sheridan, 38, 114
Sigsbee, 107
Tennessee, 38, 76
Thuban, 38
Virgo, 38
West Virginia, 13
Yorktown, 13, 16, 26
Zeilin, 38, 40, 82

Wake Island, 13, 15, 22
Warrick, Dr, 54
Weaver, Sgt, 116
Webster, Lt Gordon, RNZN, 45
Wellington, 28, 29, 32-33, 35-37, 117, 130
Wentzel, Capt George, 54
Whaley, Lt, 155
Wren, Pte Jack, 75

Yamamoto, Adml, 12-13
Yamashita, Gen, 15